AF599000

Serpentear

[*verb* /serpente'ar/ to meander,
to wind, to twist]

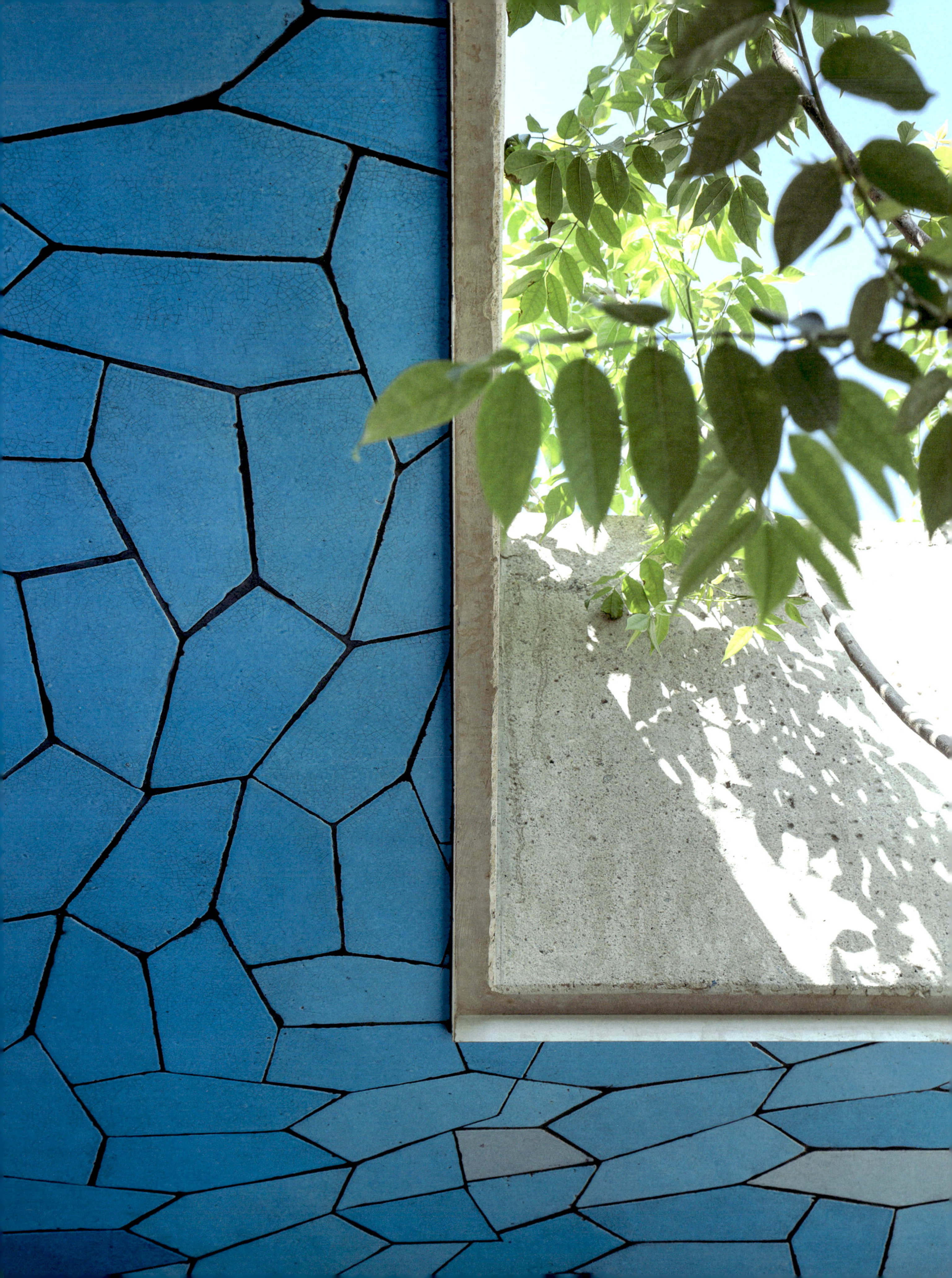

Sarah Crowner

Serpentear

Edited by Donna Wingate

Contributions by
Nikki Columbus, Quinn Latimer,
Ana Elena Mallet, Diego Matos,
and Ingrid Schaffner

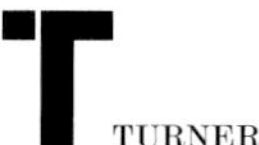

TURNER

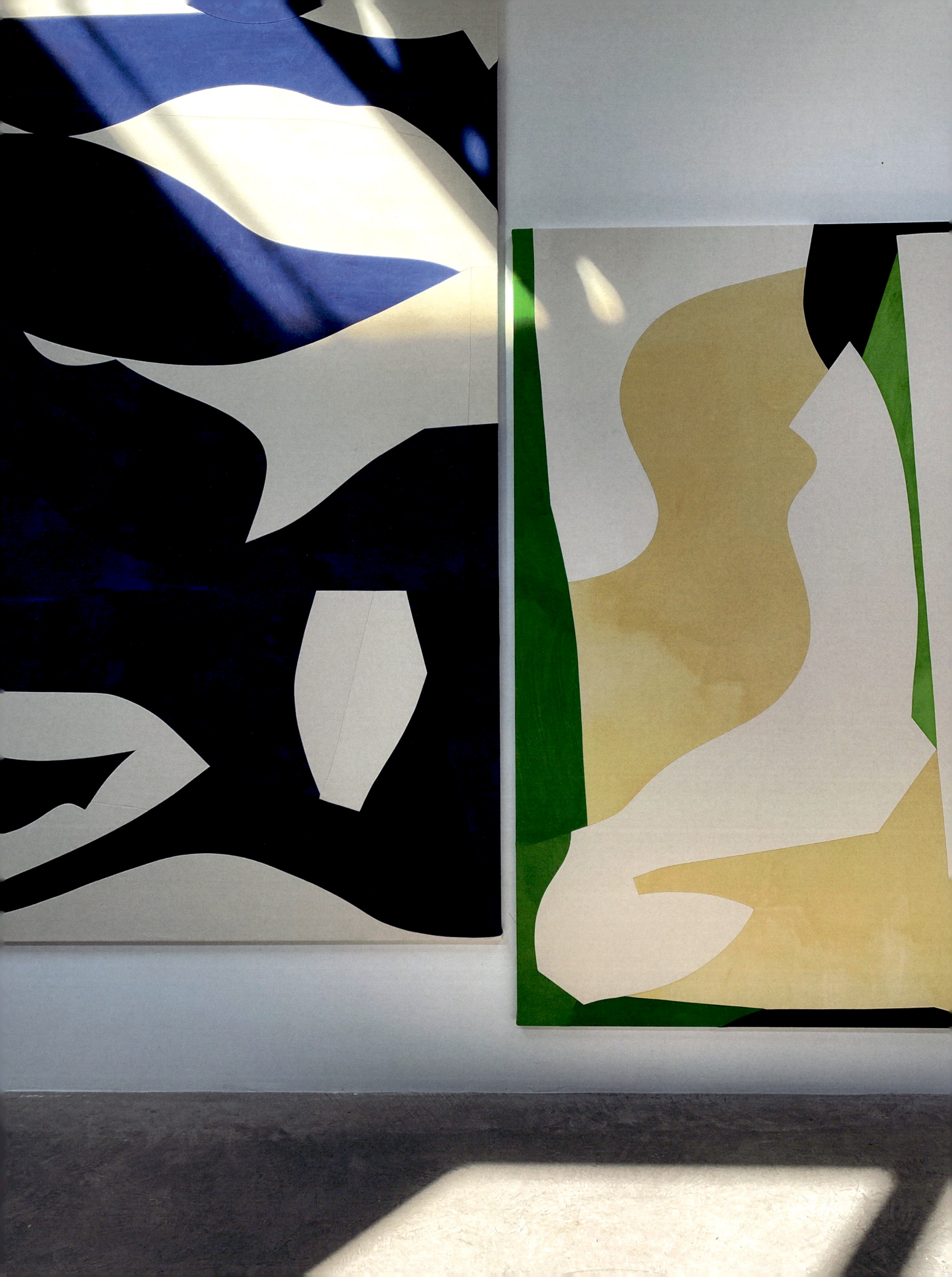

Foreword

It is Museo Amparo's great privilege to present *Serpentear*, an exciting exhibition by New York–based artist Sarah Crowner comprising two distinct yet intertwined components: her site-specific artwork *Platform (Cobalt Snakeskin)* and the accompanying presentation she has organized—drawing from our holdings of pre-Hispanic, colonial, modern, and contemporary Mexican art—to accompany a selection of her own recent works on canvas.

Crowner's monumental *Platform*—installed with great precision and occupying over three hundred square meters of the museum's courtyard—is made from glazed snakeskin-shaped terracotta tiles fabricated by Guadalajara-based Cerámica Suro, a decades-old family-owned ceramics workshop with whom she has collaborated regularly since 2014. During her work on this extraordinary project, Crowner plumbed the depths of the Amparo's permanent collection and emerged with an interpretive, personal, and deeply researched selection of Mexican art in myriad mediums and across many time periods—ranging from black-and-white contact sheets from photographer Graciela Iturbide, to Talavera pottery and eighteenth-century Mexican baroque painting, and a selection of sketches for costume designs by Juan Soriano. Organized in a manner that falls outside of traditional art historical frameworks based on categories, chronologies, or mediums, the resulting installation is a true collaboration between an artist, the museum, artworks, and history. The presentation is a unique, even revelatory engagement for viewers to experience surprising juxtapositions with immense potential for new expressions and meanings.

Throughout Sarah Crowner's career, she has consistently pushed at the edges of contemporary painting, advancing the medium into the realms of architecture, installations, performance, and artist books. This thoughtful volume, published on the occasion of her exhibition, allows us to consider the full arc of her project across these various mediums and genres, in a book and exhibition that fall outside of the exhibition catalogue and "solo show" templates. Many of her previous tileworks, paintings, and designs for the stage are reproduced and discussed here in depth, providing insight into the ways in which she has drawn inspiration from Mexican culture across disciplines and throughout the history of modernism as a whole. We also feature a portfolio of images alongside Quinn Latimer's lyrical narrative poem "Score for Three Snakes," which itself represents a kind of work within a work here in this book.

This exhibition continues the Amparo's longtime commitment to mounting architecture and design exhibitions, foregrounding the importance of imagining more livable environments. These have included major exhibitions such as *Enrique Norten: The Limits of Form* (2012); *New Territories: Laboratories for Design, Craft and Art in Latin America* (2016); *Mario Pani: Architect in Process* (2016); *Perspectives: Tatiana Bilbao Estudio* (2018); and *Clay and Fire: The Art of Pottery in Oaxaca* (2019).

We extend our profound appreciation to Sarah Crowner for her partnership and generosity, and to Ana Elena Mallet, who worked so closely with the artist on organizing the exhibition within the galleries and contributed an insightful essay to this publication. We would also like to thank Nikki Columbus, Diego Matos, and Ingrid Schaffner for their thought-provoking essays, Quinn Latimer for her poem, and Ryan Polich for his thoughtful design of this catalogue. The Amparo is ever grateful to our museum staff for all of their hard work, and to Cerámica Suro for producing the tiles. And lastly, our sincere thanks to Santiago Fernández de Caleya of Turner, our copublisher, and especially to Donna Wingate for her close collaboration with Sarah Crowner on the editorial and creative direction of this handsome volume.

Ramiro Martínez Estrada
EXECUTIVE DIRECTOR

Lucía I. Alonso Espinosa
GENERAL DIRECTOR

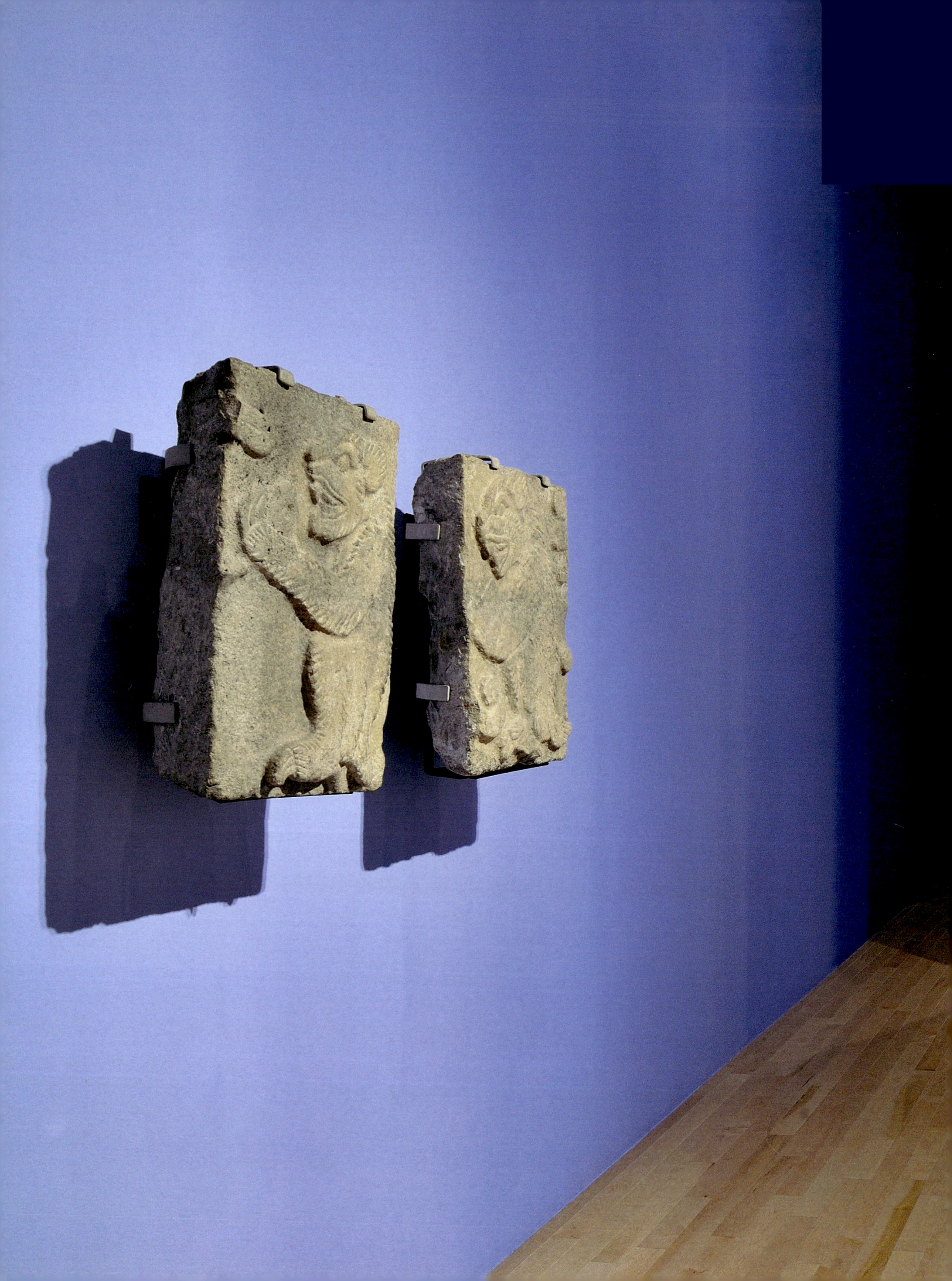

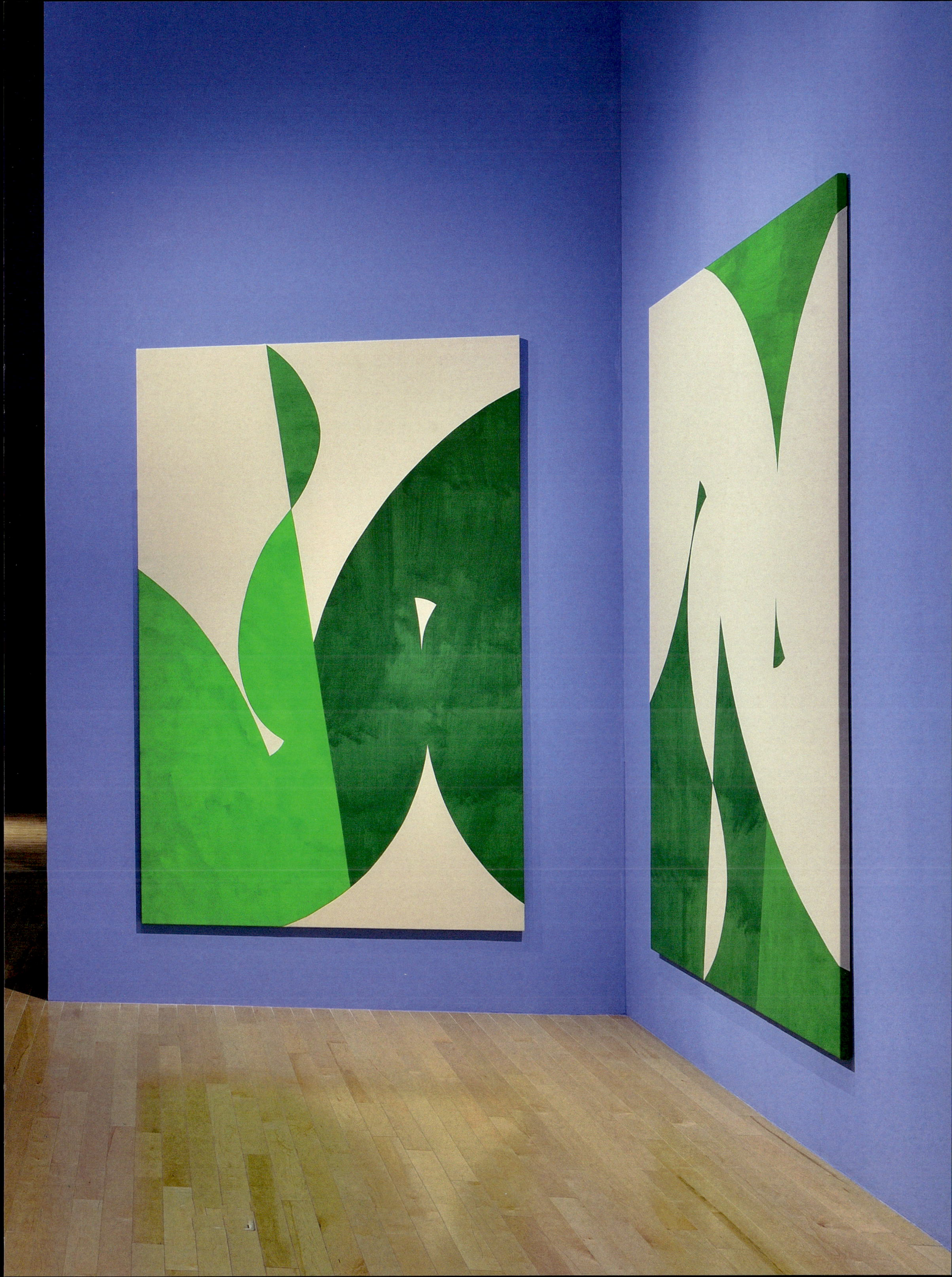

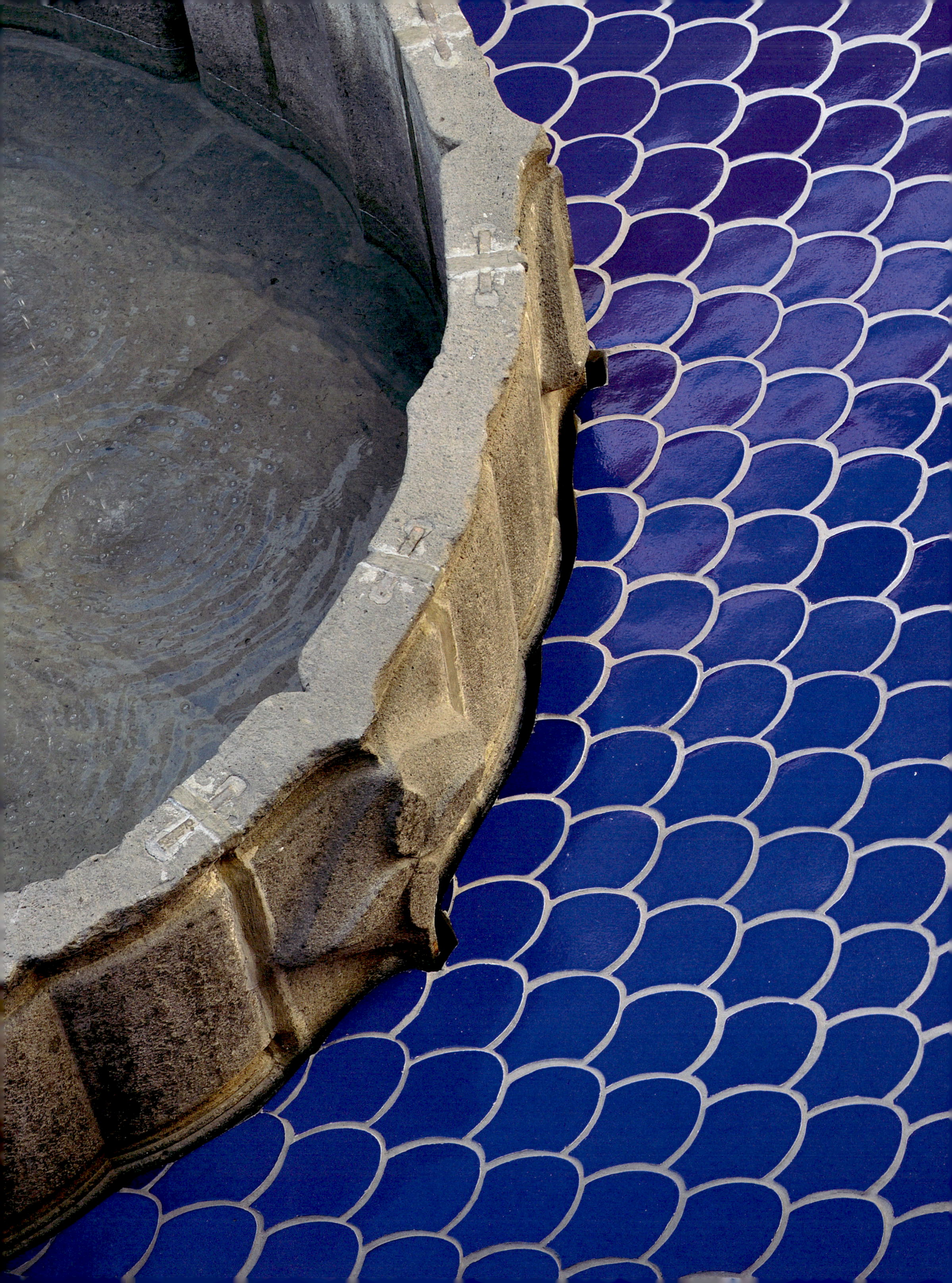

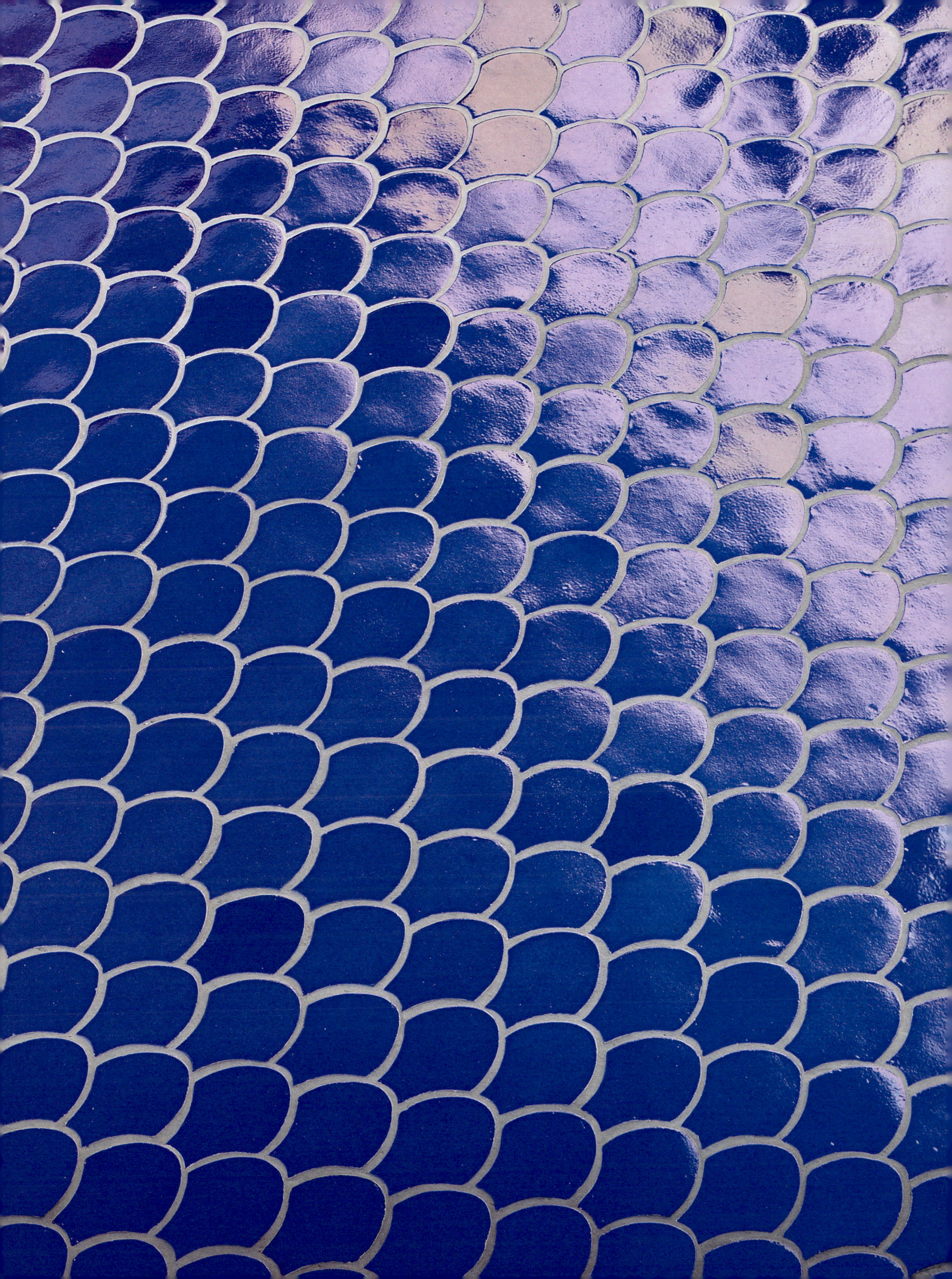

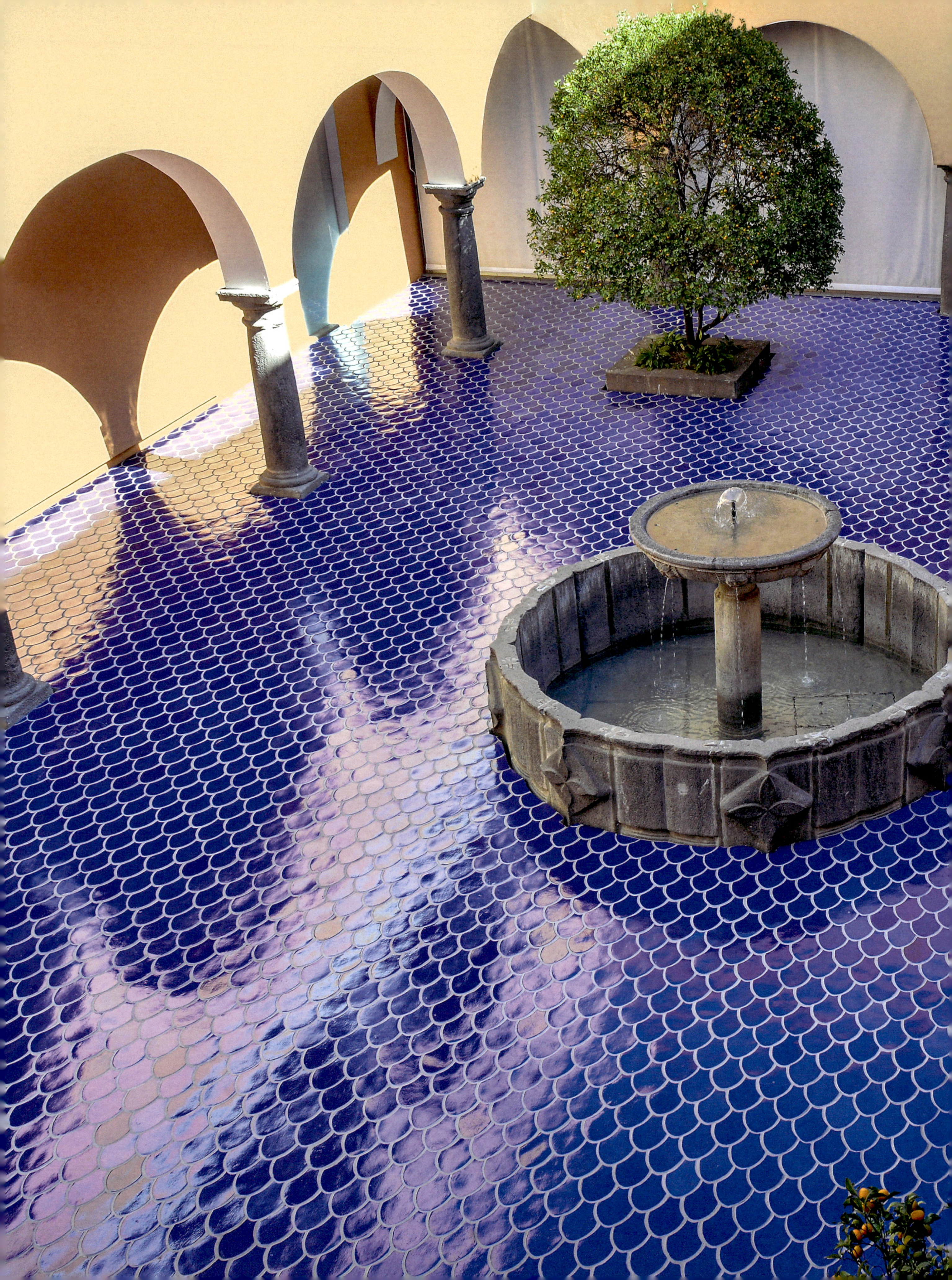

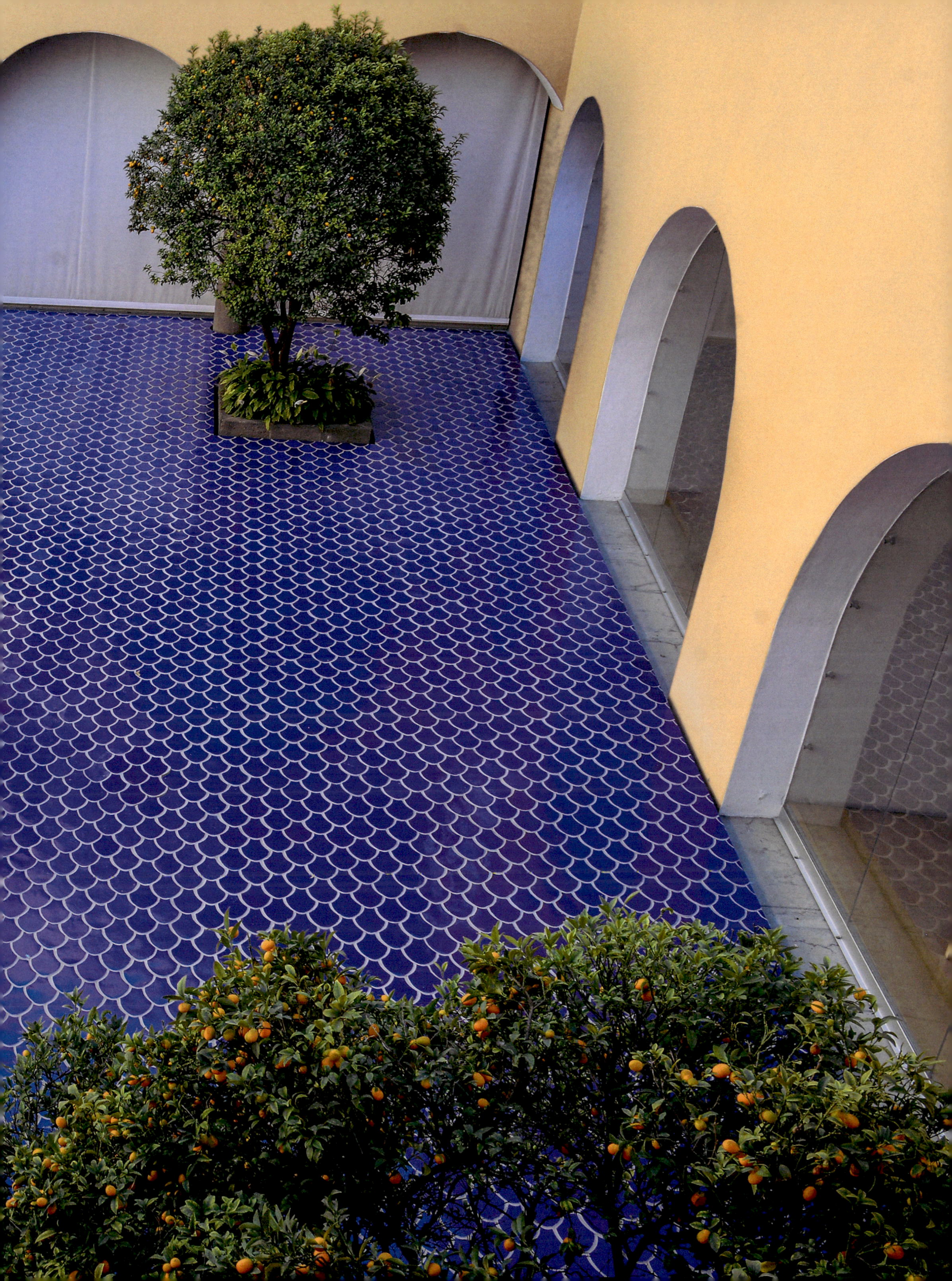

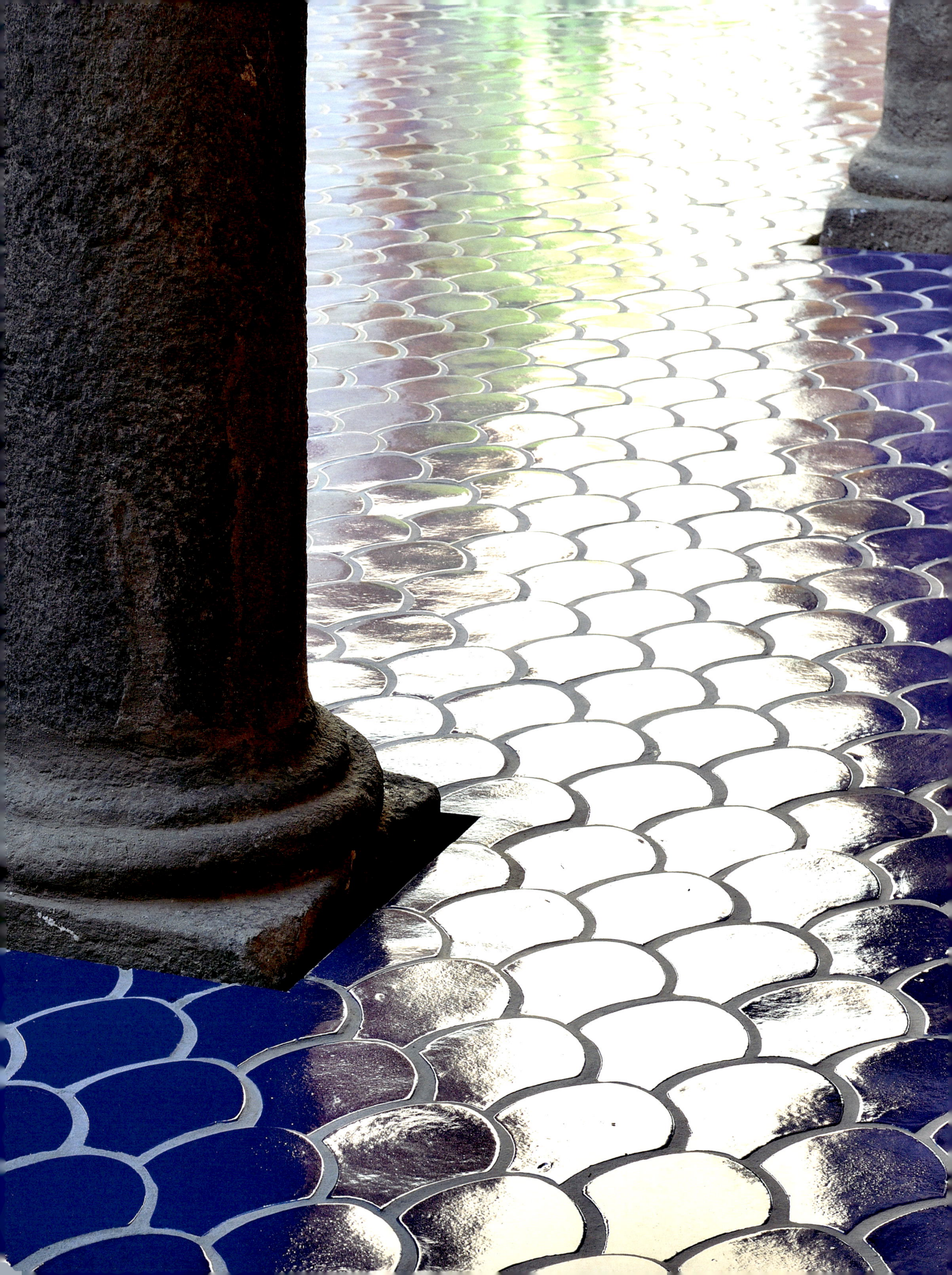

Ana Elena Mallet

Material Interfaces

Sarah Crowner's Tileworks

OUR INFORMATION AGE, dawning in the 1970s and unfurling into the broad-based industrialization of our modes of communication, reveals the ways in which different systems interact via what we might call "communication zones"—the areas and channels (and rabbit holes) that are mapped out for us. Signals are received and processed by others in order to facilitate interactions, providing a more or less adequate set of operations. In the best-case scenarios, new knowledge is generated. Our activities—real or digital—are our data patterns, and in both emotional and technical terms we might say that our existence, the conduct of our daily lives, is always registered, recorded, logged. As such, we are permanently affixed to the interface.

Sarah Crowner's artistic practice over the years has become an architecture of material matrices. Her most recent project at the Museo Amparo in Puebla, Mexico, reveals her interest in Mexico's past and present. Nestled in one of the building's colonial patios is her raised terracotta tile floor, which, notwithstanding the museum's recent renovation by the architect Enrique Norten, is a reflection of Mexico and its history. (The original building dates from the sixteenth century and has been used as a hospital, a school, and housing over the years. In the 1990s, the architect Pedro Ramírez Vázquez converted it into a museum.) Crowner's intense cobalt-blue tiles in the shape of reptile scales might recall the sea, the skin of a snake, or a mirror of water. The repetition of patterns used by the artist in this installation generates a visual effect that refers to abstract painting, architectural plans and design work, but also to natural elements and found patterns.

Crowner situates her artmaking practices somewhere between the applied arts and fine art, and has established a remarkable body of work that has consistently questioned the established hierarchical order of painting over design.[1] She creates paintings, objects, and installations that gracefully and graciously push at the edges of each of these disciplines. While the artist has long engaged with traditional techniques and materials, such as clay, wood, fabric, canvas, and paint,

Crowner completely reformulates the contexts in which they are presented and/or installed, such as modern buildings, gardens, museums, homes, stages and other performance venues, and commercial spaces. The artworks that emerge from these intersections—murals, tile-works for floors and ceilings, tapestries, swimming pools, and yes, paintings—invite us to reevaluate any previous understanding we might have of these environments, professional applications (such as design and fabrication), and artworks. In fact, our entire concept of use value relative to material form is challenged via the arc of her project.

It could then be said that Crowner works with interfaces—adjacencies that point toward the nature of their materials. Her work about, at, or on limits doesn't draw any particular conclusions—that is, it doesn't delimit or constrain any artwork for the sake of a precise result—but rather expands its surroundings via inquiries and criss-crossing borders:

> I realized the artist's job is not to prove something, but to see what can be broken and rebuilt. The subject, if we need to find a subject, might be on the surface about patterns, but really the subject is artmaking as a process, the system of moving sideways, looking at what is around you in the world and trying to make sense of that and build a new world.[2]

Installation view of *Wall (Wavy Arrow Terracotta)*, 2018. Glazed terracotta tiles, plywood, mortar, and grout; dimensions variable. Carnegie Museum of Art, Pittsburgh, PA

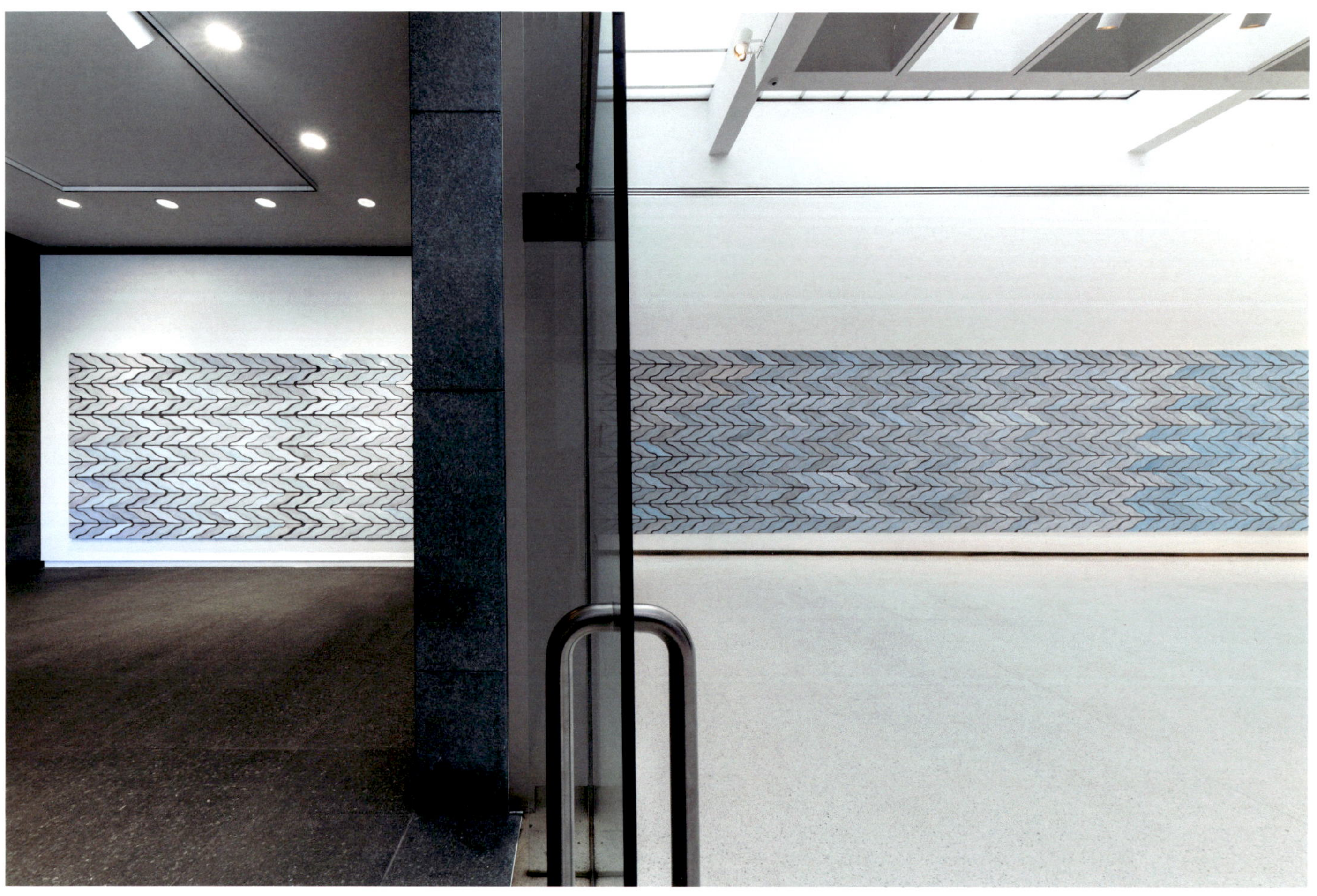

Crowner is able to link distant points together in her artworks because these flexible boundaries refer to temporality and chronology, as well as art and design. She creates organic shapes that also allude to primordial orders of nature and the sacred: straight lines, spirals, and circles can be read as forms of expressions of time throughout the history of cultures, and the circle and semicircle are astral symbols with multiple interpretations. The snake or the curved line is a symbol of water, of the primordial soup, and of the origin of life on land and sea. All of these symbols have parallels in the objects and images of Egypt, Babylon, Assyria, Peru, the Pacific Islands, and North America, including Mexico, whose stone carvings, drawings, and variety of artifacts provide a deep well of resources for the artist. For example, *Wall (Wavy Arrow Terracotta)* (2018), a wall piece extending sixty-six feet across and composed of blue tiles that vary in tones ranging from light to medium to colder shades of gray blue, appears to come to life in the daylight, creating a curvy chevron pattern that gives the illusion of braiding and wavy movement. What results is a kind of epic shorthand for the type of primitive representation one might find in a cave painting.

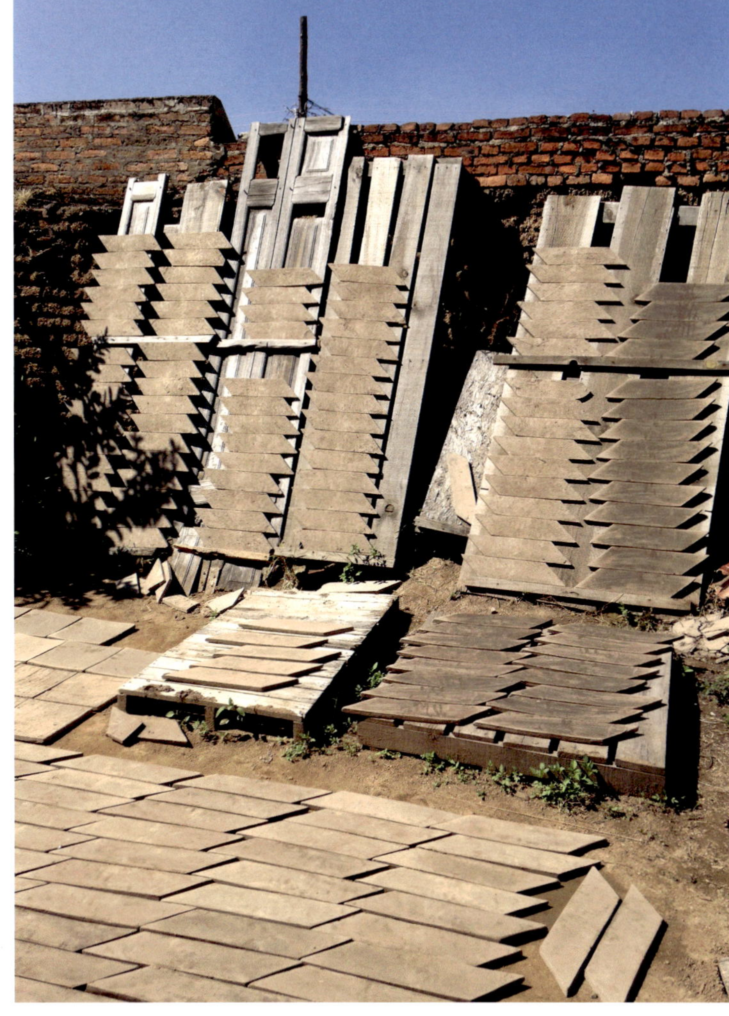

Cerámica Suro, Guadalajara, Mexico, 2013

Crowner's relationship with Mexico is an important aspect of her tilework. Seeking to expand her production, in 2013 she traveled to Cerámica Suro, a factory located on the outskirts of San Pedro Tlaquepaque in Guadalajara. Founded by Noé Suro Olivares in 1955, the workshop produced white earthenware for department stores, hotels, restaurants, and craft shops. Soon after, the workshop began to grow and develop different styles and techniques inspired by local artisan traditions for a new group of clients, especially those in the hotel business. Mosaics and tiles for facades and buildings became emblematic solutions that, moreover, were hand-finished. The painters of Cerámica Suro also became renowned for their work, while the company's color department created original shades and combinations that became very popular.

In the 1990s, Luis Miguel Suro, Noé's son and a visual artist, began to produce his contemporary artwork within the family business. Soon after, friends and colleagues had taken over the kilns, and the workshop became a place for artists to experiment with forms and techniques. When José Noé Suro Salceda, Noé's eldest son, took

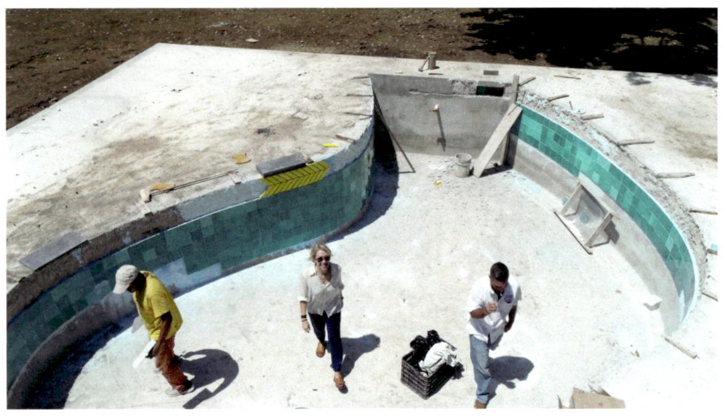

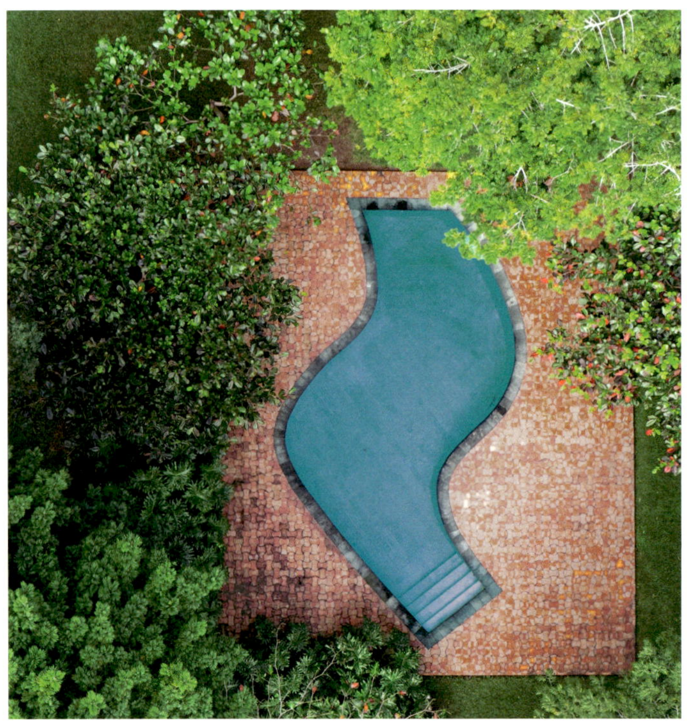

ABOVE AND OPPOSITE Swimming pool, Fundación Casa Proal, San Rafael, Veracruz, Mexico, 2018

over and converted the workshop into a factory with greater capacities, his interest in contemporary art led him to redirect production to embrace the work of applied artists and others working in creative fields, the main clients of the company today. Architects, designers, artists, and chefs now have a place that responds to their needs and where new solutions can be found, even for the most extravagant projects.

In Crowner's 2014 floor installation in the Casa Franco by Luis Barragán in Guadalajara, large white, shaped tiles produced at Cerámica Suro and blue-gray grout also created a dynamic, undulating composition. The entrance to the house looked like the jaws of a dragon from which a serpentine tiled forked tongue protruded, thanks to the pattern of Crowner's floor. Inside, the fluctuating sensation was accentuated by the contrast of the white walls with horizontal cutouts that produced a play of perspectives, very much in concert with Barragán's interest in the play between light and color within various elements of his architecture. By means of composition, the earthly and concrete served to create an atmospheric space, which visitors perceived as ephemeral. There was a practical dialogue with Barragán and his architecture—this we can say is real—and yet our understanding of the artwork was also activated in deeply spiritual and emotional terms.

A similarly engaging dialogue between disciplines, materials, and time can be seen on the floor piece, panel, and tiles that Crowner developed for the restaurant of the Guggenheim Museum in New York (2017). In conversation with Frank Lloyd Wright's iconic architecture, Crowner created a curved tile panel that responds to the museum's design but, with its bright yellow color, reacts to the concrete material and pale tones of the building, providing a counterpoint to the building's austerity and purity. Color confronts and complements, redresses and revises our perceptions of reified modernity while demanding that it, and we, pay close attention to the present.

The work that Crowner made in 2018 for the Fundación Casa Proal in San Rafael, Veracruz, extends beyond the limits of the artist's previous tile installations and the boundaries of what we know about the medium of painting. A swimming pool takes on the form of two waves, side by side, coming together to generate movement and tension. Again, the artist deployed tiled patterns and repetitions to

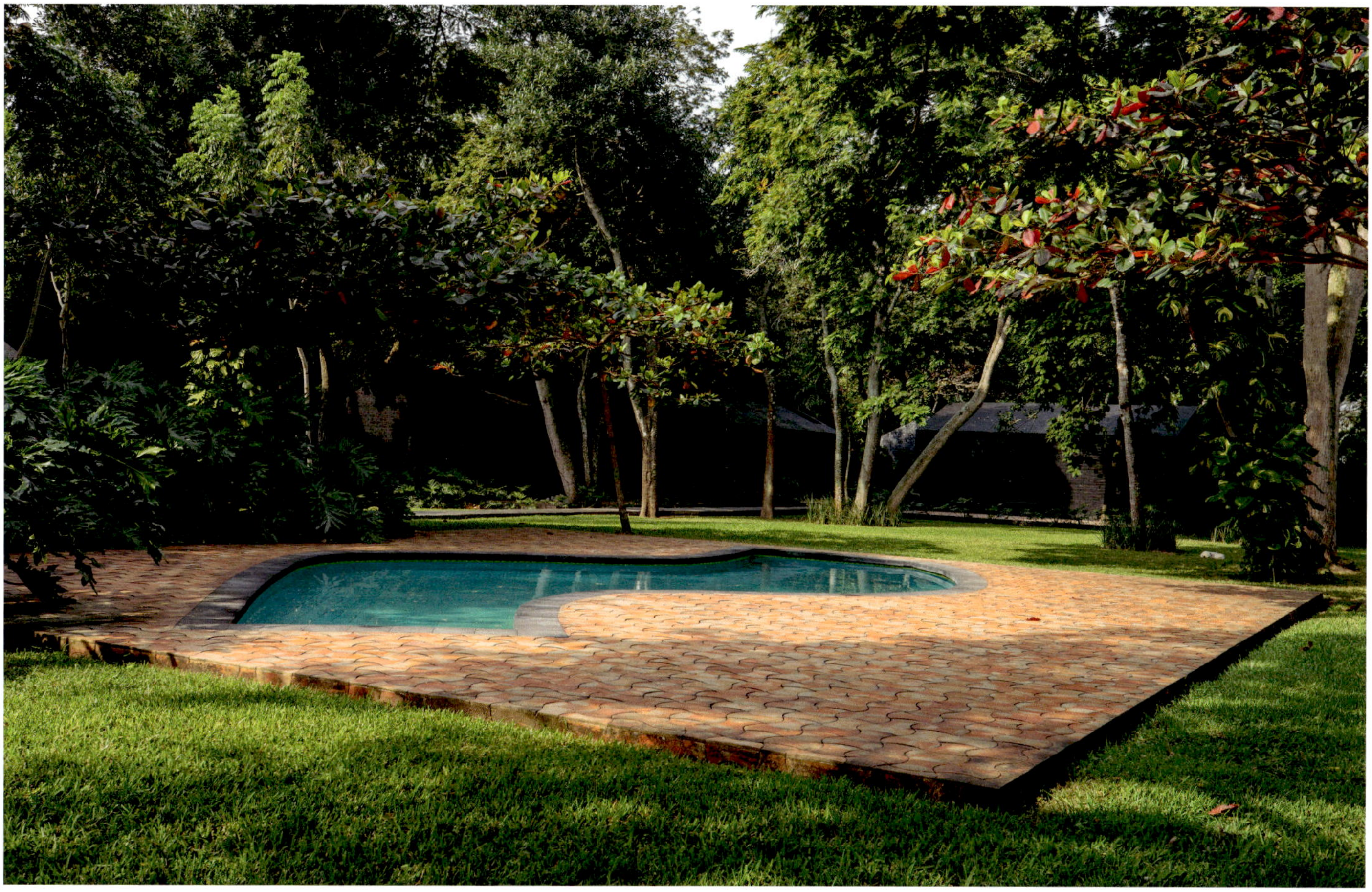

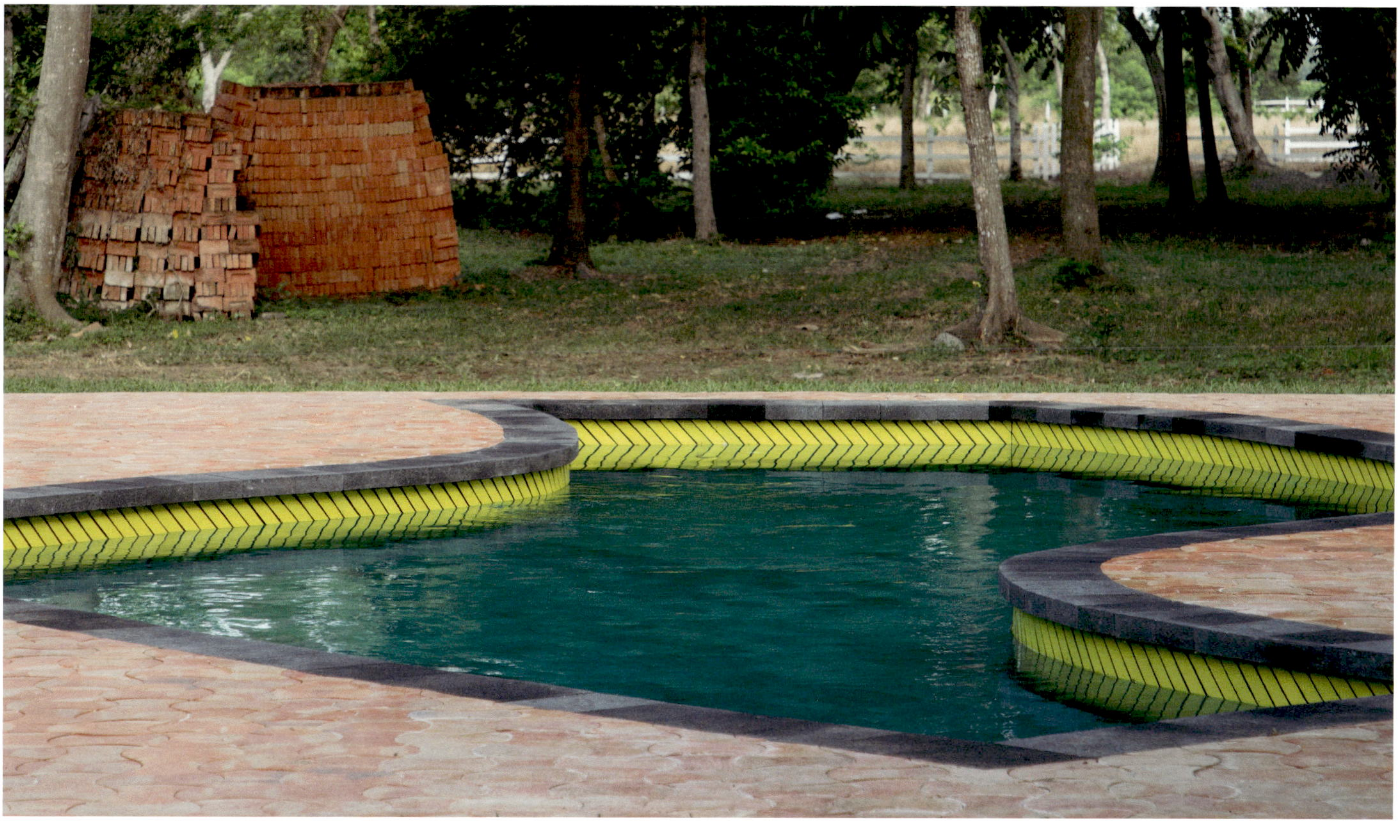

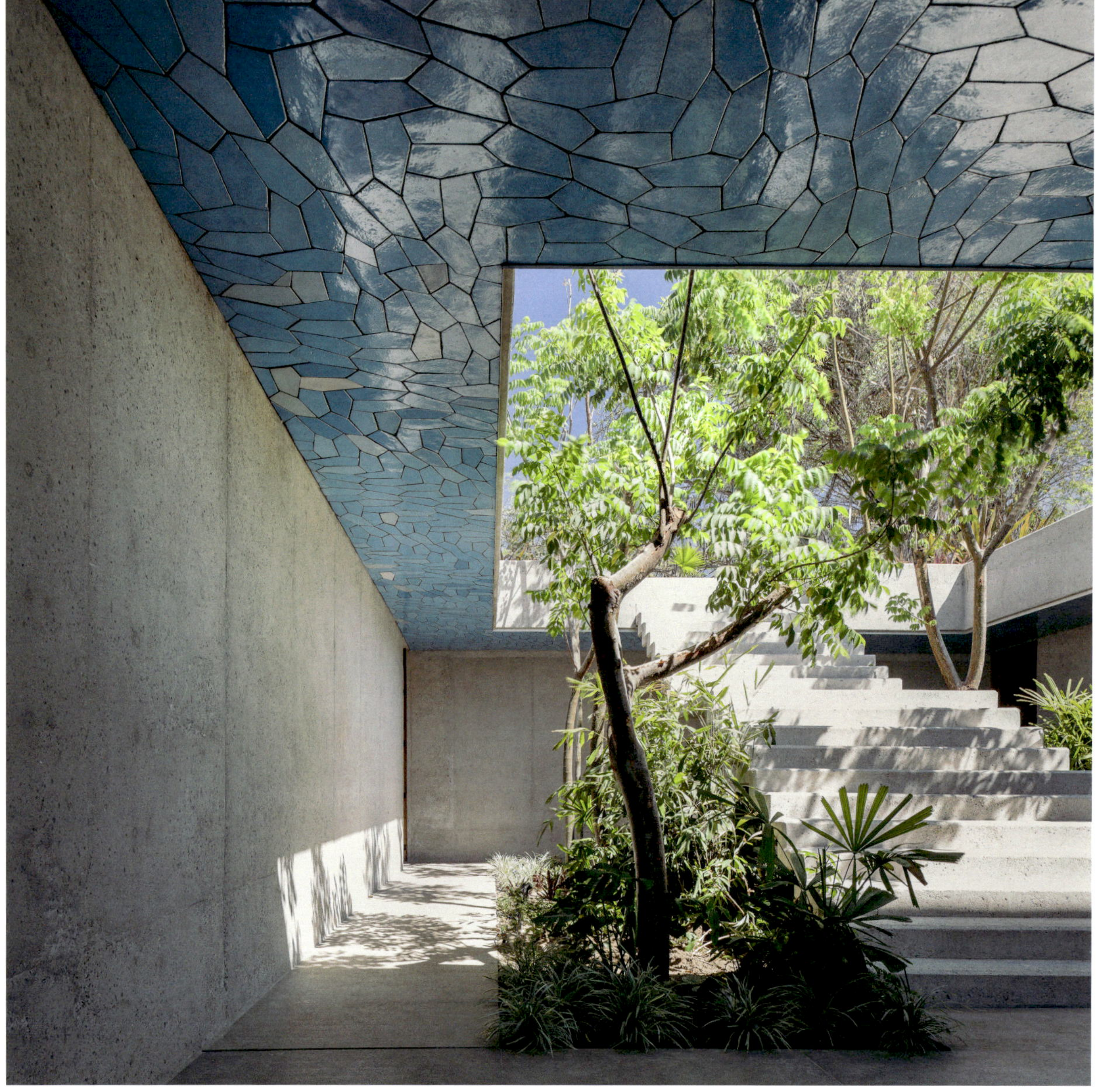

generate optical illusions. Raw terracotta frames a body of water—the pool itself is an intense blue—that is outlined with volcanic rock (a material associated with Mexican architecture) and a yellow tile border that contrasts with the background, shape, patterns, and materials. This is a delightful artwork, but it is also one that has been made to be used. We might even characterize this work as a painting, in the form of a swimming pool, that is activated by the presence of a body. As a rule, Crowner's work invites a body to become involved, whether it is the artist's own when making her work, as with her paintings composed of sewn panels, or that of the viewer, who in order to enter the work—as in the case of her swimming pool—must offer more than just their gaze.

The immersive sensation of the pool culminates in the magical setting the artist created for Valhalla, a house designed by the Mexican architect Tatiana Bilbao in Punta Mita, Mexico, in 2022. In Valhalla, the floor, Crowner's tiled ceiling, and the brilliant blue horizon of the

ABOVE AND OPPOSITE *Ceiling (Stretched Pentagons)*, 2022. Glazed terracotta tiles, plywood, aluminum, mortar, and grout; dimensions variable. Valhalla (house), Punta Mita, Mexico, architecture by Tatiana Bilbao Estudio

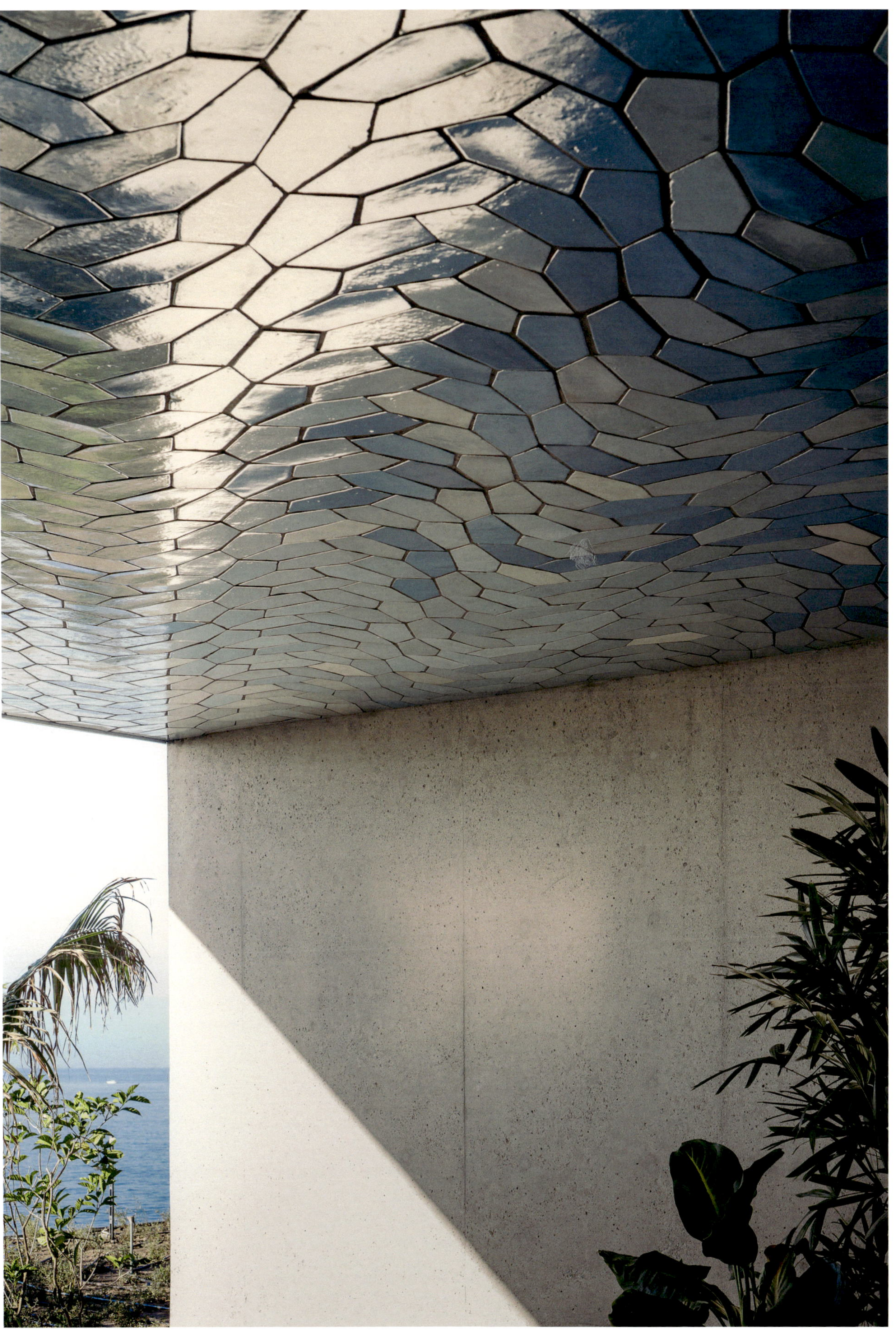

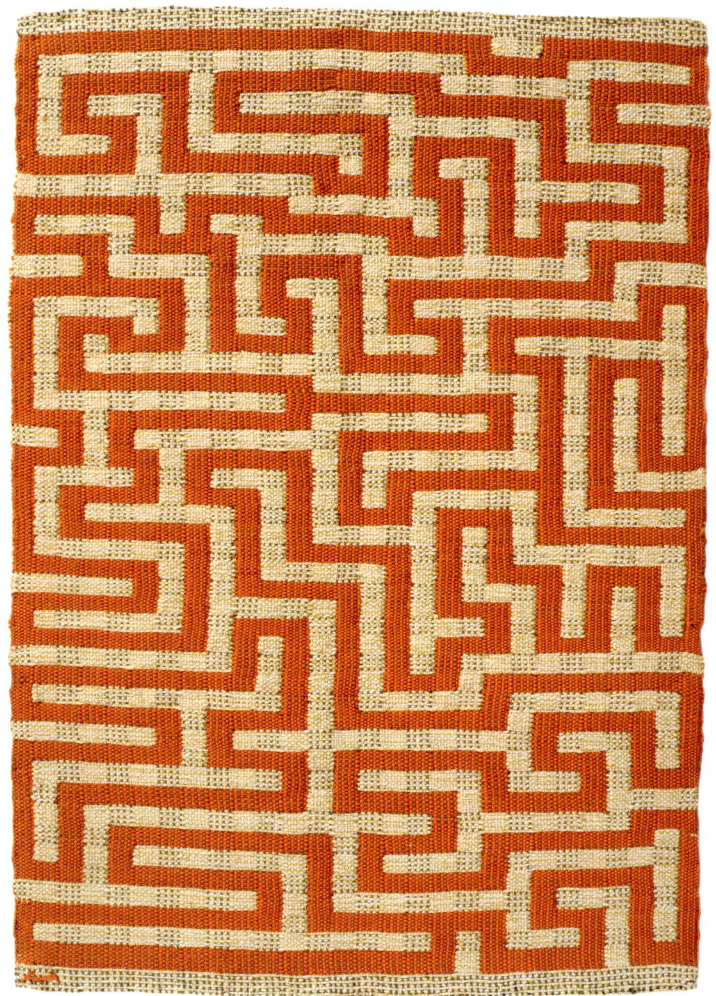

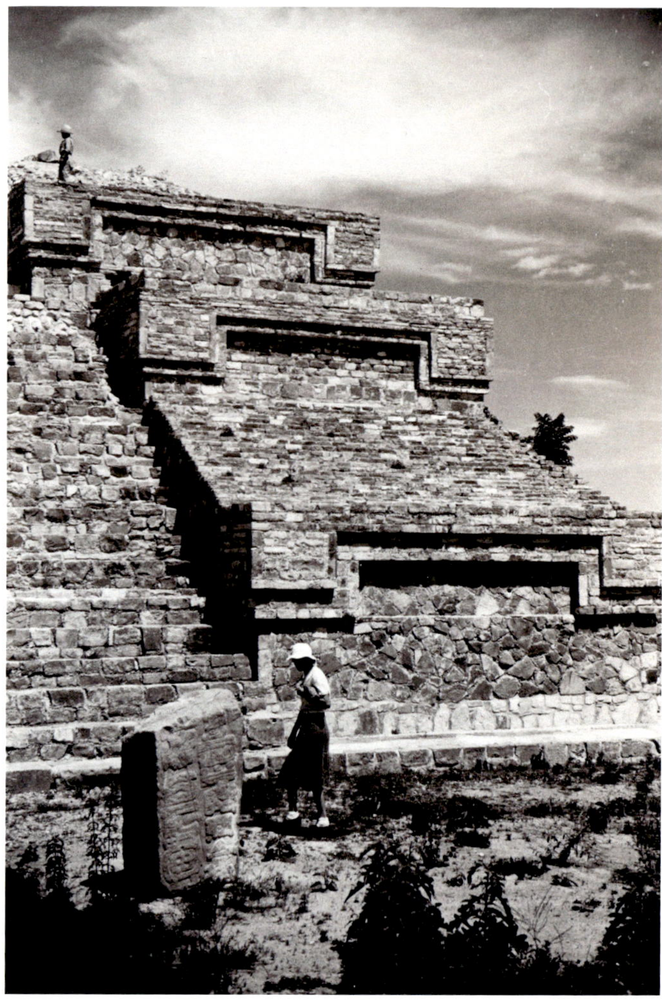

LEFT Anni Albers, *Red Meander*, 1954. Linen and cotton; 20½ × 14¾ in. (52.1 × 37.5 cm). Private collection

RIGHT Josef and Anni Albers at Monte Albán, Mexico, 1939. Gelatin silver print; 4¾ × 3¼ in. (12.1 × 8.3 cm). The Josef and Anni Albers Foundation, 1976.7.1397

oceanfront surroundings blur and merge into a singular sensation as the perception of this work changes in the shifting light throughout the day. Patterns and repetitions create an environment that frames the entrance to the house, as well as the surrounding landscape. The interior and the exterior come together to become a painting, and the viewer becomes both participant and observer.

Although color has always been part of Crowner's exploration processes, her many collaborations with Cerámica Suro have resulted in new tonal ranges that have enriched her work. Her dialogue with Suro broadened her interests and helped her develop a love for the history and culture of Mexico. Crowner now belongs to the group of foreigners who—having traveled, lived, and/or worked in Mexico during the twentieth century and, with deep respect and dedication, having been influenced by the cultural heritage, local materials, traditional craftsmanship, and visual richness of different moments of Mexican history—have managed to capture this inspiration in their work. In doing so she joins a long line of illustrious artists and designers, such as Josef and Anni Albers, Ruth Asawa, Elena Gordon, Carlos Mérida, Clara Porset, Cynthia Sargent, and William Spratling, among many others.

FOLLOWING PAGES *Ceiling (Stretched Pentagons)*, 2022. Glazed terracotta tiles, plywood, aluminum, mortar, and grout; dimensions variable. Valhalla (house), Punta Mita, Mexico, architecture by Tatiana Bilbao Estudio

And so a seemingly utilitarian floor—as basic a requirement for human movement as our feet, the wheel, and the earth itself—at the Museo Amparo provides us with an experience that is at once exactly the same and entirely different: it simultaneously collapses our understanding of use value and our sense of perception as the interior merges with the exterior, the contemporary fuses with the historical, the structural grounds the contemplative, and the artisanal humanizes the commercial/industrial. Crowner's tileworks function as an interface between time, materials, mediums, artistic movements, perceptions, disciplines, illusions, and definitions. For viewers, this extends the notion that art exists beyond a determined hegemonic space and can function as a living, beautiful, useful, and mutable work. All the while, art and design come together and generate a complete work of art that requires our direct participation. Faced with the experience of living, encountering, and inhabiting these artworks, spectators become active participants/users.

NOTES

1. Sarah Crowner, email correspondence with the author, February 28, 2022. "My work falls between the applied arts and the 'fine arts,' and poses questions about design versus painting, and the way the work can be both at once . . . somewhere between art and craft, or between a quilt or a tapestry and a painting. I like to question these ideas, and the relation between craft or design (handmade for a utilitarian end) and art (non-utilitarian)."
2. Crowner, email to the author.

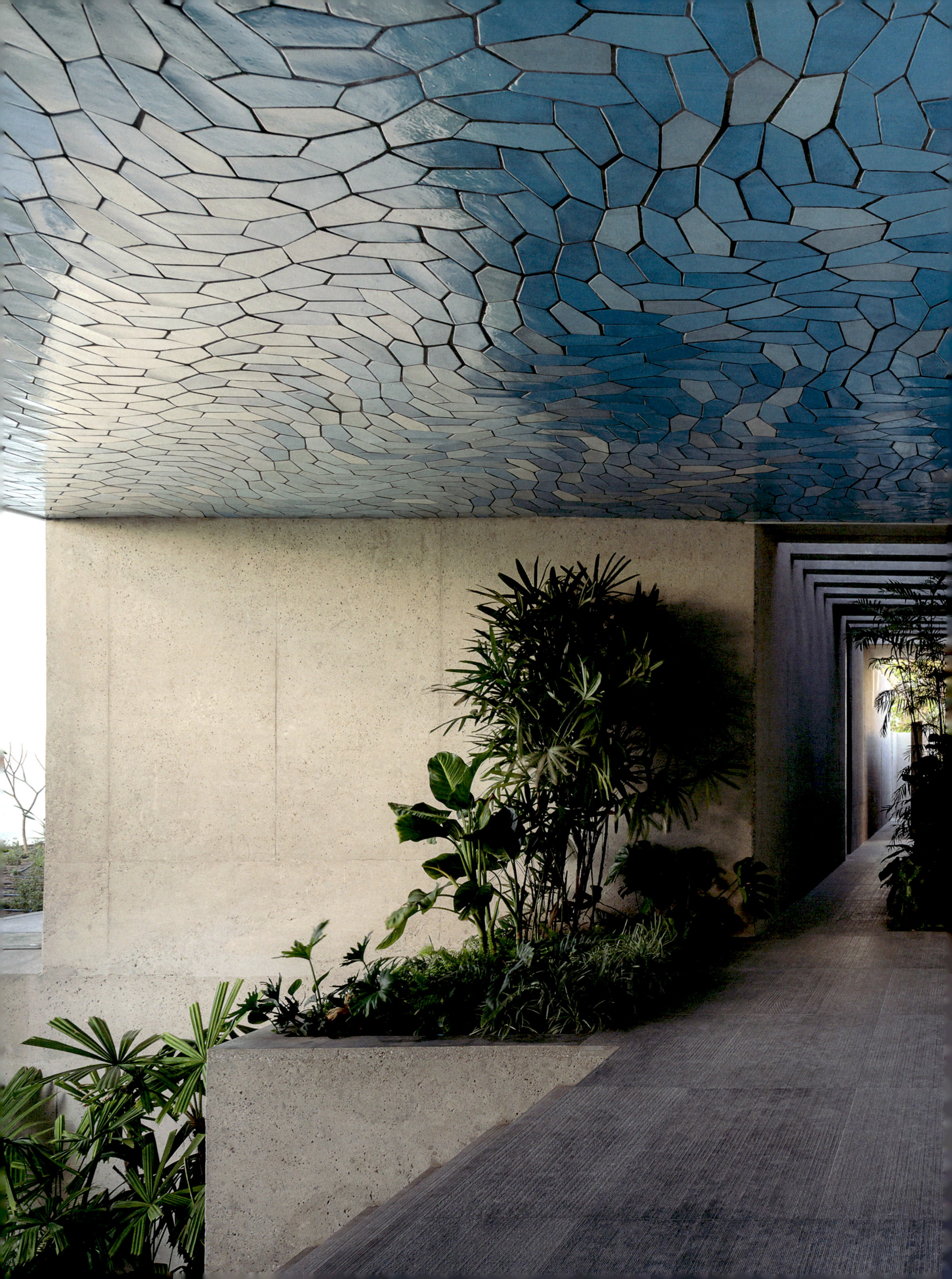

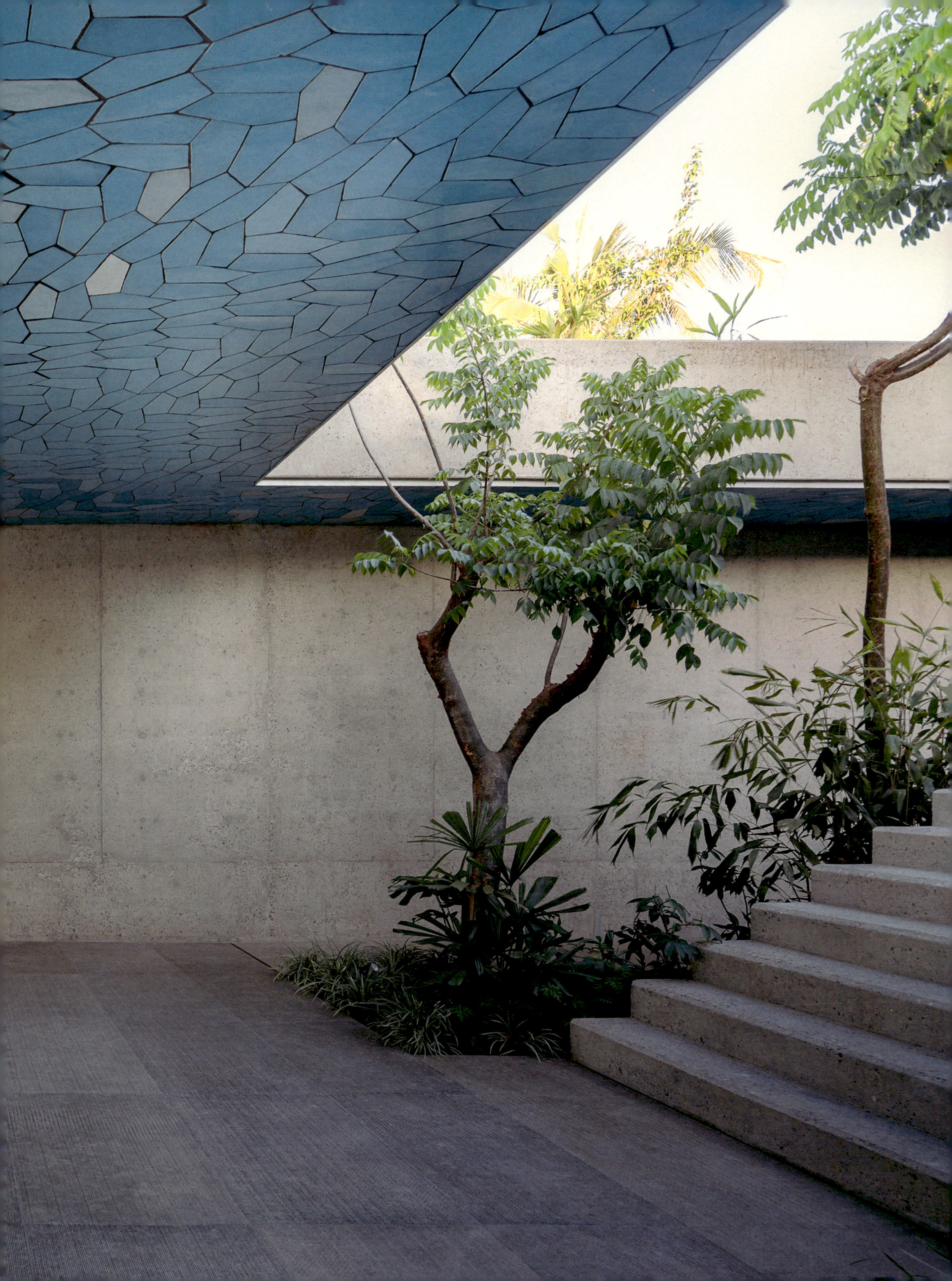

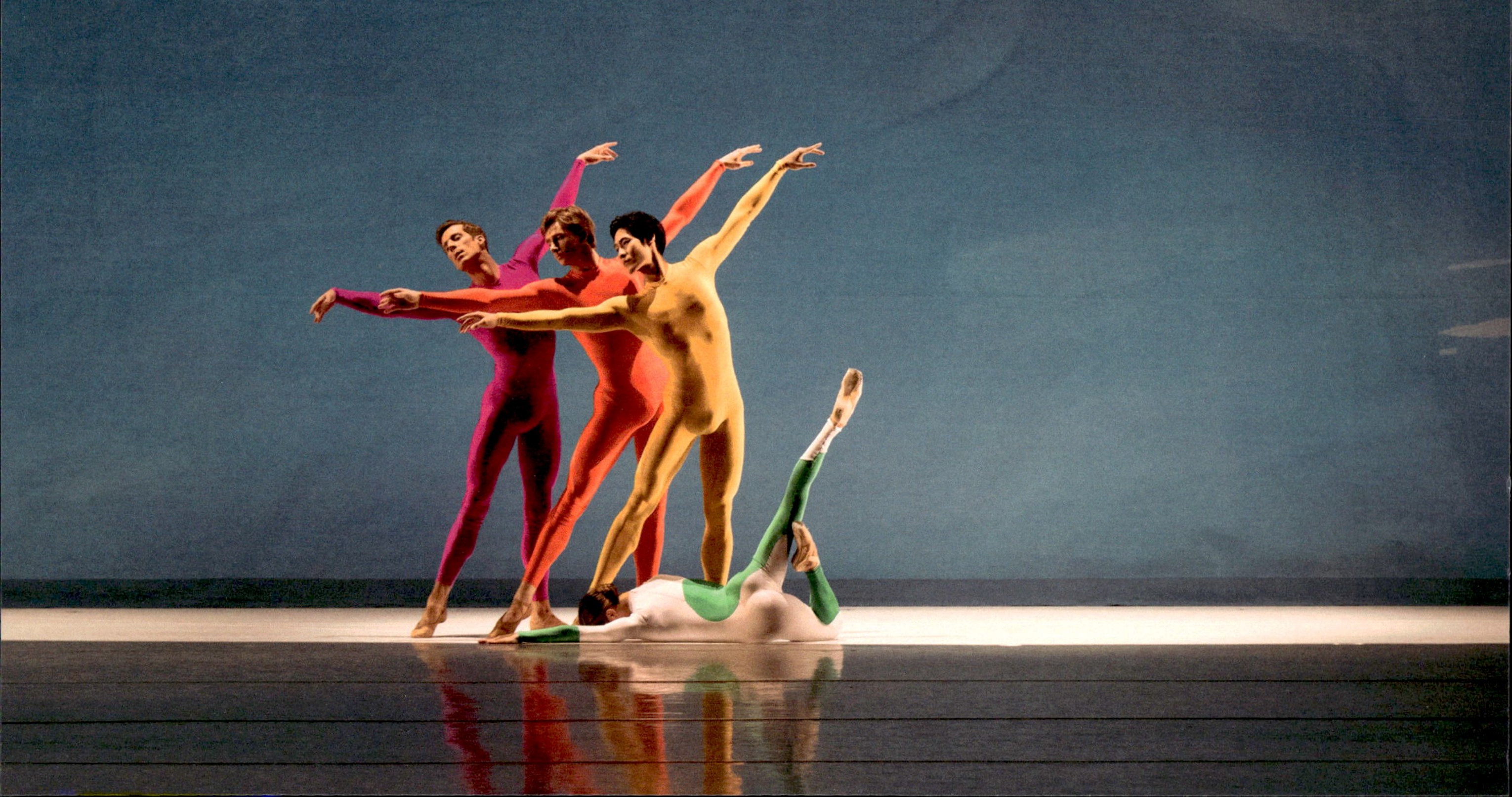

Nikki Columbus

Sarah Crowner in Five Acts

Blaine Hoven, Aran Bell, Joo Won Ahn, and Christine Shevchenko in *Garden Blue*, 2018. Sets and costumes by Sarah Crowner, choreography by Jessica Lang. American Ballet Theatre, New York

I. Quotes of Paint

WHEN SARAH CROWNER DESIGNED a stage for a 2013 lecture and performance series at Wiels, in Brussels, she took inspiration from local artist Marcel Broodthaers.[1] The late Belgian conceptualist and poet frequently decontextualized and abstracted typographic symbols, but he had a special fondness for the comma. Transposing this form into three dimensions, Crowner's plywood platform *Score* (2013) extends nearly ten feet across and stands one and a third feet high. Equally, however, the curving shape of the comma could be read as a single quotation mark—an *inverted* comma—which serves (in American English) to punctuate a quote within a quote. Viewed from one perspective, the platform appears to open the quote; walk 180 degrees around, and it closes the quote. A quotation mark is an apt form for a stage, demarcating the arena of performance. Yet as an artwork itself, set within an art space—a container within a container—a quote within a quote is even more fitting.

The shape of *Score* could also be seen as a self-reflexive commentary on Crowner's own paracitational practice, which frequently draws from the history of modernism for source material—in particular, geometric abstraction from the 1920s to the 1960s. While this is a widely recognized strategy among her generation (and the one before), Crowner's approach stands apart. Her tone and method are far from the postmodern parody of Ryan Gander and Jonathan Monk, the research-intensive work of Jill Magid and Simon Starling, or the recovery and reactivation sought by Paulina Olowska and David Maljković. Rather, Crowner has frequently described her process as "using art history as a medium," implying that her artistic precedents are something plastic to be pulled around and reshaped.[2] Her citations are typically partial, fragmented, and rearranged, not only invoking geometric abstraction but continuing its formal explorations.

Crowner began this line of inquiry in 2009 with the painting series *Superficie Modulada, 1956 (Parts 1–3)*. Based on a colorful geometric work on paper by Brazilian artist Lygia Clark—a sequence of

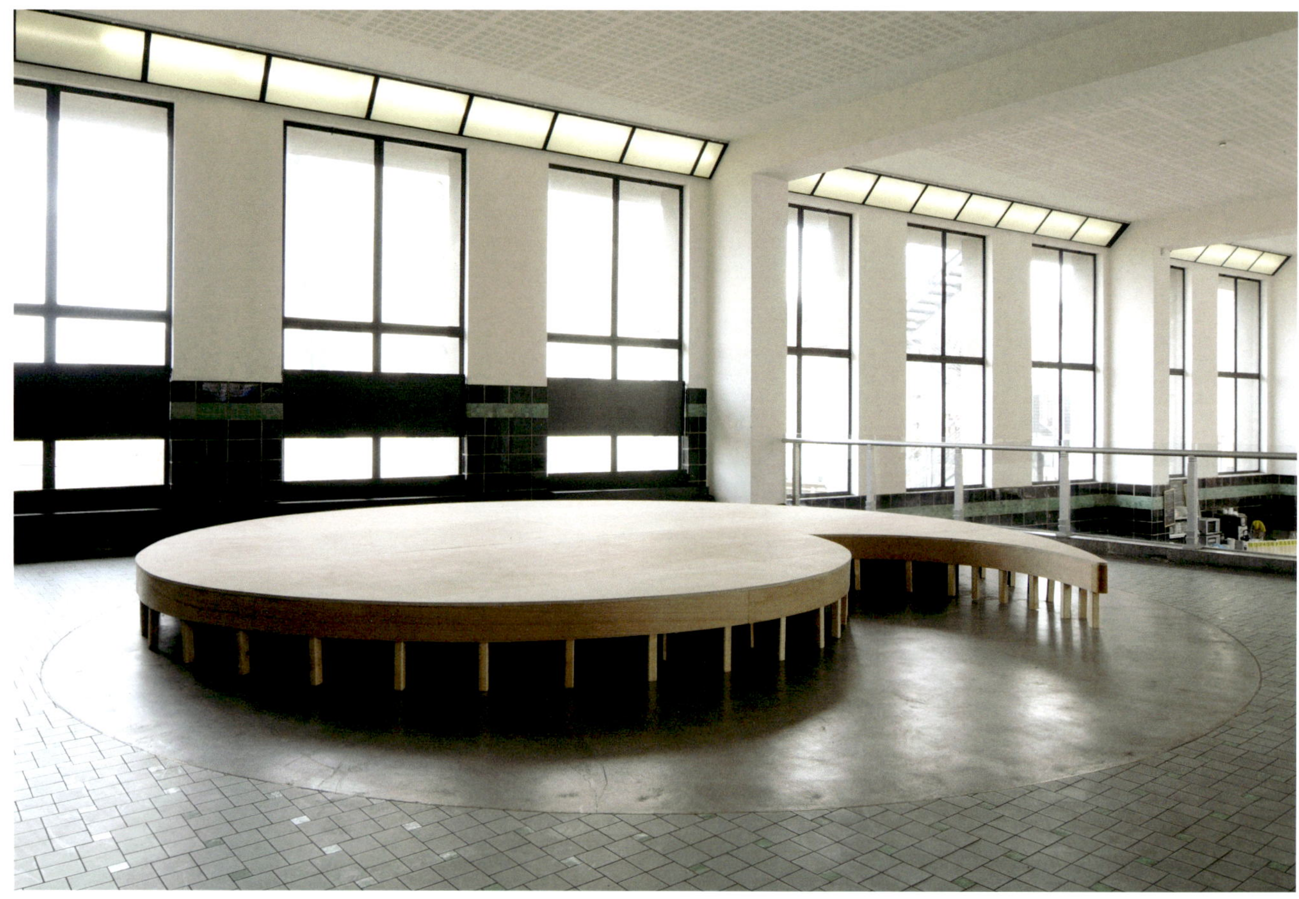

ABOVE *Score*, 2013. Plywood; 118⅛ in. diameter × 15¾ in. high (300 × 40 cm), *Experienz #2*, Wiels, Contemporary Art Centre, Brussels

OPPOSITE *Superficie Modulada, 1956 (Part 3)*, 2009. Gouache on canvas, sewn; 58 × 36 in. (147.3 × 91.4 cm). Private collection, New York

repeating, dynamic polyhedrons—the series both quotes and extends its modernist source. Crowner photocopied a black-and-white reproduction of Clark's modest painting, cropped and enlarged it five times, then divided it into its component shapes. To piece the work back together, she established a compositional process that reversed her initial dismantling. Each shape was painted onto canvas with gouache, cut out, and stitched back together with an industrial sewing machine. From the one work by Clark, Crowner created three paintings, gray-scale enlargements of details of the original—excerpts or quotes, if you will. Yet the result, as Crowner has said, is "no longer a Lygia Clark painting."[3] The final paintings cease to resemble the work of Clark and are clearly "Crowners," products of the recombinatory logic of twenty-first-century cut and paste. Yet the paintings remain recognizably *modernist* in their clarity of commitment to the power of line and form. The modular nature of Clark's Concretismo—the mid-twentieth-century Latin American school of geometric abstraction that built upon European Art Concret—anticipates and allows for Crowner's method, which unearths patterns and permutations that, in a sense, were already there.

II. Stage Presence

Clark would go on to abandon her two-dimensional "superficial modulations," proclaiming "the death of the plane" and shifting to work

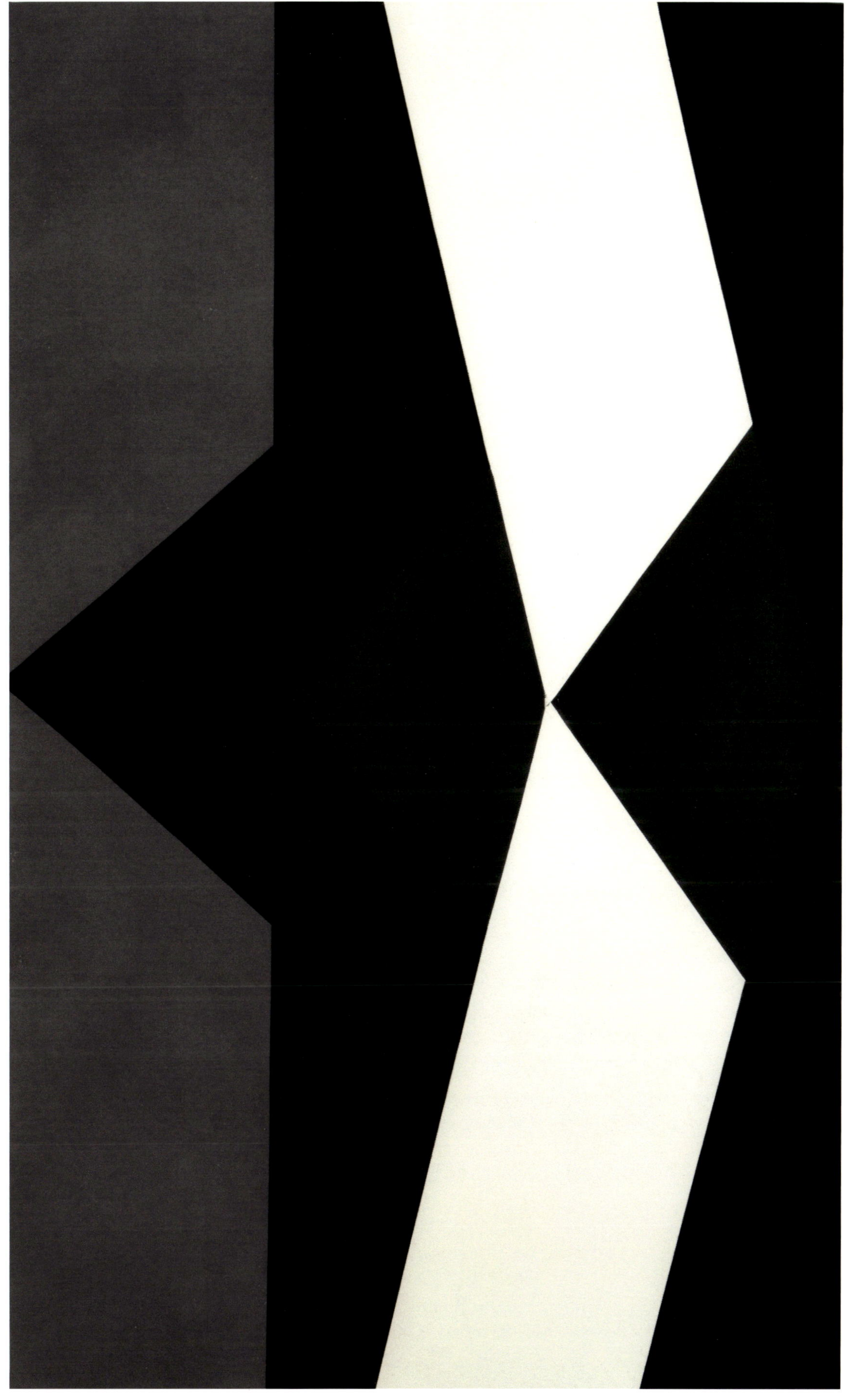

in three dimensions—in the same space-time as the viewer.[4] The Neo-Concretismo movement, which she cofounded in 1959, theorized the idea of an active spectator whose interaction with the artwork would determine its meaning. As fellow Neo-Concretist Hélio Oiticica argued, the artist "no longer [acts] as a creator for contemplation, but as an instigator for creation."[5] Crowner, too, began to reimagine her paintings in three dimensions in order to involve the viewer, whose presence would contribute to the work. While *Score*, as a standalone stage intended for performances, remains unique in her oeuvre, platforms have become an increasingly visible element within the exhibition installations that the artist devises to present her paintings. Over the last decade, the platform has moved beyond a display device to become a literal stage for performances by dancers and musicians.

As an architectural feature, the platform first appeared in a 2011 solo exhibition of paintings titled *Ballet Plastique*. Crowner's geometric abstractions on display were not modernist quotations but instead invoked theatrical models, building on a recent work that had unintentionally resembled curtains opening onto a stage. The artist thought of the paintings in *Ballet Plastique* "as backdrops, or proposals for backdrops, for an undefined performance or theatrical event."[6] The allusion to performance in the paintings was underscored by her decision to raise most of the gallery floor with a plywood dais. Visitors who wanted to examine Crowner's stitched canvases more closely were obliged to step onto this platform, eight inches off the ground. In doing so, viewers of *Ballet Plastique* became more visible to other visitors and, in turn, more aware of being viewed. With this foregrounding of attention onto the perceiving body, the paintings slid from focal point to backdrop, a foil to the onstage viewers who "assume the position of performers."[7]

Another way of expressing this mode of spectatorship is in quotation marks: the viewer became a "viewer," an actor consciously playing the role of beholder. The relationship between the viewer and the work of art was centered as a dynamic space of spectatorial self-consciousness. The viewer's position oscillated between subject and object—looking at the paintings, being looked at looking at the paintings. Multiple vectors of attention were produced through the simple addition of changing the floor to a stage.

In 2014, Crowner moved away from this bare-bones nod to activating the viewer—plywood, after all, was the preferred material of Minimalist sculptor Robert Morris, as well as of numerous relational artists of the 1990s. In its place, she developed a more aesthetically considered device to stress embodied viewing, one that was itself conceived as an extension of painting. Crowner began to reimagine the platform itself as a work of art—"a painting that you could walk on, stand on, dance on, or run across and lie down on."[8]

Invited to exhibit at Travesía Cuatro, housed in Mexican architect Luis Barragán's 1929 house Casa Franco in Guadalajara, Crowner decided to work with a local ceramic factory, Cerámica Suro. In the resulting show, *Interiores*, she replaced the plywood dais with a raised expanse of glazed white and cream terracotta tiles, connected by contrasting lines of dark grout. The raised sea of tiles, like frozen waves, began outside the gallery and flowed from room to room, asserting the floor as the dominant aesthetic gesture of the interior. The conspicuous gap between floor and walls also served to underscore Crowner's gesture as a "floor"—a self-conscious representation (or quotation) of a floor.

The tiled platform's assertive staginess, as well as the optical effect of its black-and-white hues, had the effect of making the walls recede into pale neutrality, along with the sewn raw-canvas paintings that hung upon them; for the most part, these subtle paintings announced themselves only through thin wooden frames painted with pops of blue or red.[9] But as the viewer walked across the tiles to study the paintings more carefully, the canvases reemerged into the foreground, their seams visible: in Crowner's words, "the painting comes alive as you move up next to it, realizing it is an object rather than an image."[10] The parallels between the floor and wall works then became apparent. Both are abstract wholes created out of individual parts, quietly drawing attention to the carefully wrought intersections of seams and joins.

The movement of the viewer, whose corresponding shifts of attention cause the works to fluctuate between figure and ground,

Installation view, *Ballet Plastique*, Galerie Catherine Bastide, Brussels, 2011

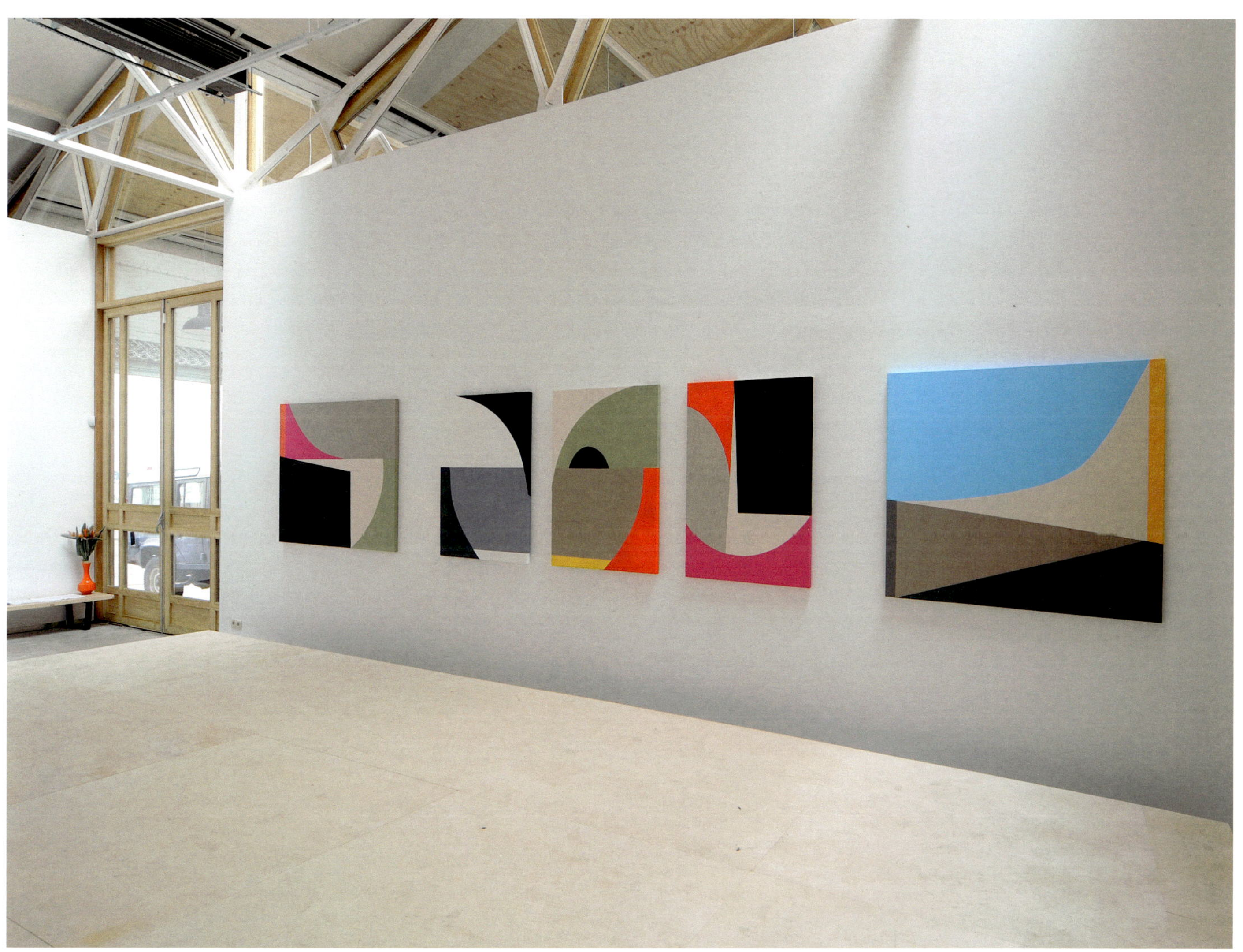

recalls a description of the early work of Venezuelan artist Jesús Rafael Soto by Italian semiotician Umberto Eco:

> These structures are kinetic because they use the spectator as a motor. They reflect the movement of the spectator as well as that of his eyes. They foresee his capacity to move and solicit his activity without constraining it. They are kinetic structures because they do not contain the forces that animate them, they borrow their dynamism from the spectator.[11]

It is only by moving through the display system of raised tiles to view the sparsely hung paintings that the viewer animates the work.

Crowner continued this interplay of figure and ground in her first solo museum exhibition in the United States, *Beetle in the Leaves* (Massachusetts Museum of Contemporary Art [Mass MoCA], North Adams, 2016). The title alludes to a mid-1960s house by the Italian architect Gio Ponti (Lo Scarabeo sotto la Foglia, or the Beetle under the Leaf), which features a distinctive interior designed by Nanda Vigo. The entire space—floors and walls alike—is smothered in white square tiles, lending a clinical mood to this mid-century home. Designed for an art collector, Vigo's tiled surface forms a backdrop—a stage—for the owner's collection of similarly monochrome abstractions.[12]

The centerpiece of Crowner's show at Mass MoCA was the nearly one-thousand-square-foot *Platform (Pentagon Leaves)* (2016), a raised expanse of hand-painted cement tiles in subtle shades of white, with the occasional lemon yellow or raw gray interrupting the pattern. Blanketing the floor like a thick litter of petals that have fluttered to the ground, it stopped just short of a freestanding L-shaped white wall upon which one painting was hung: the striking blue-and-white canvas *Rotated and Stretched Stems* (2016), which quotes a 1934 gouache by Sophie Taeuber-Arp.[13] Crowner's installation echoed Vigo's staging of the private art collection but also consciously displayed the viewer, whom the artist imagined becoming part of the composition.[14] At the same time, Crowner refrained from replicating the immersive environmentalism of Lo Scarabeo. Instead, as with *Interiores*, the tiled floor

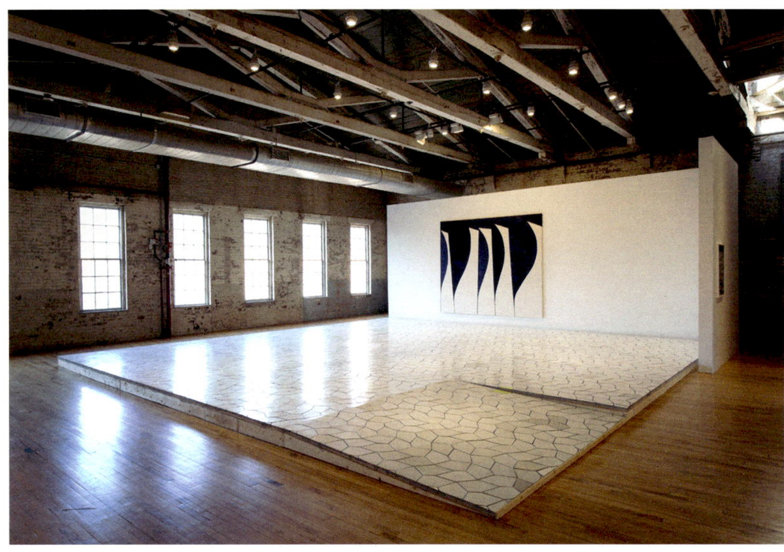

Installation view, *Beetle in the Leaves*, Massachusetts Museum of Contemporary Art, North Adams, MA, 2016

called attention to the existing environment—in this case, the brick walls and wooden floorboards of Mass MoCA's postindustrial hangar. One interior was set within another, a container within a container.

III. Action Painting

Alongside these experiments with floors and stages, Crowner began to reimagine what is hung perpendicular to them. In 2011—the same year as her first wooden platform—Crowner made *Curtain (Vidas Perfectas)*. This work was once again a quotation. She adapted a theater curtain by Polish artist Maria Jarema, originally made in 1956 for Kraków's avant-garde Cricot 2 theater. Jarema's curtain is a jumble of geometric shapes crafted from pieces of linen that are stitched together; except for its pale and faded palette, it already resembles a work by Crowner. Fascinated by this curtain's clear relationship to abstract painting, Crowner re-created it in bold hues of pink, red, yellow, and black, with the goal of employing her version in a theatrical context as well as exhibiting it independently as a work of art.

Performance view, featuring *Curtain (Vidas Perfectas)*, 2012. Serpentine Gallery, London, 2012

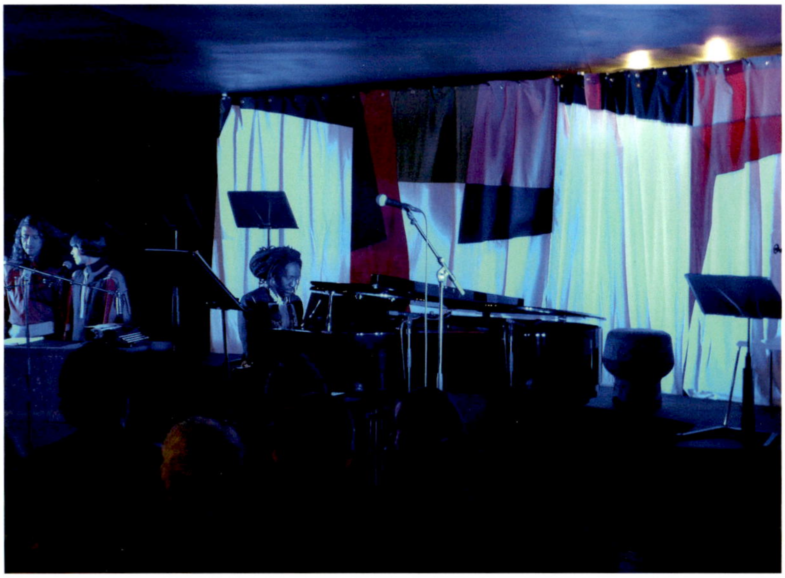

Traditionally, the role of the curtain that hangs from the proscenium arch is to separate the audience from the stage, the real from the imaginary, but Crowner immediately transformed its use by placing her *Curtain* firmly within the theatrical realm. The work first appeared as an element of a set design for Alex Waterman's production of *Vidas Perfectas* (2011), a Spanish-language adaptation of Robert Ashley's television opera *Perfect Lives* (1983) that premiered at the Irondale Center in Brooklyn. By moving her painting onstage—where it served as a backdrop for the actors and a ground for English subtitles—Crowner changed its relationship to viewers. Seated at a distance, audience members watched her work in relation to the actors who performed before it for far longer than the normal viewing time of a painting in a gallery.

The following year, as the opera production toured, Crowner remade the linen curtain in sturdier canvas, renamed it *Kurtyna Teatru (After Maria Jarema)*, and exhibited it alone as an artwork—moving it back into the foreground and the space-time of the viewer.[15] But Crowner then invited dancers to perform in front of *Kurtyna Teatru* in the gallery space, continuing the curtain's shifting status between figure and ground.[16] Even as a backdrop, however, the curtain played a quietly determining role in these performances, which were specifically choreographed in response to it. In Stockholm, choreographer and dancer Anna Pehrsson created physical movements that echoed the angles in the two-dimensional work, while in Warsaw, performer Iza Szostak identified a rhythm in the curtain's geometric shapes, layering her own "dynamic form" atop them.[17]

The result is another quotation of a quotation, as Crowner cites Jarema and the choreographers cite Crowner, translating her abstract forms into the language of movement. Although these performances place the work at one remove from gallery visitors, interrupting their field of vision, at these moments it is the dancer's presence—not the viewer—that is the kinetic dynamo of the work. The dancer becomes a kind of stand-in for the ideal integration of the viewer.

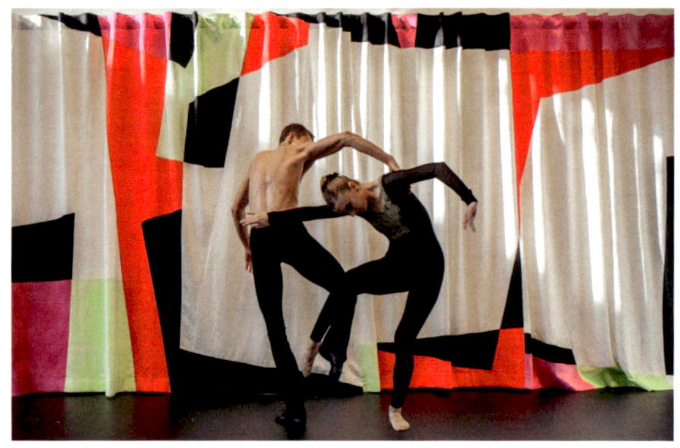

Boston Ballet II members performing before *Curtain (Vidas Perfectas)*, 2012. Museum of Fine Arts, Boston, 2015

IV. Pattern Recognition

If *Curtain (Vidas Perfectas)* is both an autonomous work and a backdrop, implicitly delineating a performance area, Crowner's Mass MoCA exhibition made this explicit, as the tilework *Platform (Pentagon Leaves)* and the canvas *Rotated and Stretched Stems* together created a display apparatus for various performances. When contemporary music group Bang on a Can gave a recital, for example, the audience sat on the tiles, sharing the same raised space as the performers. For *Post Tree* (2016), a collaboration between composer James Hoff and choreographer and dancer Carolyn Schoerner, museum visitors sat in chairs in front of the same platform.

Post Tree marked a decisive development in Crowner's practice, bringing together analogues for her compositional process into one interdisciplinary collaboration. Where Crowner uses scissors and a sewing machine to disassemble and reconfigure preexisting works, Hoff broke down digital audio files into source code and then added in the code of computer malware to disrupt the music's regular rhythms. Again, Crowner's work was formative. Hoff describes his music composition, also titled *Post Tree*, as "a very loose interpretation [of] Sarah's work" and says he "focused a lot on textures and utilized a lot of prefabricated templates for trap and other forms of dance music."[18] The title itself comes from military history. During World War I, observation posts on the battlefield were camouflaged as blasted-out trees; an Observation Post Tree (simply known as an OP Tree) was a mimetic representation of a *specific* tree, which would be cut down overnight and replaced.[19] Hoff's music begins with a high-pitched buzz, sounding like a swarm of electronic cicadas, while the 808 drumbeats repeat the rat-a-tat-tat of a machine gun.

Schoerner's choreography was created in response to both the exhibition *and* the music. "I tried to interpret their works into dance form," she explains, by employing "distinctive, repetitive patterns."[20] For example, one recurring movement is the *battement tendu*. From fifth position, the dancer's front foot slides forward to extend *en pointe*, then slides back to fifth position; this happens twice, before her back foot does the same in the opposite direction. Repeated over and again in time to a regular beat, quietly ticking like a clock, the mechanical movements begin to resemble the swinging arm of a metronome. The *battement tendu* is a fundamental movement in ballet—another prefabricated template, like Crowner's modernist sources and Hoff's trap MP3s.

A flash of crimson against the white tiles, Schoerner's curved chest and lifted arms repeat the dark curves of *Rotated and Stretched Stems*—another oscillation of figure and ground. In less visible ways too, Crowner's work led to choreographic decisions, as Schoerner was compelled to take the atypical stage into consideration. Dancers usually perform on sprung floors (to spare their ankle joints), not glazed ceramic surfaces, and they don't ordinarily need to avoid movements where their "feet might get stuck in the small dips between tiles."[21]

While Hoff's contemporary music and Schoerner's classical choreography are both distinctively different from Crowner's modern aesthetic, their translation of her core concerns into music and movement served to underline the centrality of quotation, pattern, and repetition. The performance brought out elements of Crowner's installation that viewers might have missed, slowing down its reception from a few minutes to twenty. But the performance occurred only once. The next day, the museum was silent again, except for the polite

Performance view, *Post Tree*, on the occasion of *Beetle in the Leaves*, Massachusetts Museum of Contemporary Art, North Adams, MA, 2016. Performance and choreography by dancer Carolyn Schoerner and music by James Hoff

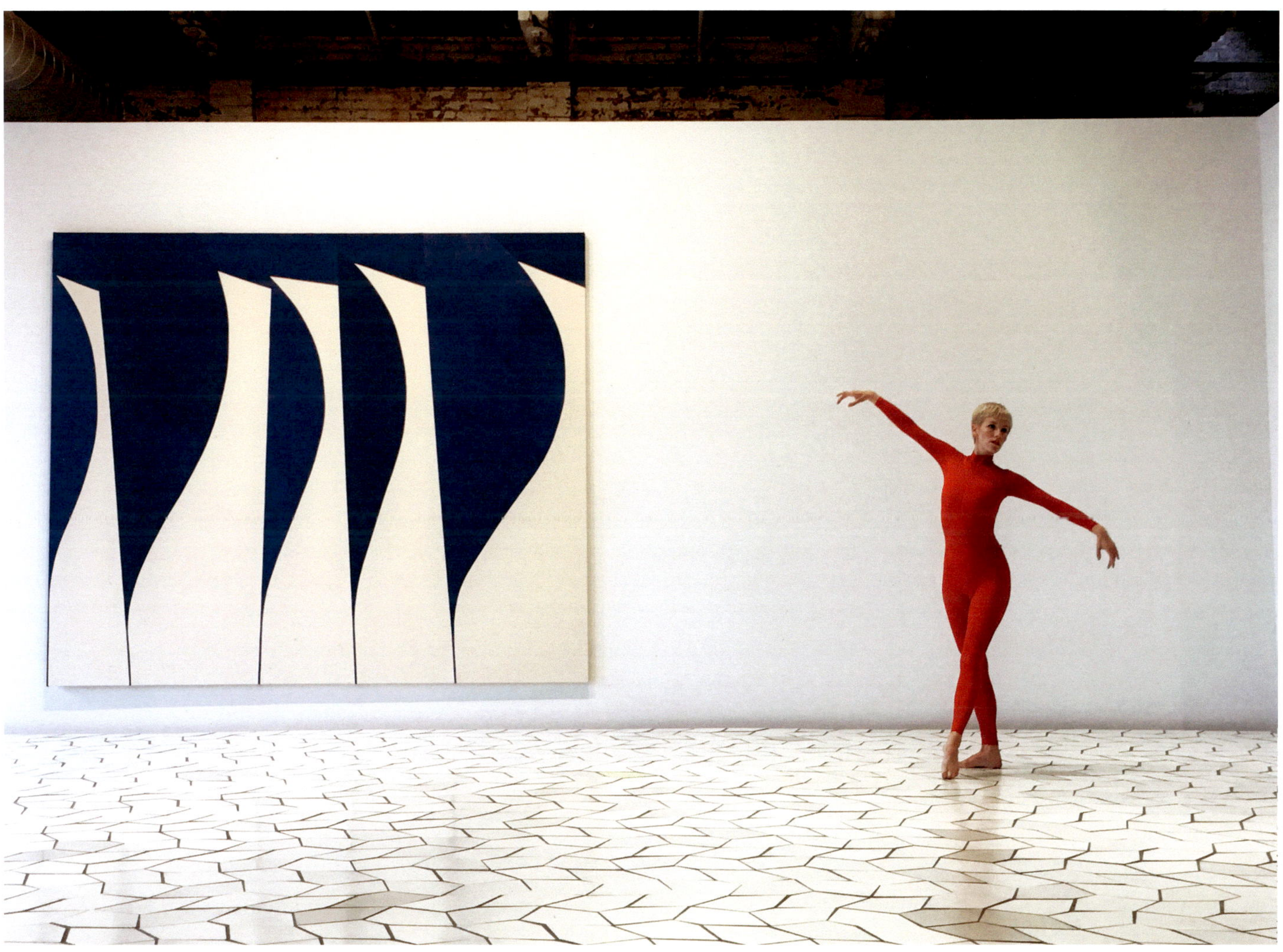

murmuring of visitors who carefully made their way onto the tiled stage before moving on to the rest of the exhibition.

V. Coup de théâtre

It was only a matter of time before Crowner's small-scale experiments with theatrical décor drew the attention of the professional dance world. In 2018, the artist was invited to collaborate with choreographer Jessica Lang on a new piece for New York's American Ballet Theatre (ABT) that would become *Garden Blue* (2018). While prominent artists have often been invited to design sets and costumes for dance—think of Pablo Picasso for Léonide Massine, Isamu Noguchi for Martha Graham, Robert Rauschenberg for Merce Cunningham—their designs either responded to the choreography or were developed in parallel. For Lang, by contrast, Crowner's design came first: "Sarah's work was the subject of the ballet," explains the choreographer.[22] In part, this was a necessary outcome of ABT's accelerated rehearsal process—only five weeks leading up to the premiere, which meant that elements like décor would have to be preplanned.[23]

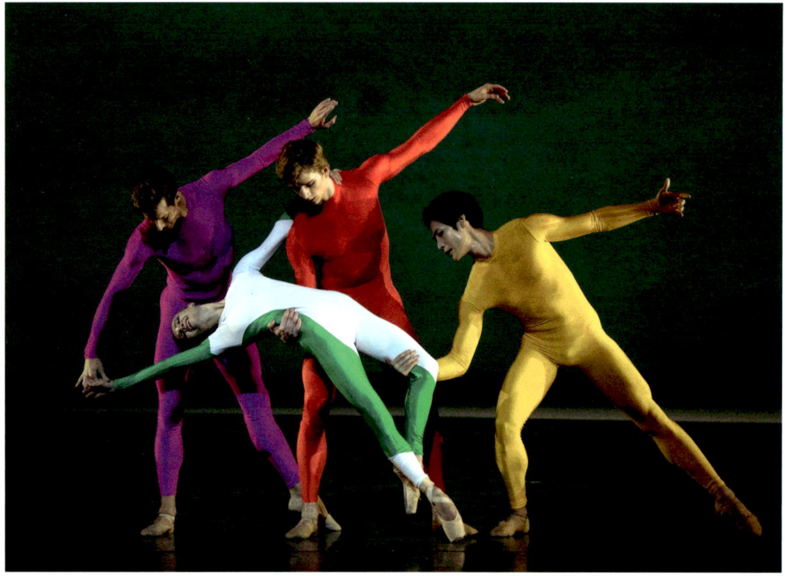

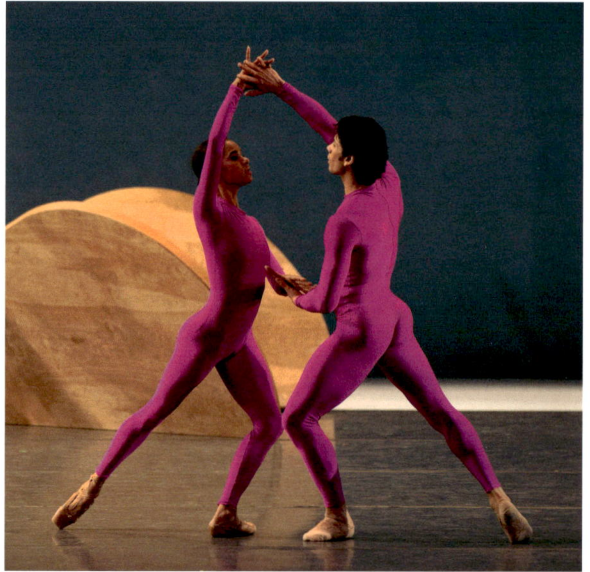

LEFT Blaine Hoven, Christine Shevchenko, Aran Bell, and Joo Won Ahn in *Garden Blue*, 2018. Sets and costumes by Sarah Crowner, choreography by Jessica Lang. American Ballet Theatre, New York

RIGHT Misty Copeland and Herman Cornejo in *Garden Blue*, 2018. Sets and costumes by Sarah Crowner, choreography by Jessica Lang. American Ballet Theatre, New York

OPPOSITE *Sliced Shapes, Violet Background*, 2018. Acrylic on canvas, sewn; 82 × 78 in. (208.3 × 198.1 cm). The Nancy A. Nasher and David J. Haemisegger Collection, Dallas, TX

Lang gave Crowner carte blanche, steering her only in terms of time and budget. This time, Crowner turned not to art history for inspiration but to nature, imagining a garden filled with flowers (dancers in brightly colored unitards of yellow, red, and fuchsia) and a weed (a single performer in green and white). The backdrop is a wash of blue, except for a narrow triangle that extends the length of one side, like a stalk or a leaf reaching for the sky. Early on, Crowner hoped to build a platform that would sit on the stage, but this was quickly deemed unfeasible. Instead, the artist designed three large props that resemble the winged seed pods of maple trees, often called helicopters or whirligigs because of the way they spin as they fall to the ground.

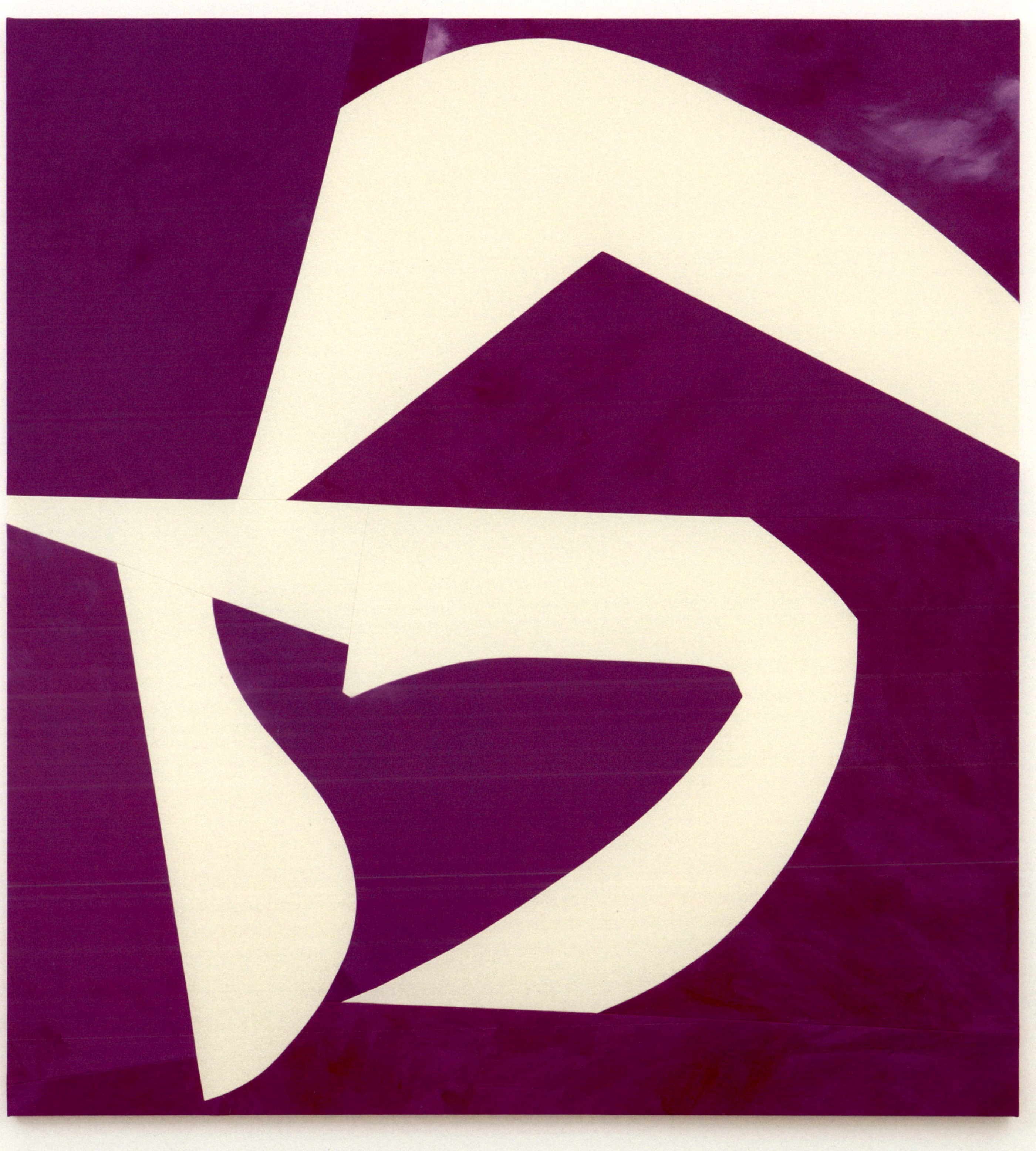

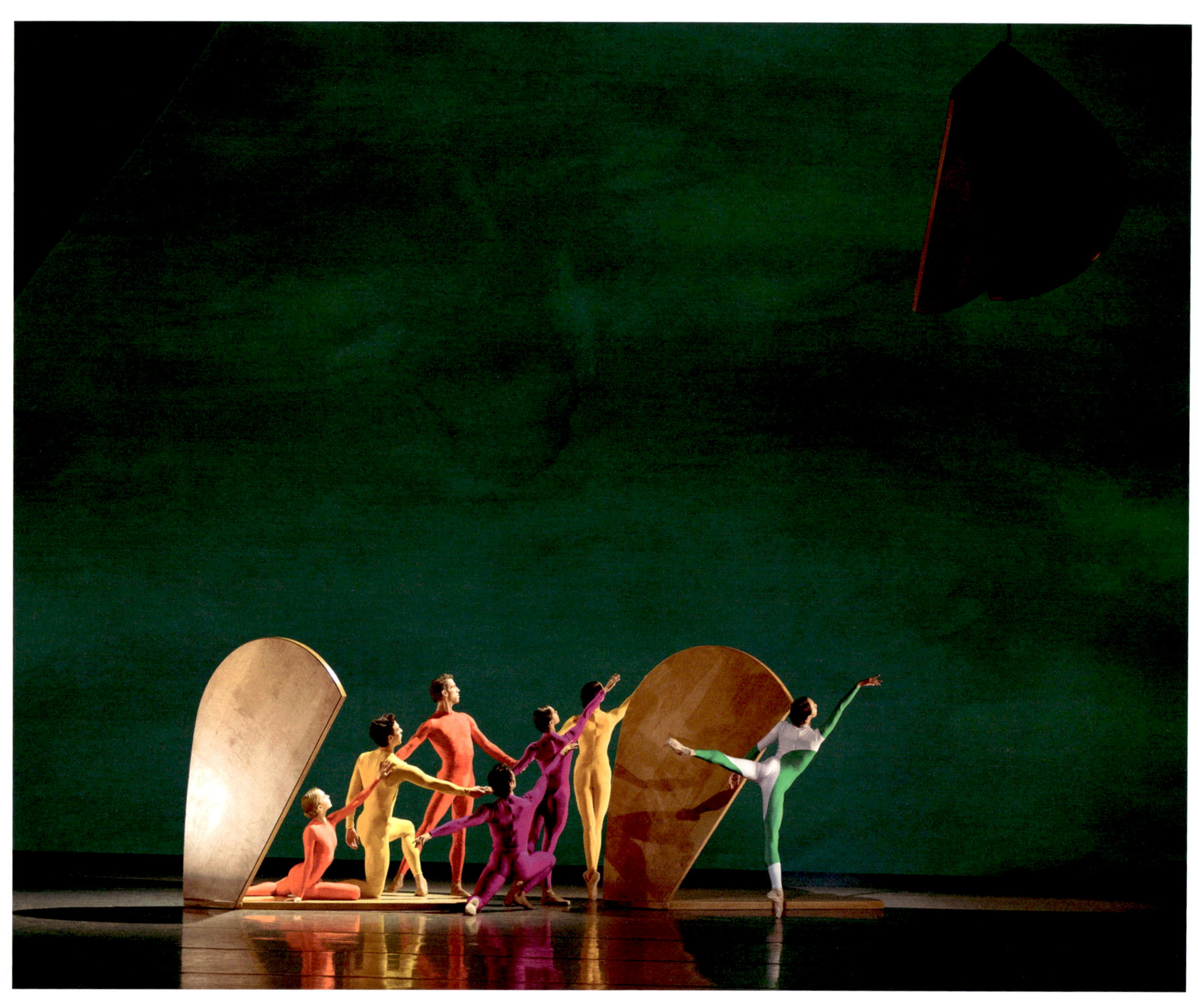

Scene from *Garden Blue*, 2018. Sets and costumes by Sarah Crowner, choreography by Jessica Lang. American Ballet Theatre, New York

Constructed of wood veneers over foamcore, Crowner's pods are sturdy but light, allowing a range of interactions between dancer and prop. While the sculptural forms cannot be manipulated like Lygia Clark's *Bichos* (1961–64), which they superficially evoke, the dancers continually turn and lift the pods, lying down on a flat side or sheltering in the crevice; one pod hangs down from above, open wings slowly twirling in the air. Although the ground directs the figures' movement, the former doesn't upstage the latter—as the old Broadway saying goes, no one ever walked out of the theater humming the scenery.[24]

Garden Blue could be seen as the culmination of Crowner's interrogations into theater—as the artist states, "it was no longer an 'experiment' or a 'proposal.'"[25] Instead, it is best understood as a lateral move into another discipline. Crowner has often spoken admiringly of artists of the historical avant-garde who worked in theater and design, without a "hierarchy among the practices."[26] One such example is Taeuber-Arp, who, as Crowner has said, "started her career as a dancer and went on to make abstract paintings, prints, stage sets, marionettes, sculptures, and architectural designs; she embroidered pillows (which she had framed and hung as paintings) and designed costumes."[27]

Rather than being the inevitable destination (and conceptual dead end) of Crowner's practice, the sets for *Garden Blue* have circled back into her art practice. For a 2019 exhibition in Hong Kong, *Paintings for the Stage*, Crowner hired the Chinese scenic painter and set designer Pink Lam to create a wall painting—a backdrop of cloudy white and blue—on which the artist hung a single work. More recently, she has created a series of domestic-scaled sculptures shaped like seed pods, such as *Wings after a Ballet (Sodalita)* (2020), carved in one piece from richly colored veined marble. Coming full circle and continuing onward—like the confidently spiraling *Score*—in these recent works, sumptuous in their simplicity of form and materials, Crowner could be seen as finally quoting herself.

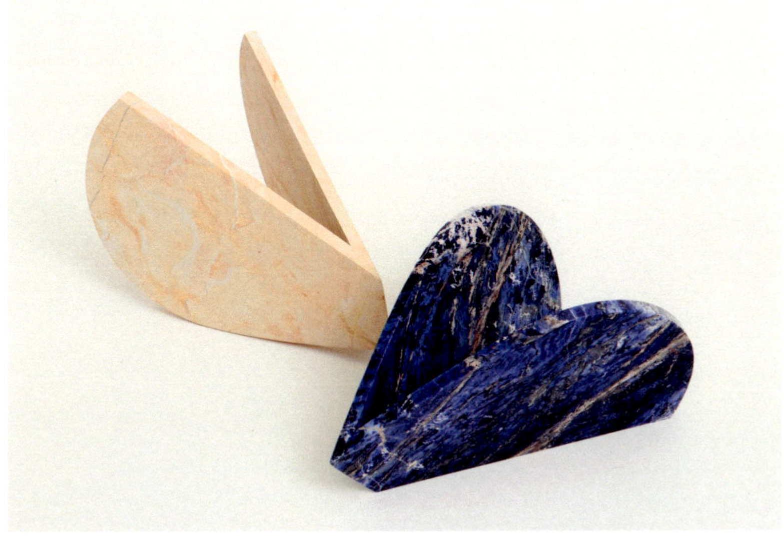

Wings after a Ballet (Sodalita) and *Wings after a Ballet (Golden Tepexi)*, 2020. Sodalita and Golden Tepexi; each 11¾ × 9⅞ × 11¾ in. (30 × 25.1 × 30 cm). Private collection

NOTES

1. The four-day-long *Experienz #2: Materializing the Social* featured "performances, choreographed actions, talks, lecture-performances, to-perform artworks, concerts and young people's workshops." See press kit and program, www.wiels.org/uploads/experienz_press.pdf.
2. Crowner, in Lauren O'Neill-Butler, "Interviews: Sarah Crowner," *Artforum* online, September 5, 2011, www.artforum.com/interviews/sarah-crowner-talks-about-her-exhibitions-in-new-york-and-brussels-28886.
3. Crowner, in "In Conversation: Sarah Crowner with Tom McGlynn," *The Brooklyn Rail*, February 2021, www.brooklynrail.org/2021/02/art/SARAH-CROWNER-with-Tom-McGlynn.
4. Lygia Clark's essay "The Death of the Plane" (*A Morte do Plano*) was published in 1960.
5. Hélio Oiticica, "Posição e programa" (1966), quoted in Alexander Alberro, *Abstraction in Reverse: The Reconfigured Spectator in Mid-Twentieth-Century Latin American Art* (Chicago: University of Chicago Press, 2017), 2.
6. Crowner, in O'Neill-Butler, "Interviews."
7. Ibid.
8. Crowner, in "In Conversation."
9. Crowner made tiled floor works for two other exhibitions in 2014 as well, in New York and Brussels.
10. Crowner, quoted in Bartholomew Ryan, "Medium as Medium," in Susan Cross and Sarah Crowner, eds., *Sarah Crowner* (North Adams, MA: Massachusetts Museum of Contemporary Art; and New York: DelMonico Books / Prestel, 2017), 30.
11. Alberro, *Abstraction in Reverse*, 114.
12. The collection of Giobatta Meneguzzo largely comprised works by the Zero Group, of which Nanda Vigo was a founding member.
13. In *Rotated and Stretched Stems* (2016), Crowner's quotation is not only rearranged but purposely warped. As the exhibition curator describes, "she photographed the book upside down, with just a small corner of the work visible, its original shape distorting as it arced over the curled page." Susan Cross, "Beetle in the Leaves," in Cross and Crowner, *Sarah Crowner*, 38.
14. Crowner, in Ryan, "Medium as Medium," 30.
15. Crowner also made another canvas version for the touring production, which she titled simply *Curtains* (2012), because she found the linen too "droopy."
16. And perhaps middle ground: at the Institute of Contemporary Art, Philadelphia, the original *Curtain (Vidas Perfectas)* was actually deployed *as* a curtain, covering a large window in the second-floor gallery, to create a more focused environment for a reading room.
17. For Crowner's description of Pehrsson's choreography at Galerie Nordenhake (2012), see her "Sideways Glances: Painting and Dancing," in Bill Bissell and Linda Caruso Haviland, eds., *The Sentient Archive: Bodies, Performance, and Memory* (Middletown, CT: Wesleyan University Press, 2018), 143–44. For a description of Iza Szostak's performance at Zachęta National Gallery of Art (2013), see "Zwiedzanie Wystawy I Performans," zacheta.art.pl/pl/kalendarz/zwiedzanie-wystawy-i-performans. In addition, when *Curtain (Vidas Perfectas)* was exhibited at the Museum of Fine Arts, Boston, in 2014, the Boston Ballet II company was invited to perform in front of it.
18. James Hoff, email to the author, April 3, 2021.
19. The first OP Trees were created in 1915 by the French army's camouflage unit, overseen by Parisian society painter Lucien-Victor Guirand de Scévola (who is also credited with coining the term *camouflage*). See Hanna Rose Shell, *Hide and Seek: Camouflage, Photography, and the Media of Reconnaissance* (New York: Zone Books, 2012).
20. Carolyn Schoerner, email to the author, April 15, 2021.
21. Schoerner, email to the author.
22. Jessica Lang, email to the author, June 26, 2021.
23. Lang, email to the author.
24. The backdrop is, of course, literally upstage from the performers.
25. Crowner, email to the author, January 31, 2021.
26. Crowner, quoted in Bartholomew Ryan, "Painting as Score: Sarah Crowner on *Format*," *Sightlines* (Walker Art Center) online magazine, November 20, 2012, walkerart.org/magazine/painting-as-score-sarah-crowner-on-format.
27. Crowner, "The Blind Man," Triple Canopy website, 2012, www.canopycanopycanopy.com/contents/the_blind_man. In addition, scholars have commented on the similarities between Taeuber-Arp's early compositions and choreographer Rudolf von Laban's Kinetography, a form of dance notation that employs abstract symbols. For more on this, see Flora L. Brandl, "On a Curious Chance Resemblance: Rudolf von Laban's Kinetography and the Geometric Abstractions of Sophie Taeuber-Arp," *Arts* 9, no. 1 (2020): 15, mdpi.com/2076-0752/9/1/15/htm.

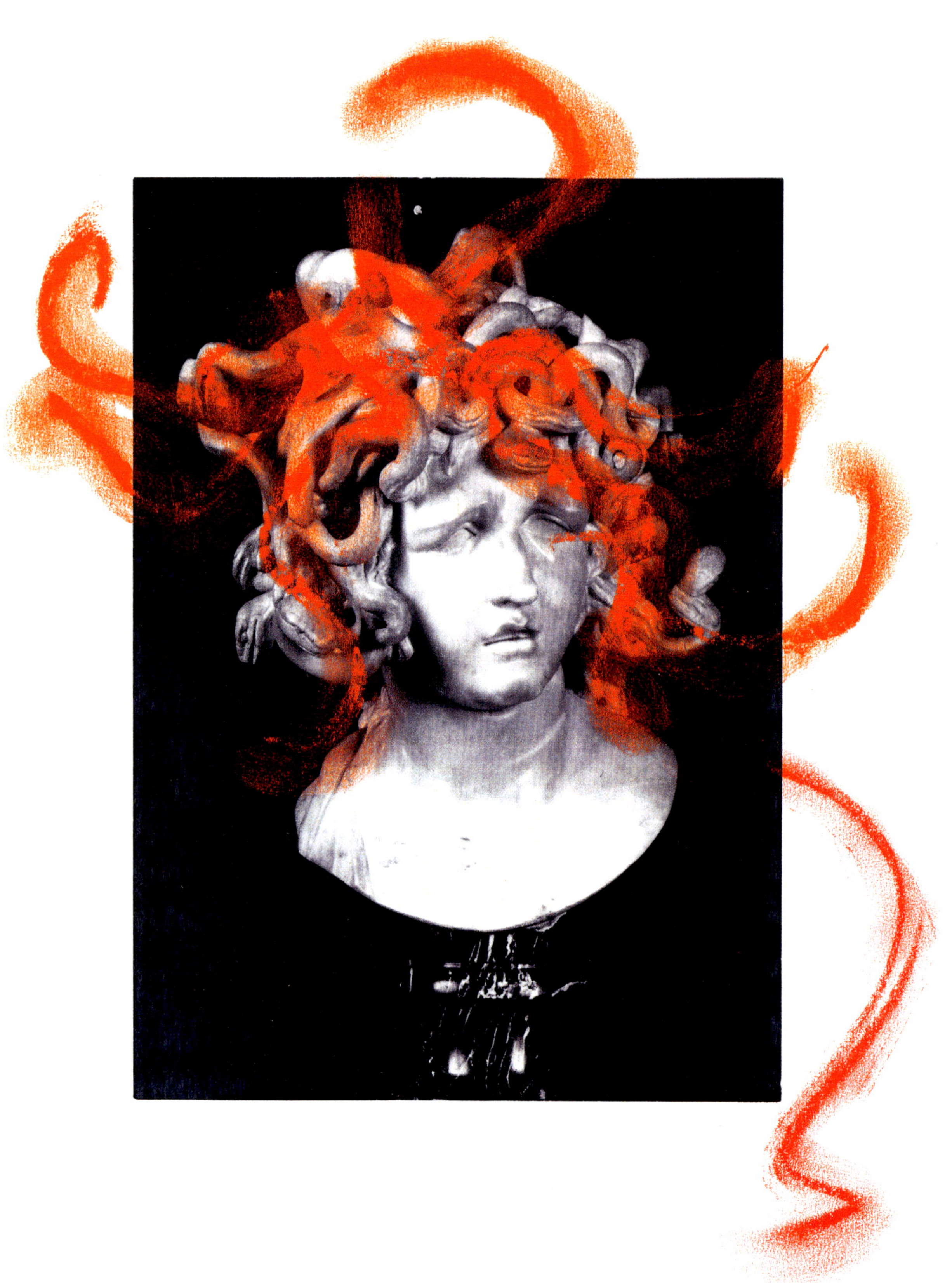

Quinn Latimer

Score for Three Snakes

First Snake (pre-litany)

The snake as a symbol of healing in a broken world or the snake as violence, for healing "naturally" suggests the destruction that must happen before it can take place. The snake as a symbol of the fluidity of form and the endlessness of matter. The snake as mouth, as consumer, consumption, consummation, construction. The snake as loop, as refrain, as algorithm, as repetition. The snake as sleight of hand, as mirror image, as surface for projection, as stage and some serpentine movement across it. The snake as trick pony. The snake as image-system. The snake as art history and collective memory. The snake as politics and political history, as iconography, as nonviolence, as symbolic sacrifice, as irrigation and lines both liquid and electric. The snake as symbolic power. The snake as art object. The snake as architecture. The snake as temporal affect and theory. The snake as ludic song for justice. The snake a snake—for real this time. The snake as time.

Untitled, 2020. Pastel on printed paper; 11 × 8½ in. (27.9 × 21.6 cm). Collection of the artist

Second Snake (body)

You should have seen it coming: sidewinding, its eyes like a colon, its teeth some semicolon, its body a series of—what—commas. If the painter works the wall, the ceiling, the floor like a score, her grammar of forms as serpentine and levitating as some algorithm borrowed from both the moderns and the ancients, to what timeworn surface should we apply our analysis? The cool concrete or cold tile or tight canvas, the warm wood planks of the kitchen or forested terrace, the pebbled contours of some holding wall? Holding what, though, not our laconic, slithering bellies. Coolly sliding over each surface, as our hands do. You think, you see: skins or sculptures, waters or worlds. Or painting. Such curved bodies and their glacial antecedents; the lake and the concave belly beneath, for instance. And the world below that. You should have seen it coming. The snake's *s* indicates levels: under world, over world, spirit world, another world. Meanwhile your body an *s* swiping the grass or the river of grass, its blue and green waters, red and black reflections. The snake is holding you, you always knew this. The one you held in your wet palm in the mini-mall as a shaking child, the one you wrote as a mute adult on the ancient island path, the serpent's lime-green limber body coiling and unspooling like electricity under your mineral gaze. The snake instructs: I am the upper limit. It sings, in a loop, as refrain: I am the lower limit. Look at my likeness, my levels of. An armature for the world: space and image, architectonic and art history, cosmology and infrastructure and language. All knowledge forms: pre-litany, body, coda. Some switchback trail, not snakelike but actual animal. The snake says: Level up. It sings its soft pigments as iridescence, its hard scales as transparent.

Third Snake (coda)

In the photograph, the spectators lean into the enormous bird sculpture, its graphic, kaleidoscopic surface exerting some hypnotic and gravitational pull, turning their human bodies into a sketch of ugly, perplexed wanting. In another image, glistening fish are laid out at market, in repeated lines just touching, all tightly woven textile or electrified score, ambient and all over. Like the outdoor ceiling, near the water, in which tiles loop and crest and arch and glitch, blue as some skin. Some skin. In each image I see the snake's scales slide past, offering the body of the world, on loop, from above and below. In the paintings, though, there is some glitch: the scales are like teeth, excised from the mouth of the world. The serpent's heavy body, all integument, is fragmented, in close-up. It is flat and graphic as the snake's bite. Well. In an early poem, you wrote about the image of two black eels gleaming in a bowl placed next to the photographer's blurred body. Inside their porcelain, the eels were two black rainbows coiled to match the curve of their perimeter. You asked: Whose hands hold this picture? Whose eyes? You wrote: The coiled eels circle the blue water of my iris, tighten around the black pupil at the shrinking center of my world. So. Should that still hold true, so should this: The serpentine body is a poetics, a sentence, sacred medicine, bird, fish, eel, image, a ceiling, a limit. The snake might be a bowl, ancestral, and a silvering photograph, postwar. It is a world, worlds. It is a river. Two men float down it. Violence. Their bodies are found in the flooded forest on the snake-river's banks. Their loved ones say: They have moved to another level of the world. We mourn them, our mourning song as long and looped and medicinal as the snake's sentence, its expert wish for justice. The snake holds the men in its coils, its tendrils. The snake as time, as memory. Take off your skin, the snake instructs them. Remake the world.

FOLLOWING PAGES Installation view, *Plant Based*, Galerie Nordenhake, Berlin, 2021

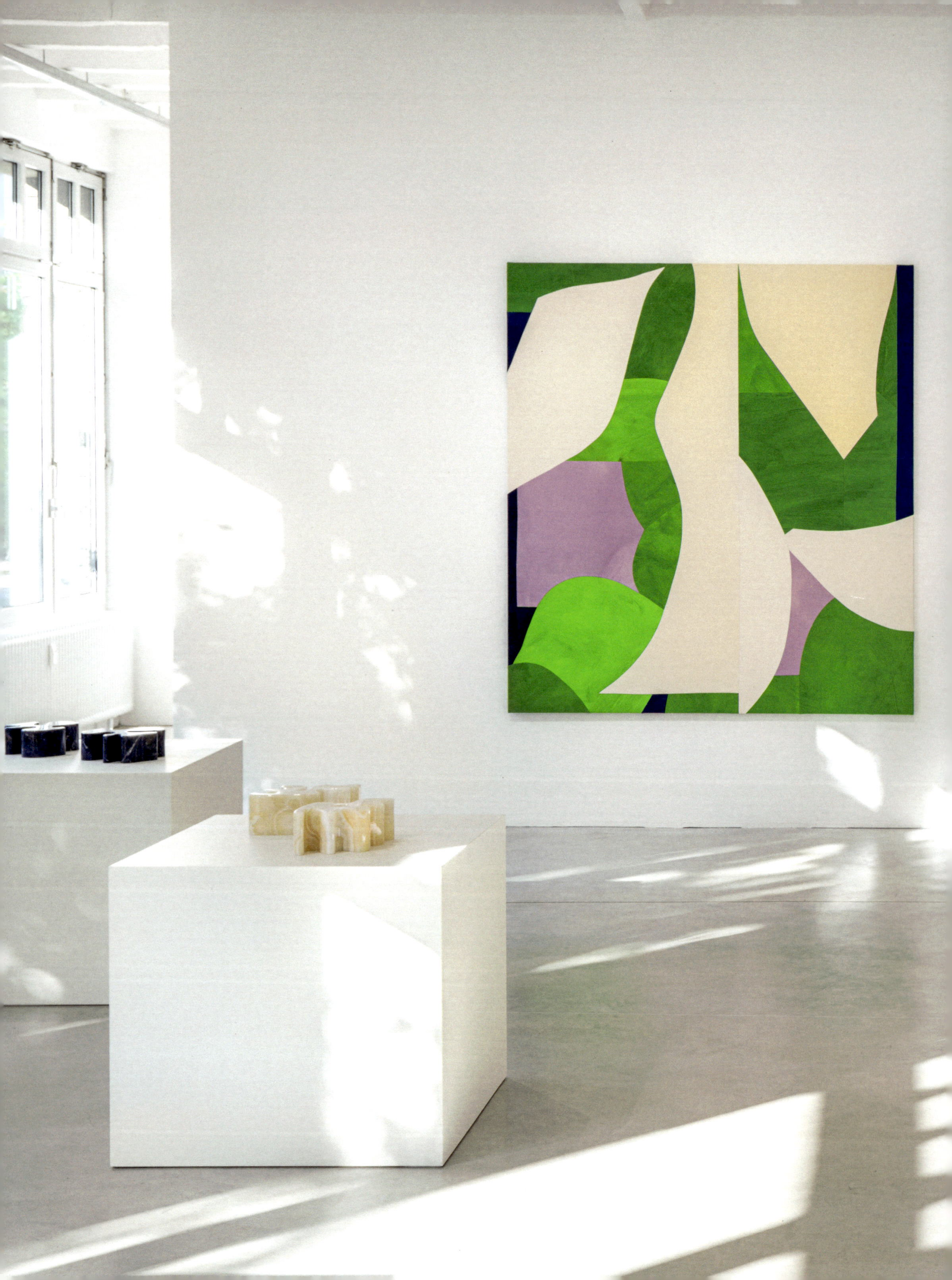

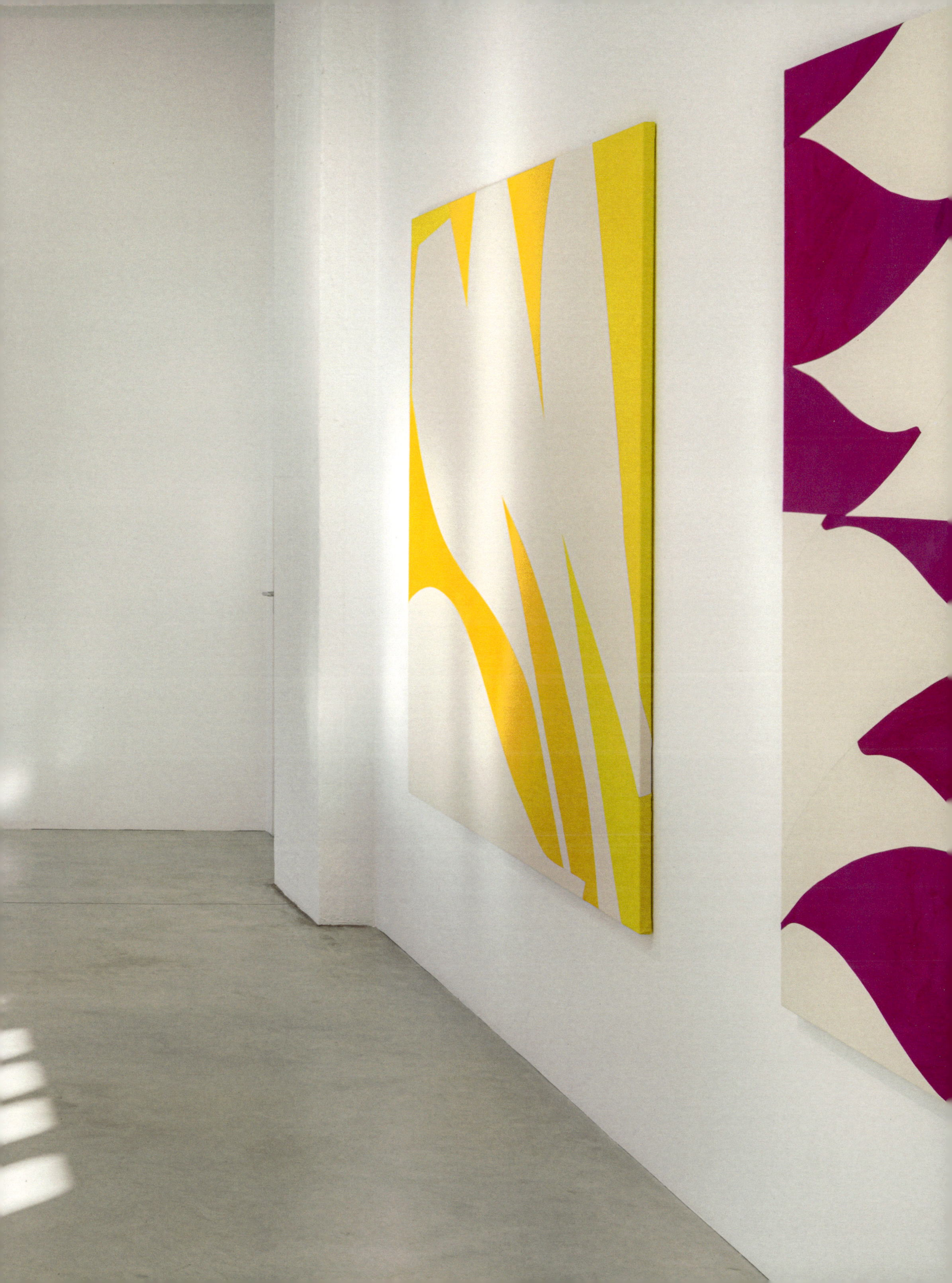

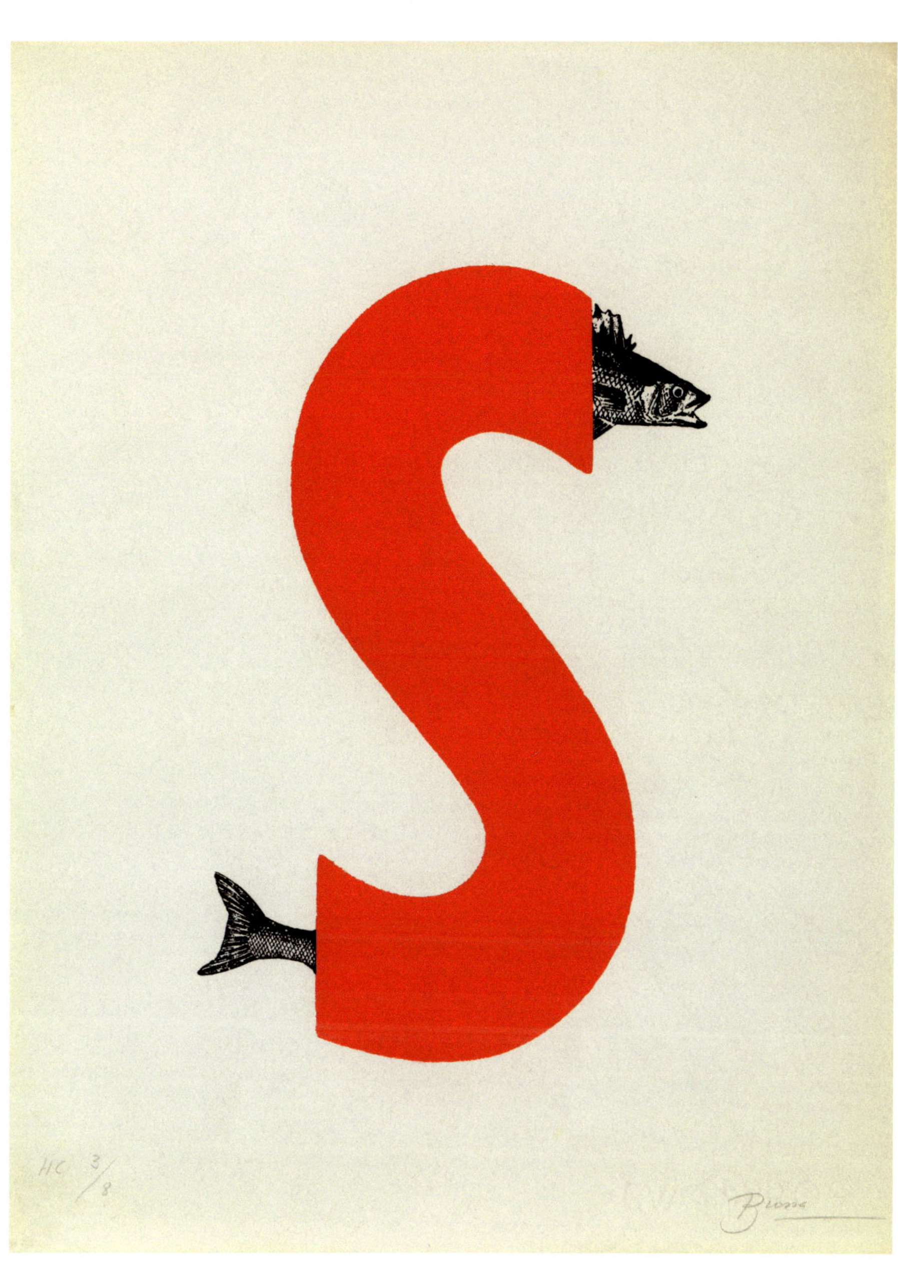

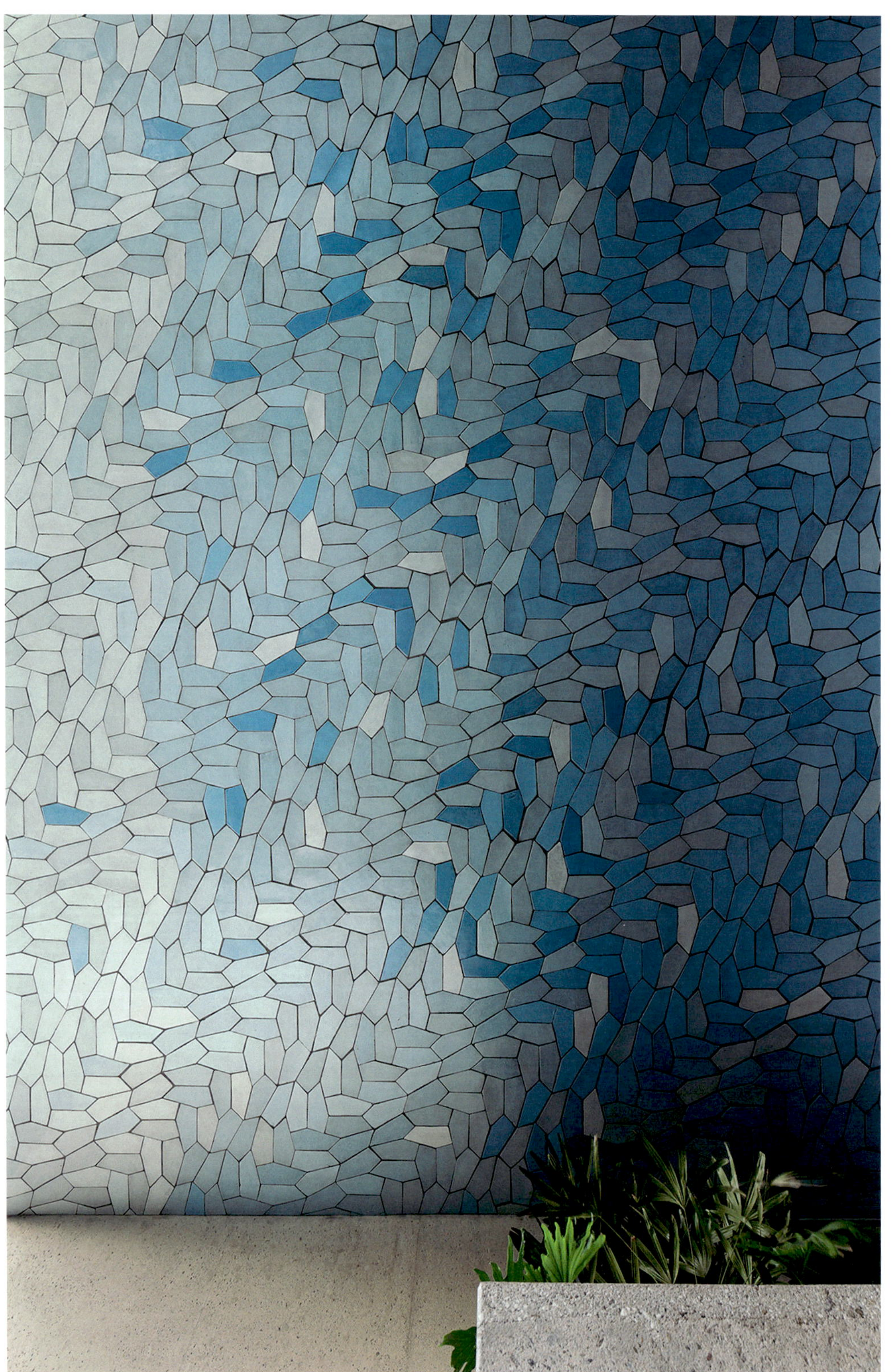

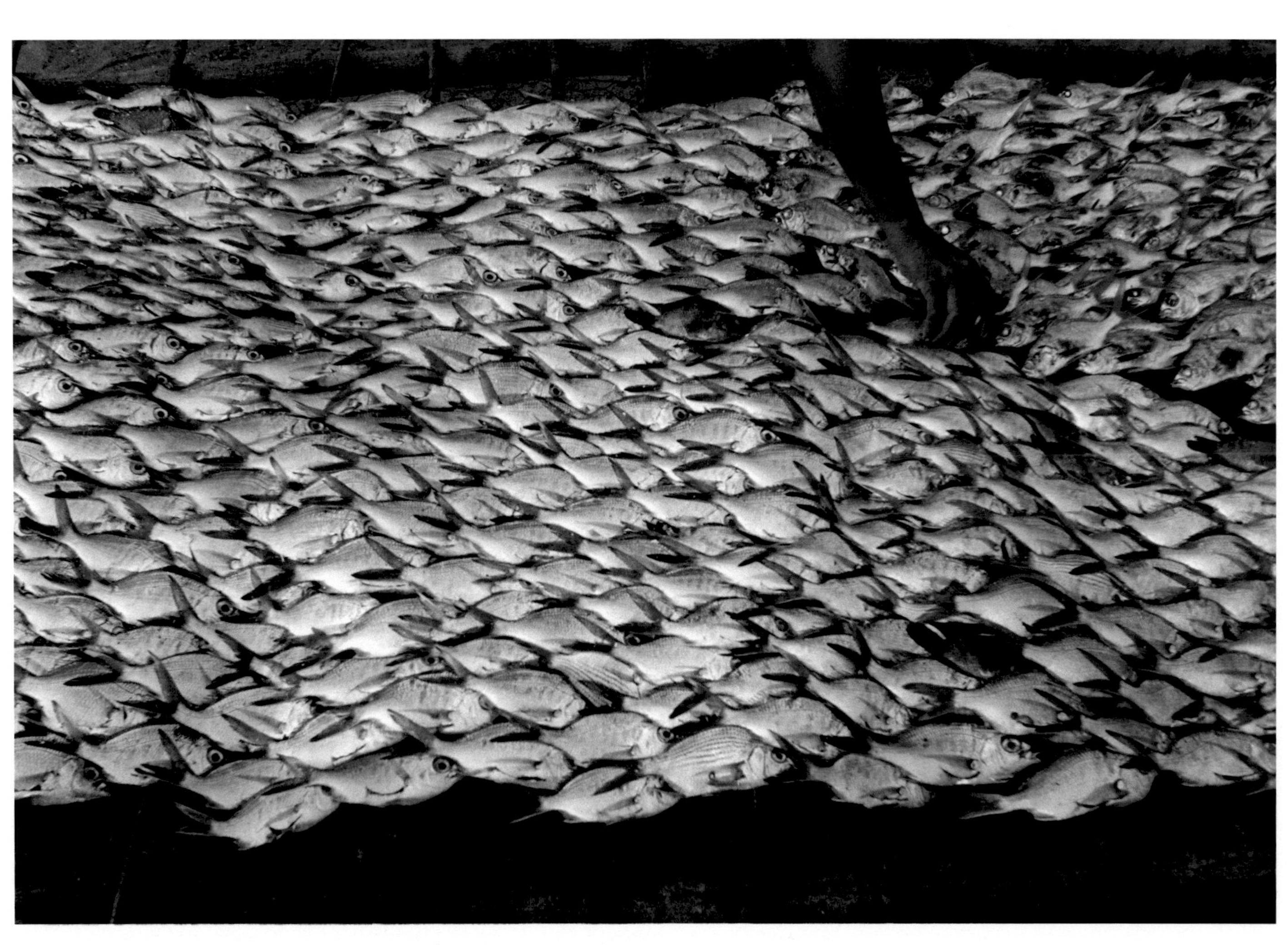

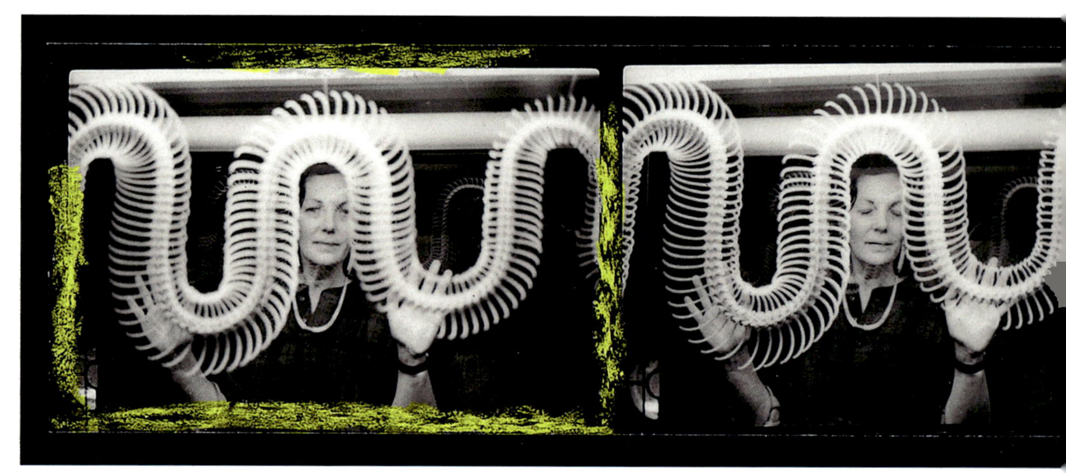

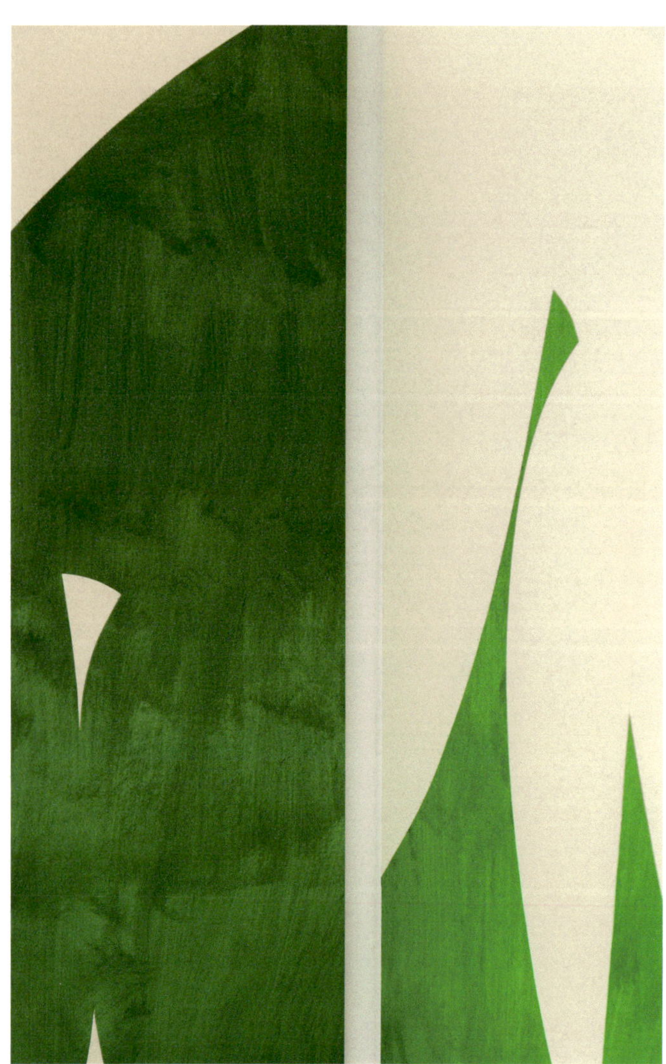

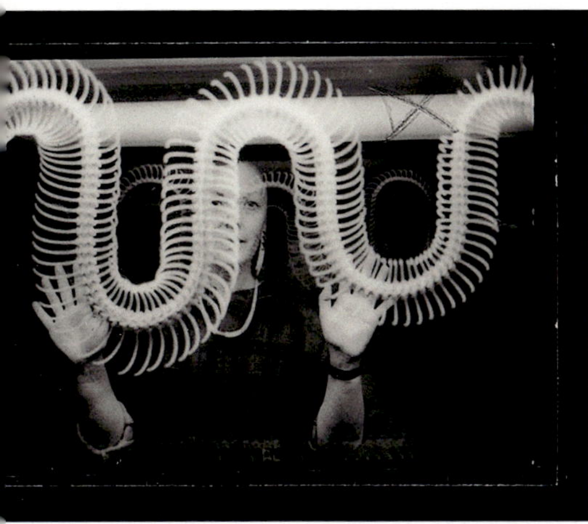

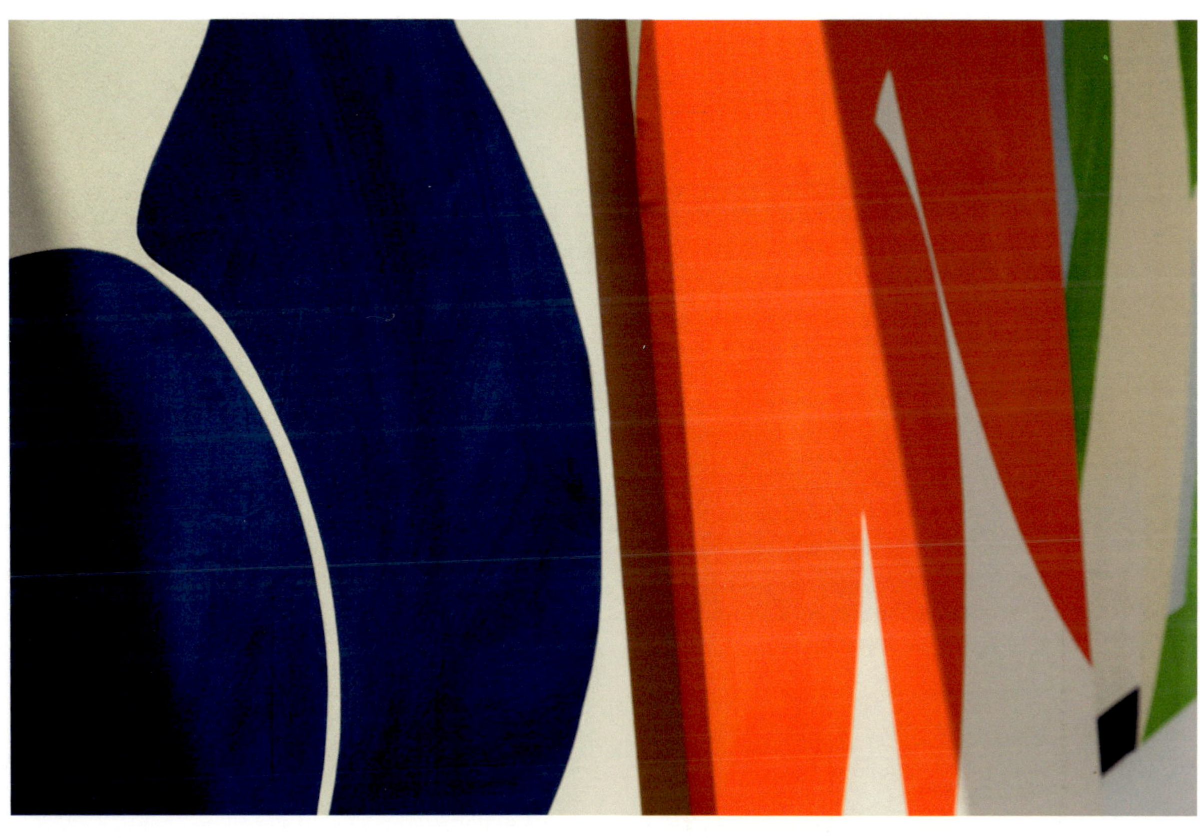

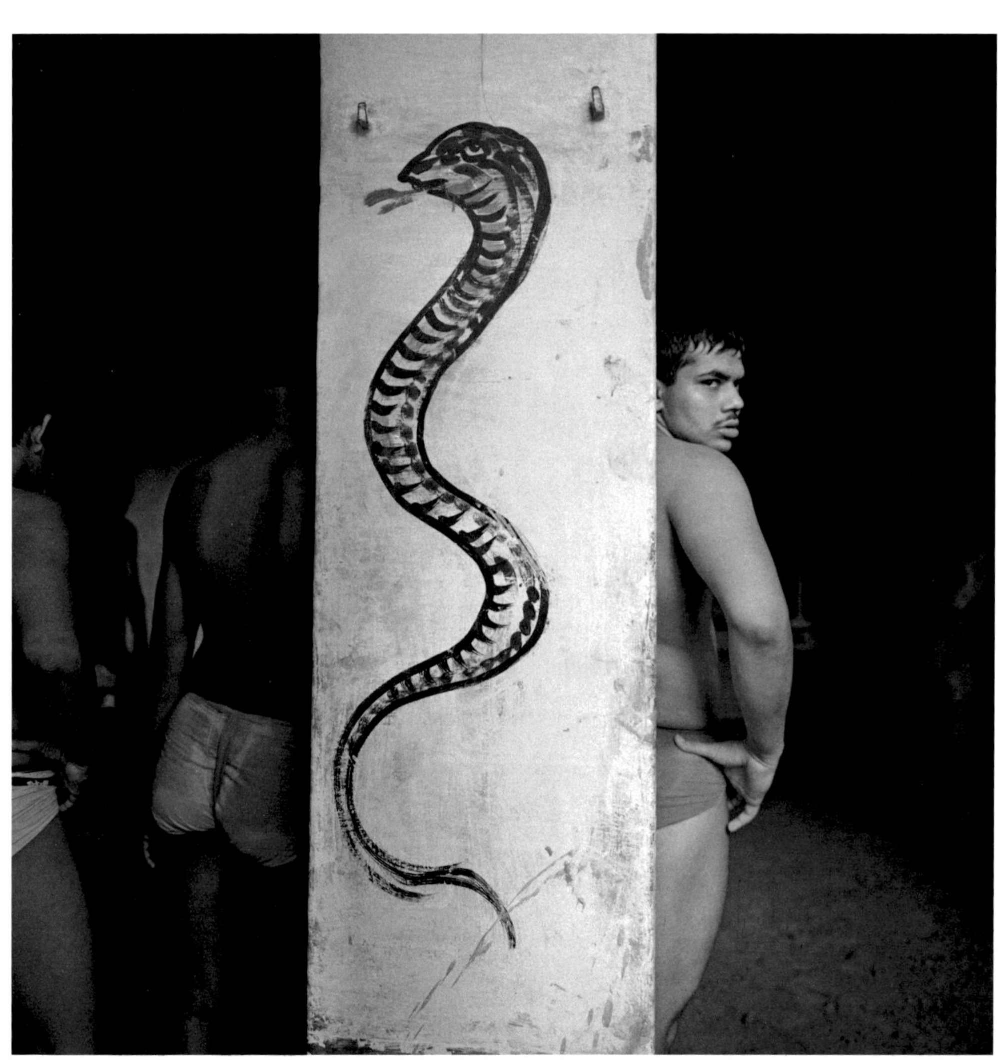

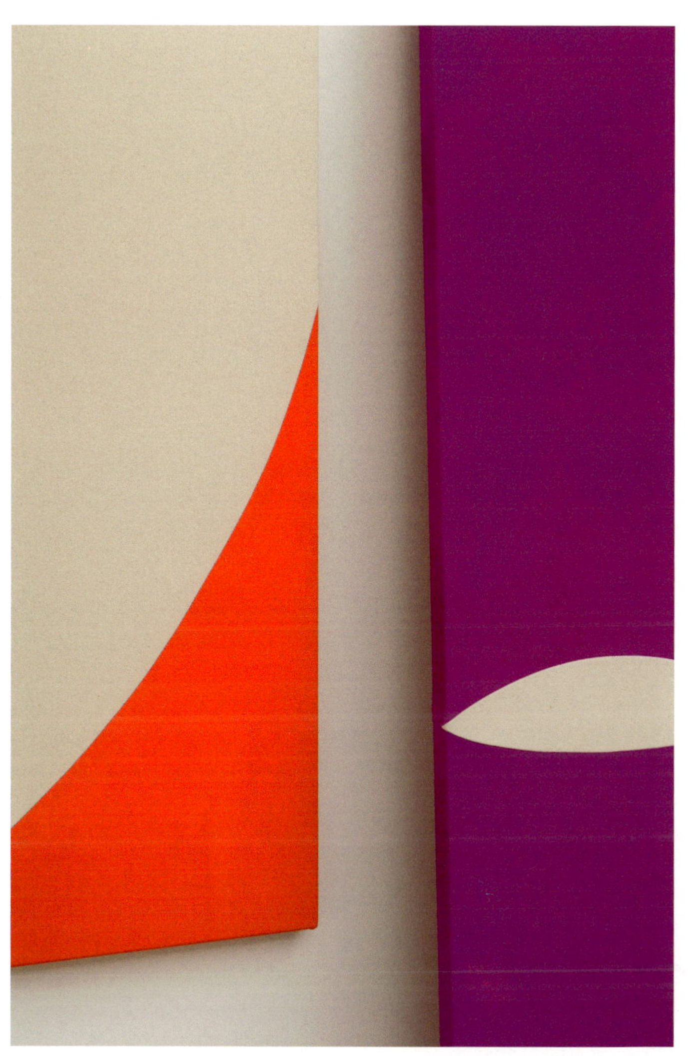

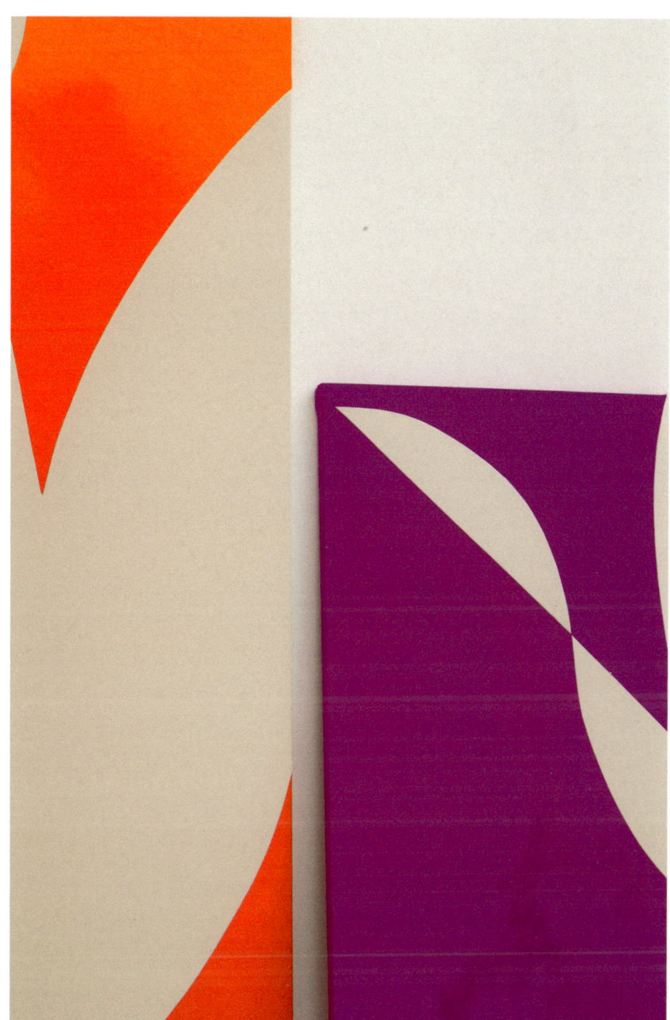

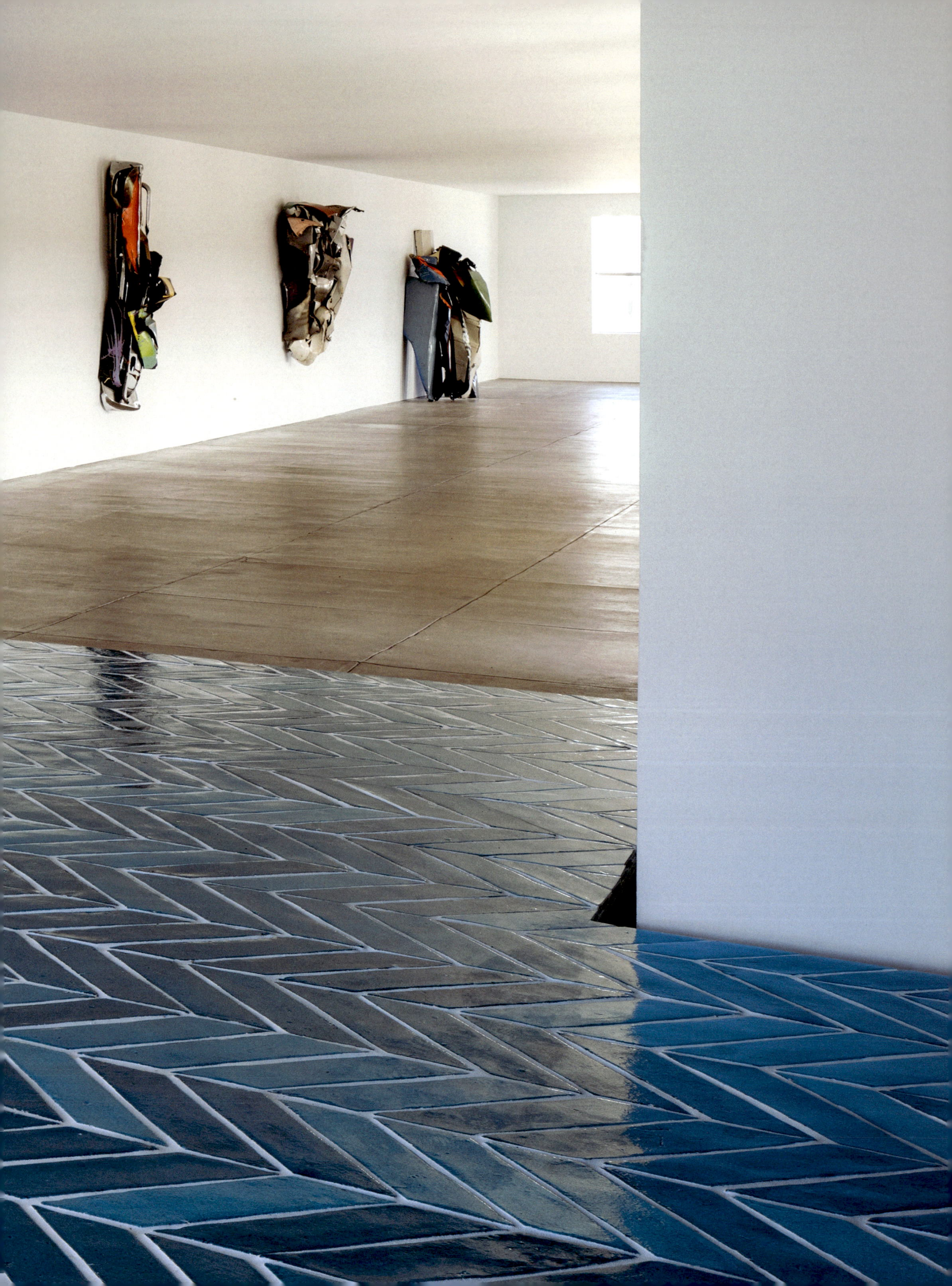

Ingrid Schaffner

Emotional Architecture

Installation view, *Platform (Blue Green terracotta for JC)* (foreground) and works by John Chamberlain (background), Chinati Foundation, Marfa, TX, 2022. Background, left to right: *Paddy's Limbo*, 1976–77 (painted and chromium-plated steel; 51 × 27 × 21 in. [129.5 × 68.6 × 53.3 cm]); *One Twin*, 1979 (painted and chromium-plated steel; 65 × 55 × 26 in. [165.1 × 139.7 × 66 cm]); and *Electric (Electra) Underlace*, 1979 (painted and chromium-plated steel; 85 × 62 × 33 in. [215.9 × 157.5 × 83.8 cm])

Mexico City

HOW SMOOTHLY A LINE from Mathias Goeritz's fervent "Manifesto of Emotional Architecture" curves its way from Museo Experimental El Eco's courtyard in Mexico City in 1953 to Sarah Crowner's magnificent installation in the courtyard at the Museo Amparo in Puebla today. It is an albeit involute journey, traveling by way of these two artists' distinctive engagements with avant-garde art histories and interdisciplinary practices, as well as their shared belief in the power of forms to move, to stir, to elevate, and to connect interior and exterior conditions, people, and passions. Advance one step closer, and be prepared to discover that Crowner's painting at the Museo Amparo is a massive tiled platform, designed to be walked on. And watch out for snakes. Crowner likens the tongue-like tessellation of her ceramic tiles to the scales of a serpent, the very creature Goeritz summoned in this line from his manifesto, asserting that his own artwork be understood as emotional architecture:

> Sculpture, such as the *Serpent* in the courtyard, had to become an almost functional architectural construction (with openings for the ballet)—without ceasing to be sculpture—linking and giving an accent of restless movement to the smooth walls.[1]

Goeritz's *La Serpiente* (*Serpent*) was an integral element of the Museo Experimental El Eco, which he conceived as a total work of art and created as a space for the avant-garde. Privately commissioned, the museum opened in 1953 to host an interdisciplinary program, which had already begun "its activities, that is, its experiments, with the architectural work of its own building."[2] In other words, the building itself was a manifesto, "written" in concrete and launched in opposition to the numbing effects of being "crushed by so much functionalism"; the Museo Experimental stood for an affective artistic alternative to the International Style by providing creative space for emotions. Prioritizing feeling over function, Goeritz pointed to the pyramids, temples, and cathedrals to give precedents for a museum that appeared to have dedicated only a minuscule amount of space to exhibitions. The portioning of what was already a diminutive plan into a small building relative to a large outdoor patio was, he argued, "necessary to complete the excitement once obtained from the entrance." This being a long narrowing corridor, "ending almost at a point," the entrance also had the impractical aspect of being the museum's main gallery.

Open for less than a year, the Museo Experimental El Eco could be considered a failed experiment except that—after operating for a period in drag as a gay and lesbian bar, an Elizabethan theater, an anarchist theater, and an underground music club—the building itself eventually resumed its museum identity. El Eco, as it is now known, reemerged in 2005 under the auspices of the National Autonomous University of Mexico as "an inhabitable sculpture," wherein Goeritz's founding principles of experimentation continue to thrive, sometimes quite audibly. (In 2015, as part of a larger commemoration of Goeritz's centennial and El Eco turning ten, the New York–based visual artist Terence Gower had the words of "Manifesto of Emotional Architecture" set to music. Performed by the young gospel singer Rachel Sharples, Gower's work amplified an integral aspect of Goeritz's design to build into everyday civic life the abstract dimension of "spiritual elevation.")

The construct of emotional architecture, in addition to giving physical and symbolic presence to light, color, shape, and scale, also incorporated sculptural values of plasticity and touch. Goeritz extolled his building's inexact planes and irregular angles, along with the "strange and almost imperceptible asymmetry" that he equated with living things, like trees. Not alone in his sensibilities and beliefs, Goeritz calls out by name in the manifesto a number of architects, artists, and engineers, as well as one musician, and acknowledges trade workers like masons, plumbers, and laborers, as well as the students of the Guadalajara School of Architecture. As a declaration of the role of the collective in bringing forth the aspirations of emotional architecture, the Museo Experimental El Eco was an interdisciplinary and socialist project from the ground up.

One of those named in Goeritz's manifesto was the renowned architect Luis Barragán, who, in turn, invited the sculptor to collaborate on what would become one of modern Mexico City's most notable urban landmarks, *Torres de Satélite* (1957–58). Soaring up from an island in the middle of a major traffic artery, five towers of colored concrete visually pulse with the speed of passing cars. Goeritz referred to the prismatic monoliths as "plastic prayers." In the spirit of which, Barragán invited Goeritz to create the altar for what would certainly be the architect's most sacred of commissions, the Capuchin Convent Chapel (1954–63). A sculptural mass of square planes, covered in gold leaf, Goeritz's altar shimmers next to Barragán's wooden cross, which rises freestanding from the floor with heartbreaking elegance. The composition of the chapel seems starkly similar in its elements to those of the courtyard at El Eco. Striking too are the differences between building a house of God and a house of dadaism. The devout Catholic Barragán's emotional architecture yielded spaces of perfect solitude, fit for contemplation. A man self-described as without faith, whose artistic spirit was awakened in 1930s Berlin, Goeritz turned his devotions to building a tiny temple for avant-garde experimentation, collaboration, and play.

Brooklyn

Behind a metal gate in Red Hook, an industrial Brooklyn neighborhood, and against a backdrop of shipping yards with distant views across the East River to Lower Manhattan, is Sarah Crowner's studio. It is part of an atelier compound of small buildings owned by artist Cassandra MacLeod, who wished to establish a live/work environment to share with artist friends. Surrounding a garden courtyard are a communal kitchen, individual studio spaces, and a ceramic studio, next door to which two men were in the process of installing a printing press. When I visited the artist in November 2021, there was a peaceful and purposeful vibe to this enclave, where, as it happens, the best place to get to know Crowner's painting practice turned out to be the ceramic studio.

Crowner maintains that it was working with the elemental material of clay that taught her how to build an abstract painting. This seems sensible enough, though the route is curiously funny. Given that Crowner grew up on the West Coast, where clay has long been accepted as a fine art material, it's not at all surprising that Crowner knew of Beatrice Wood's work—especially considering Wood's pottery studio was in Ojai, where Crowner's grandparents lived and her parents also now live. It was less Wood's ceramics than her legendary life and historical reputation as the "Mama of Dada" that inspired Crowner to create a group of utterly absurd bottomless vessels. Each of these is based on a different chapter in Wood's autobiography and is titled with a name from her avant-garde coterie of friends: Constantin Brancusi, Marcel Duchamp, Mina Loy, and Anaïs

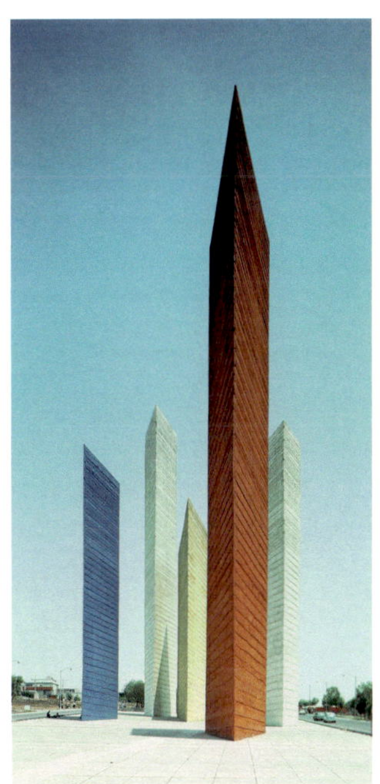

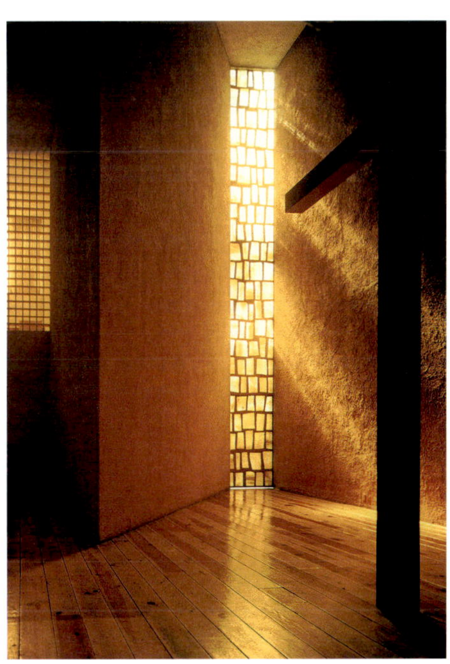

LEFT Luis Barragán and Mathias Goeritz, *Torres de Satélite*, Naucalpan de Juárez, State of Mexico, 1957–58. Undated photograph, ca. 1960

RIGHT Luis Barragán, Capuchin Convent Chapel, Tlalpan, Mexico City, 1954–63. Transept window designed by Mathias Goeritz. Undated photograph, ca. 1960s

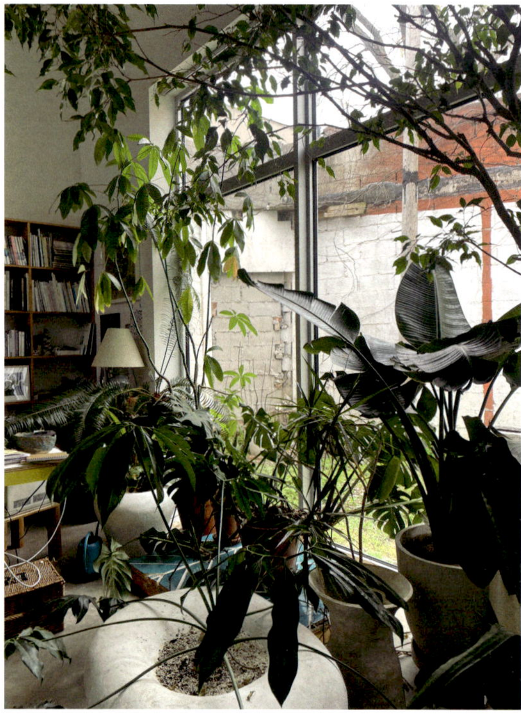

ABOVE Studio view, Brooklyn, NY, 2022

OPPOSITE Installation view, *Post Jacaranda*, Galerie Nordenhake, Mexico City, 2019

Nin; her spiritual guide, the theosophist Jiddu Krishnamurti; and her husband, Steve.

Formed as if sketched by hand from raw clay, the first of Crowner's ceramics bears little resemblance to the ceramic tileworks and wheel-thrown wares she has most recently been making. "I turn to functional pottery when I'm tired of painting or frustrated by it."[3] Fully equipped with materials, wheels, wedging tables, and a kiln, the ceramic studio is well used, judging from the small sculptural pieces of glazed clay that line every ledge, fill a wall of shelves, and spill into plastic buckets on the floor. Ever accruing, this collection of colorful oddments constitutes an archive of material references; it was established as such by another studio mate, Ester Kislin, and has grown as a collective endeavor. "I really like oxides," says Crowner, who seems drawn by the archive into shop talk about grogs and clay bodies, Mason stains, and how glaze "stands up." Pea green is her favorite color, she notes, picking up what looks like a tangled stem of clay and pointing out how the pooling turquoise glaze thins into a metallic sheen.

Bringing the outdoors in is a recurrent move in Crowner's pursuit of abstraction. In her painting studio, one is immediately struck by the profusion of plants. The front of the space, which is naturally well lit by a wall of windows and a skylight, has become a temporary conservatory for hearty philodendrons, a towering ficus, and other leafy specimens in very large pots. Green was one color Barragán never used in his architecture, leaving that to nature. He did design an entire house in Mexico City, Casa Gilardi (1975–77), around one jacaranda tree and painted the courtyard purple to complement its flowers. And so did Crowner calibrate the palette of the paintings of her 2019 exhibition in a Mexico City gallery to the flowers of the potted young

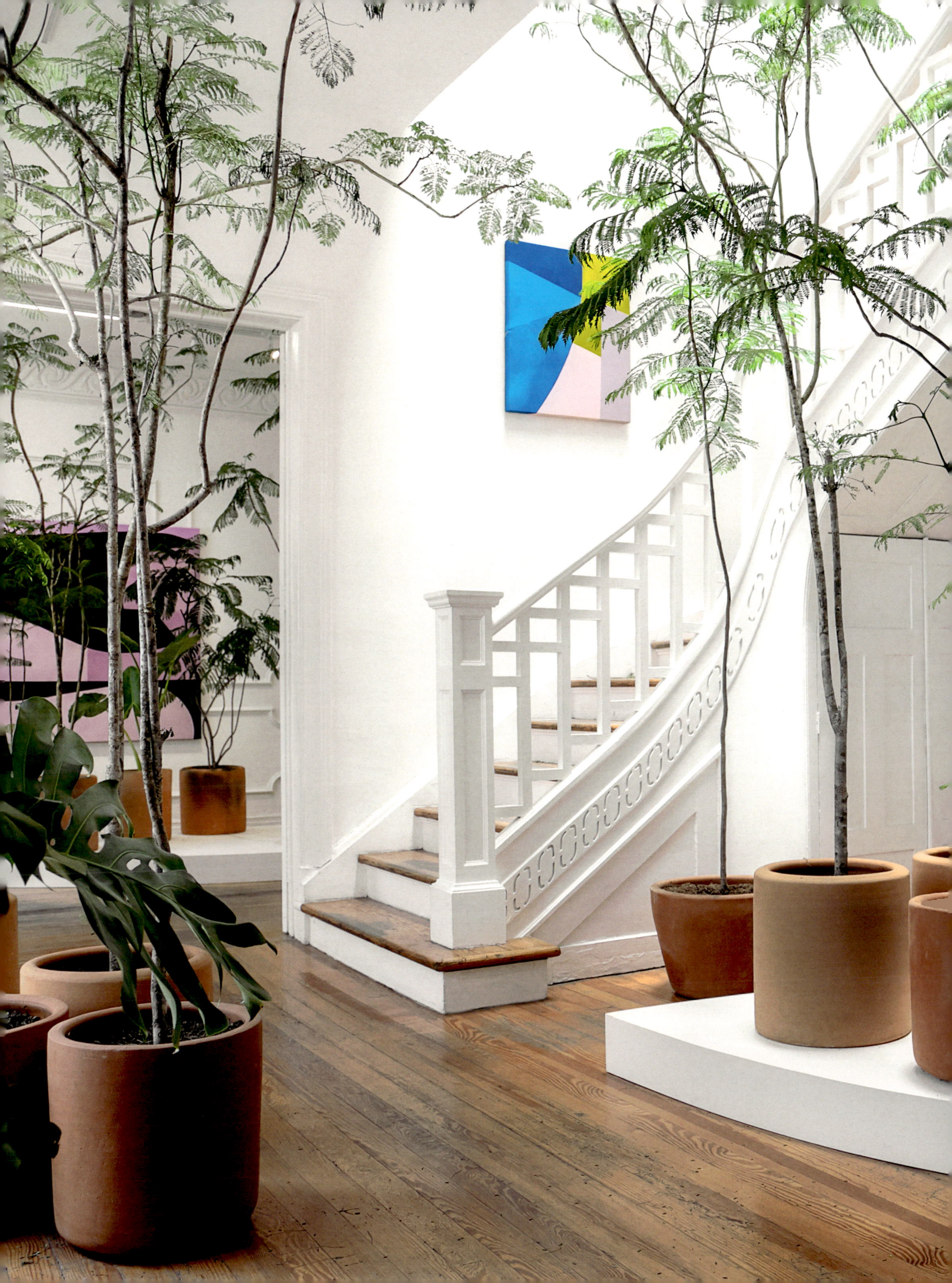

jacarandas she had installed so thickly in the rooms that viewers had to navigate the greenery to view the violet canvases.[4]

Among the paintings underway in her studio was an arresting composition of brilliant red bands flanking an almost pictorial central panel. With serrations of green on an ocher ground, the panel had achieved a level of resolution in its own right; however, it was just too small to fit the already existing stretcher. Crowner's solution—adding bold margins—also resulted in a visual structure that she strongly relates to the work of Henri Matisse. "I love his use of verticals," she said of an artist who clearly inspires her deeply and on many levels—from his famous use of paper cutouts to "sculpt" color to his endless capacity to draw new figures and grounds from the leaves of a philodendron. One of her recently completed works appears to have absorbed the essence of Matisse's Nice—the doves, the nudes, the leaves and petals, the swimming pool—into an undulation of sapphire, viridian, and white smooth forms. She described another nearby canvas as the negative spaces of "Dufy's leaves" isolated and amassed into a big green pattern, which she had abstracted from the work of Matisse's fellow Fauve Raoul Dufy. Crowner was already eyeing this work for the chopping block.

"I like it when they're a bit off, a bit strange," Crowner said, speaking of what her compositions strive for, something unbalanced. Our focus shifted from the wall to the floor, where Crowner wrestles her work into beguiling elegance. Building on her work in clay, her process begins with the wet work of creating a palette of painterly monochromes on raw canvas. Next comes the cutting. Sometimes she works with a paper pattern (over the years, Crowner has created quite a kit of curves) or scraps of previous works. Other times, she goes at it freehand, shearing shapes from the painted canvas with very sharp scissors. Then there is the *couture*, French for "sewing," but like the art form in fashion, its construction can verge on sculpture. Working on a big drop cloth, Crowner arranges her shapes on the floor. Walking around the composition, with no predetermined sense of up or down, she pins, she pauses, she moves around pieces, then she stops to sew.

Stiff and wrinkled, the painted fabric sections resist flattening. The curves of Crowner's highly tailored seams also make it impossible for the artist to have any real sense of how a work is coming together until it has been ironed. At this point, the canvas is as likely to be cut up and ripped apart as it is taken to the next stage (of being stretched and hung on the studio wall for contemplation) or, potentially, returned to the cutting table for further work. Crowner has been working this way for over fourteen years and now experiences the process of sewing her paintings at varying velocities: working quickly and slowly, intuitively and reflectively, as she balances art and craft. She knowingly points toward her trusty Juki, the industrial sewing machine that makes all of this possible.

Summer (with Margins), 2021. Acrylic on canvas, sewn; 78 × 72 in. (198.1 × 182.9 cm). Private collection

Guadalajara

In pursuit of new possibilities for painting, Crowner created her first three tiled platforms in 2014. Of these, the most ambitious was the

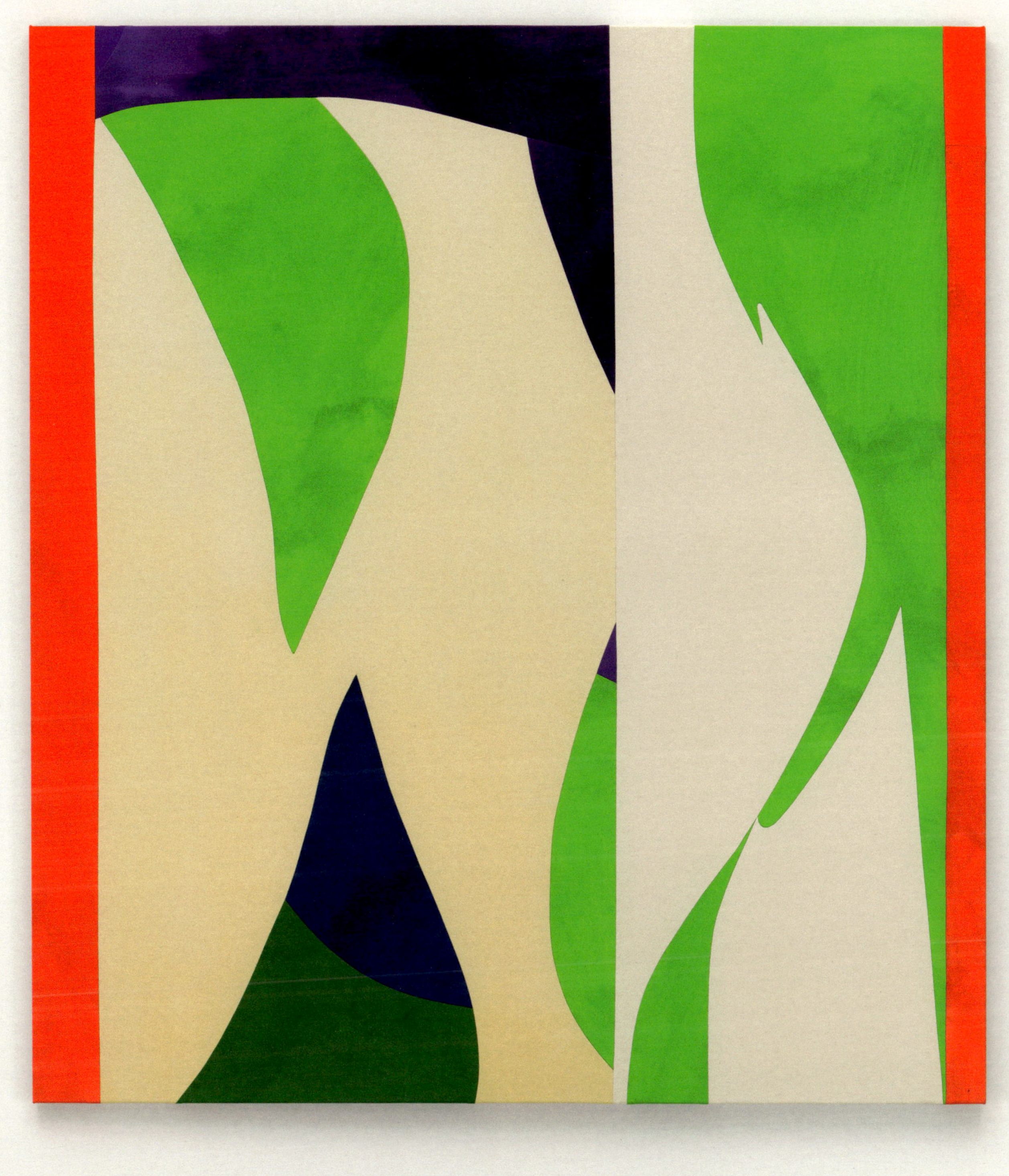

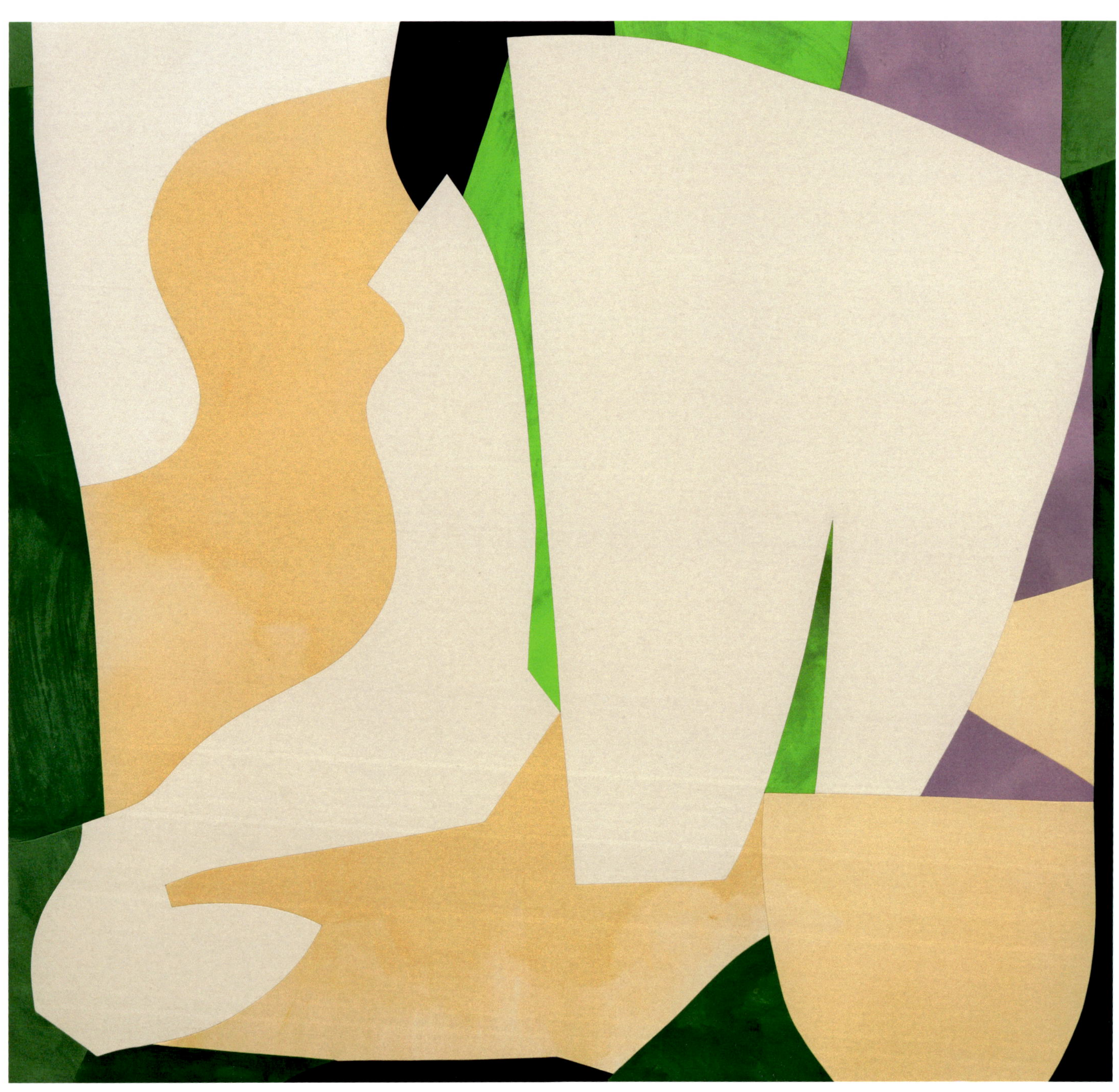

ABOVE *Spring*, 2021. Acrylic on canvas, sewn; 86 × 92 in. (218.4 × 233.7 cm). Private collection

OPPOSITE *Reclining Forms, Open and Closed*, 2022. Acrylic on canvas, sewn; 90 × 70 in. (228.6 × 177.8 cm). Zmijewski Collection, New York

FOLLOWING PAGES Studio view, Brooklyn, NY, 2022

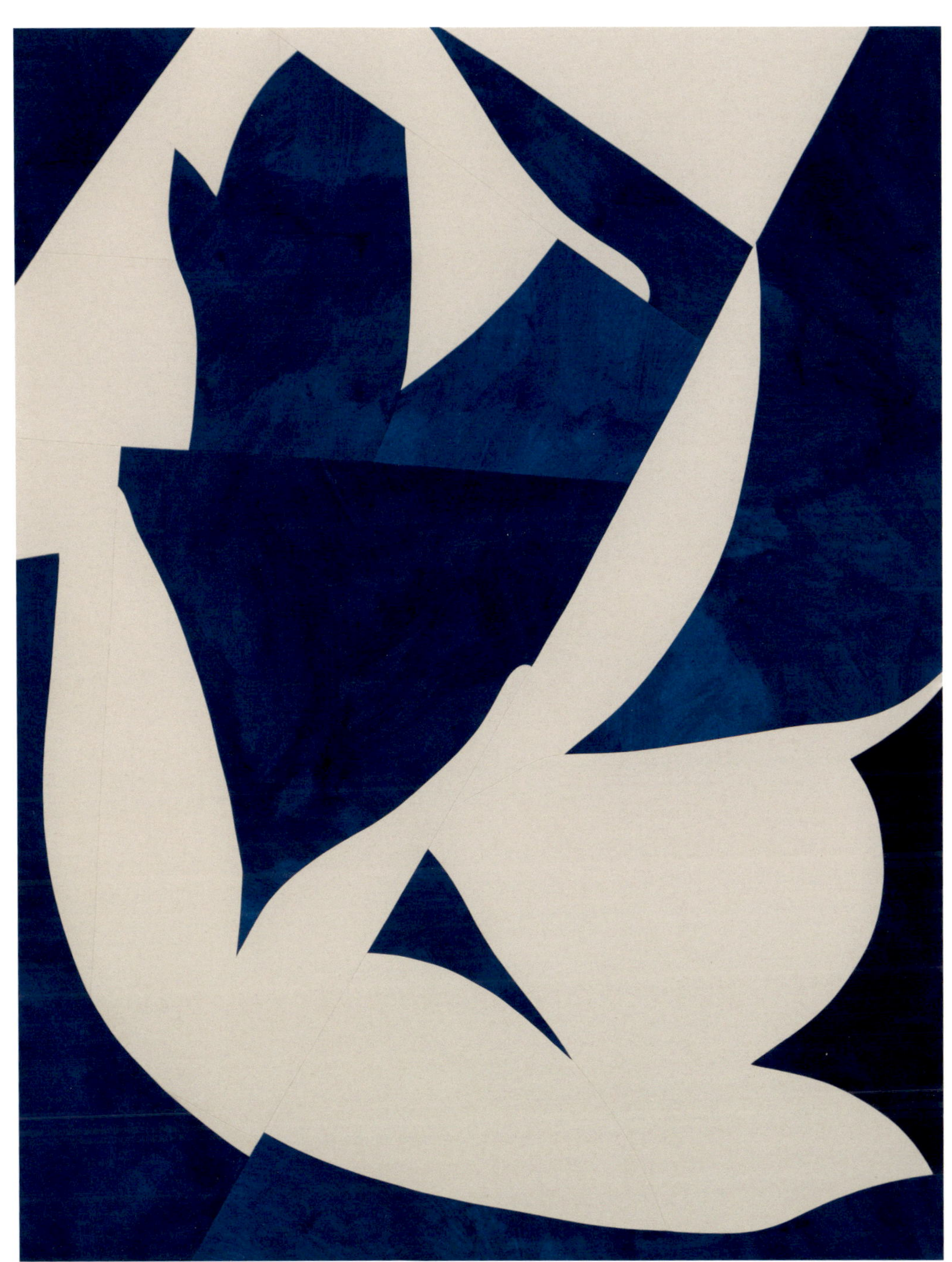

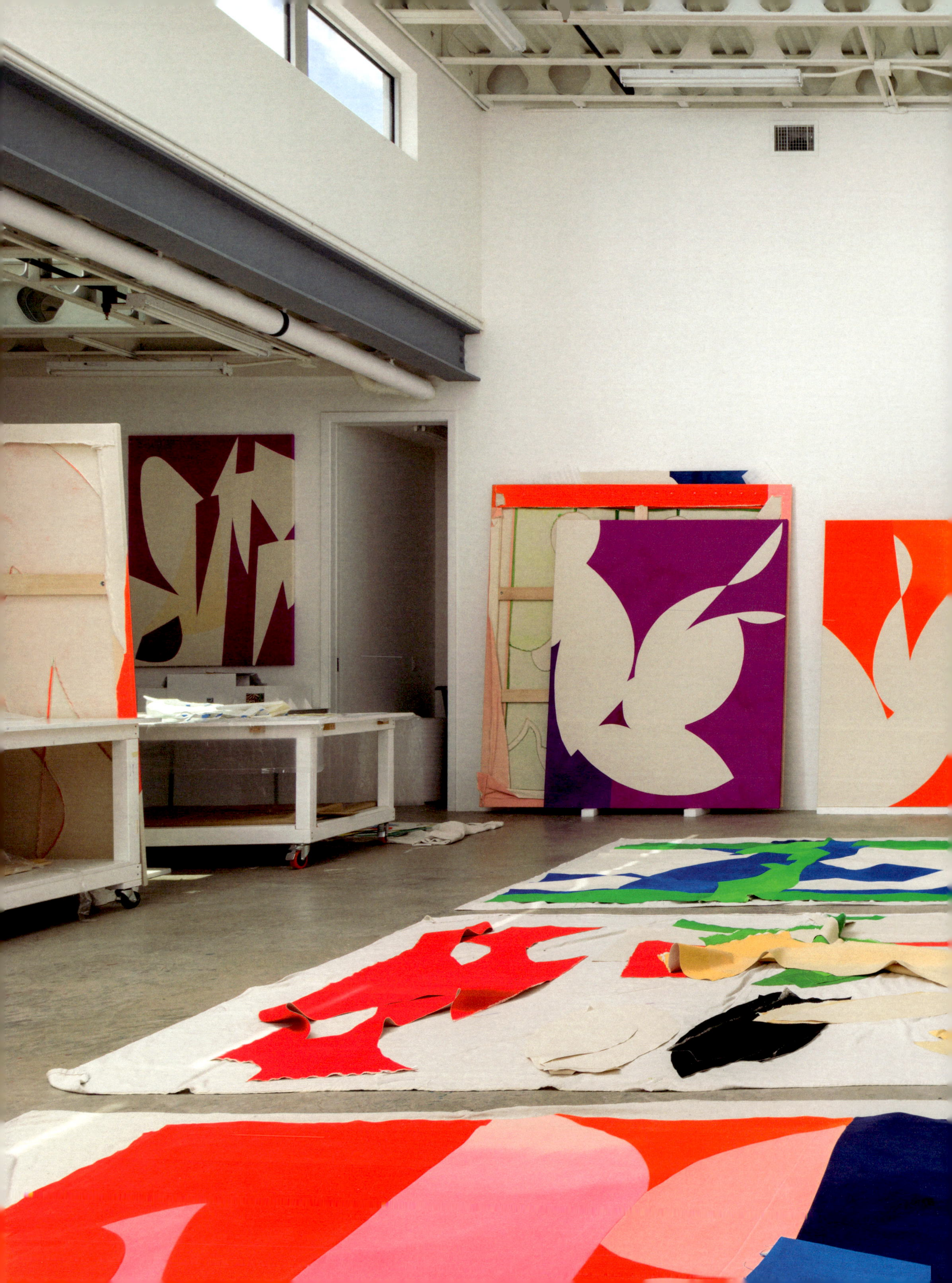

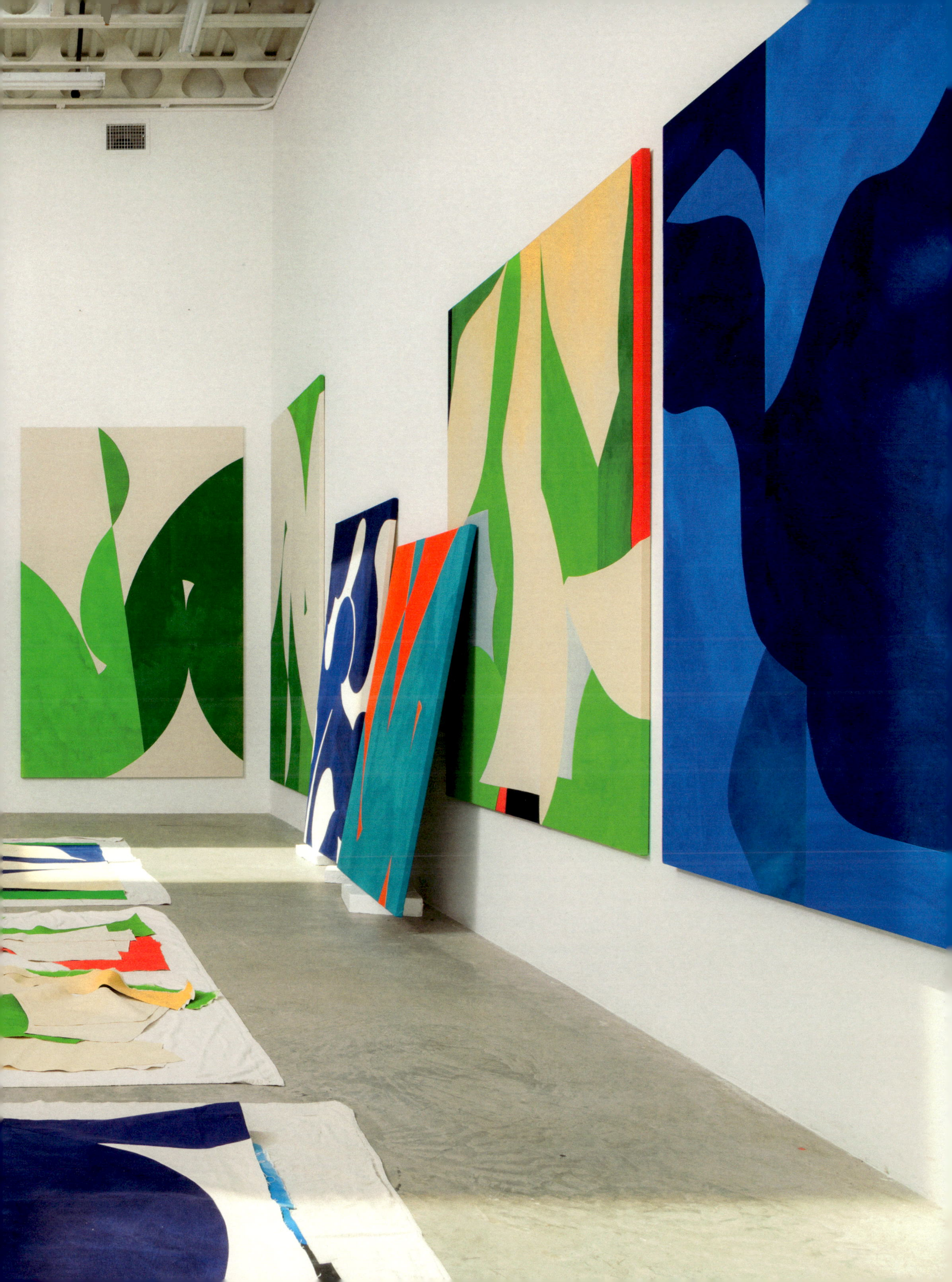

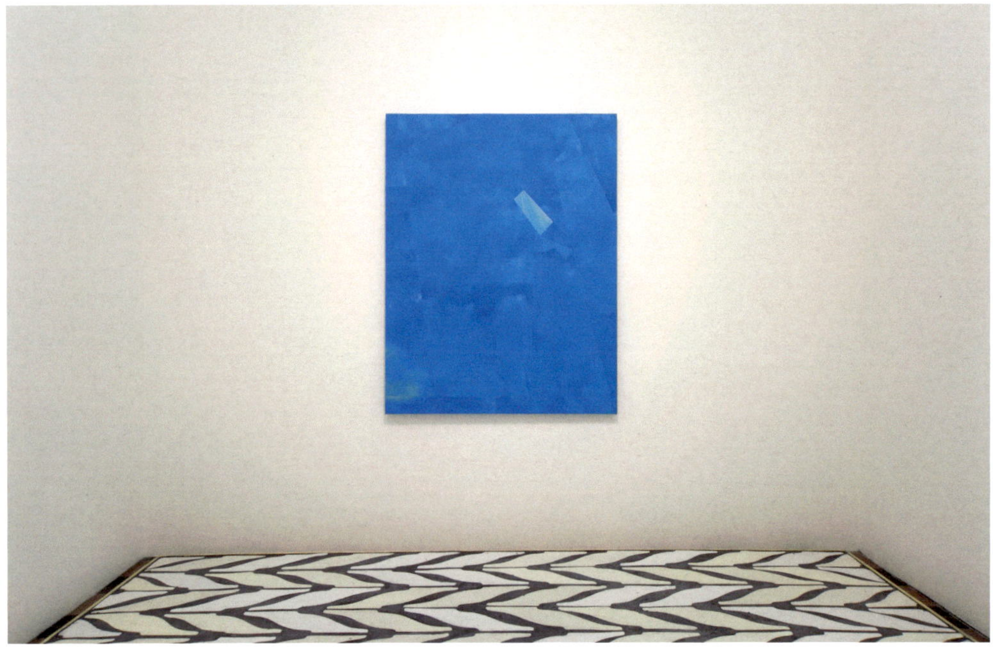

ABOVE AND OPPOSITE Installation views, *Interiores*, Travesía Cuatro, Guadalajara, 2014

main feature of *Interiores*, a site-specific installation for a house by Luis Barragán. Now home to the contemporary art gallery Travesía Cuatro, Casa Franco (1929) is one of several private commissions that constitute the architect's earliest work in his hometown of Guadalajara. Modern in style yet Mexican in materiality, what tinges there are of the architect's signature work to come were set aglow by Crowner's bold and sensitive intervention. Covering the entire ground floor in pale-colored wavy arrow-shaped tiles, her painterly project had a cabling effect, pulling the viewer from room to room, from street to garden. The house became a vessel through which light, pattern, and people flowed—or floated.

As site-specific installations, Crowner's platform paintings are enormous barge-like constructions that begin with the building of a raised wooden floor upon which the tiles can be set. Once completed, though only a mere six inches off the ground, the platforms pose a thrilling rise.[5] Getting on a stage to perform the act of looking, mounting a pedestal to put oneself on display, breaking art's taboo of *don't touch*: all of these inhibitions are crossed at once by the viewer. Stepping up onto Crowner's painting, one enters a plane where color, pattern, line, surface, and even sound become vibrant and tactile, right beneath one's feet.

At the Barragán house, the haptic drama was further heightened by a prolonged near kiss. Covering the floors without touching the walls, Crowner's work was separated from Barragán's architecture by a narrow gap. Within this margin operated one of art's great signifiers: a band of wood running around the platform and finishing the edge effectively read as a house-sized frame around the painting on the floor. In a more conventional relationship to the architecture, other frames were hanging on the walls. Installed throughout the house was a series of six monochrome paintings. Composed of painted shapes, stitched together and tautly stretched, these canvases were so delicate in hue as to appear almost totally ambient with the whiteness of the rooms. One exception was a window-like painting in shades of sky blue. The floor too was barely blushed by the pale pink and yellow of Crowner's tiles. In contrast to the decisive quiet were the strong symmetry and sense of movement that color, along with line, also gave to the installation as a whole. The dark lines of gray grout undulated coolly underfoot. At eye level, the picture frames were painted such intense fluorescent colors they glowed.

Emotional architecture's opposition to cold functionality finds correspondence with Crowner's desire to bring the warmth of embodiment and utility to painting. "It's using your body to receive painting; it's a bodily experience," she explained of her tile paintings, which have also taken the form of ceramic murals that invite viewers' hands to touch walls of color.[6] She has also pushed the reception of her canvas paintings into more durational encounters, though not in such immediately tactile ways. "I'm curious about the impact of time on our experience of painting," she told an interviewer in 2011. "If you walk into a gallery or museum you might experience a painting for as little as one minute . . . [but] what if you were seated in an auditorium 'watching' that painting—perhaps with dancers moving in front of it—for, say, forty-five minutes?"[7] As it turns out, this wasn't just speculation on Crowner's part. When her friend the composer, performer,

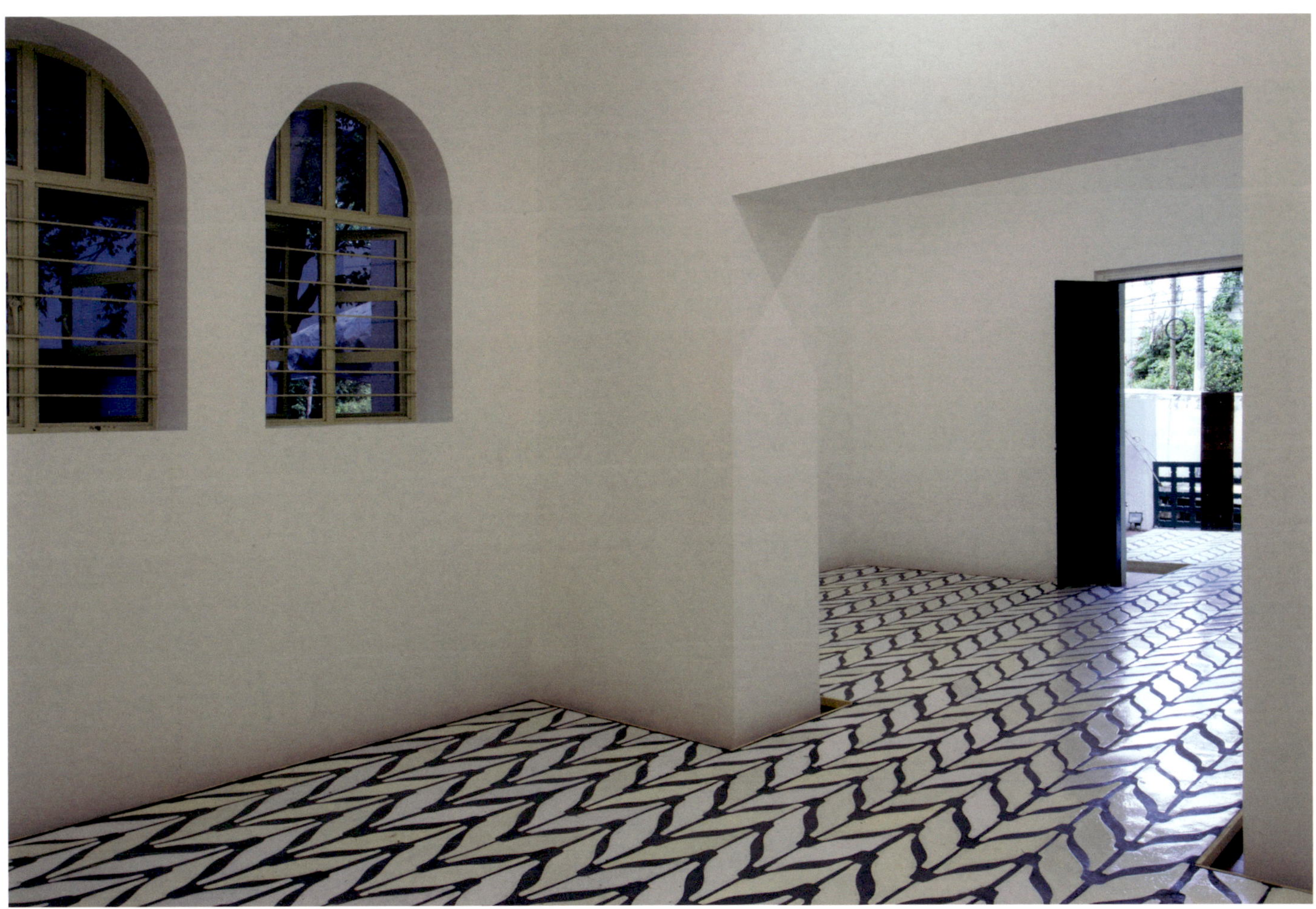

producer, and scholar Alex Waterman invited her to contribute to his Spanish-language staging of Robert Ashley's 1983 opera *Perfect Lives*, Crowner was ready to see her painting perform. Set in the desert between the US and Mexico, *Vidas Perfectas* (2011) was minimally staged with a brilliant curtain on a largely empty stage. In the black box of the Irondale Center in Brooklyn, Crowner's soft linen drapery, with its stark shapes and bright colors, appeared less a backdrop than a painterly presence. Also performing more discreetly on stage was an enameled sculptural object, a geometric sliver of blue; this was the bench Crowner took it upon herself to design "so the actors would have something to sit on."

With Openings for the Ballet

To become emotional implies movement, motion, stirring, change. No wonder, then, that dance lay at the heart of Goeritz's "Manifesto of Emotional Architecture." Remember how he described his *La Serpiente* in the courtyard? The sculpture, he wrote, must create "openings for the ballet." And dance reciprocated, by making the museum a sculptural proposition, plastic with movement and feeling. Photographs taken in the courtyard show Walter Nicks's El Ballet Negro[8] performing in, around, and with Goeritz's monumental zigzag of black metal—making the sculpture and the space both exuberant and alive. Other photographs, taken in the museum's corridor gallery, show a young

Walter Nicks's dance company El Ballet Negro performing at the Museo Experimental El Eco, Mexico City, 1953

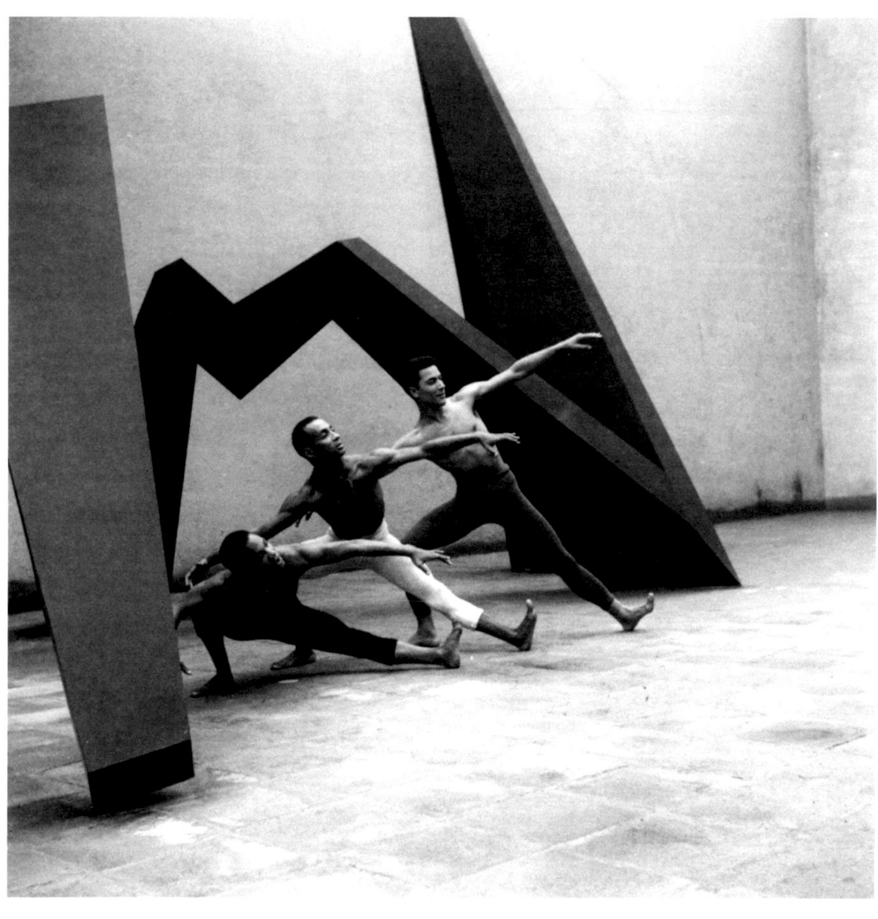

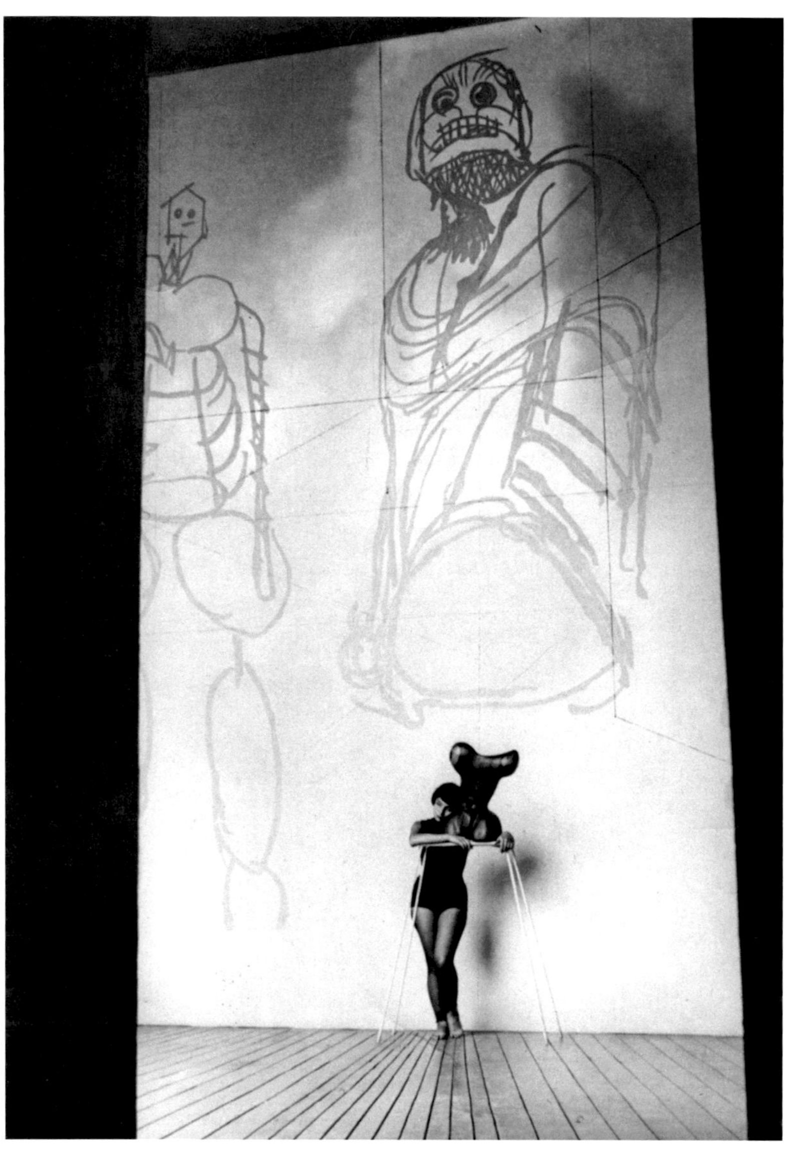

Pilar Pellicer performing at the Museo Experimental El Eco, Mexico City, ca. March 1954

Pilar Pellicer dancing her own choreography, rising statuesque before a mural by Henry Moore—her arms extending the gestures of his drawing's lines. These historic photographs of Ballet Negro and Pellicer were taken during the 1953 inauguration of the Museo Experimental El Eco. Inaudible is the music, a percussive composition by the Russian-born Mexican composer Lan Adomián, that played throughout the entire museum.

"My great love." That's how Crowner has referred to dance and her interactions with it through her art. *Post Tree* was commissioned as a new piece by choreographer Carolyn Schoerner with music by James Hoff for Crowner's 2016 exhibition *Beetle in the Leaves* as part of a series of events that took place in one of the galleries.[9] The dance was an almost sculptural montage of stuttering classical ballet moves. Performed by Schoerner, her elongated limbs in a red leotard, atop the geometric white tile of Crowner's platform with the attenuated blue shapes of her paintings in the background, the event was a total composition. For *Garden Blue* (2018), a ballet by choreographer Jessica

Lang commissioned by American Ballet Theatre, Crowner designed the costumes and an interactive set. The dancers moved around large wooden shapes, which they picked up and responded to on stage; it was as if her paintings, platforms, and color palette had come to life. Crowner draws deeply on nature for her art's feelings and form, and these lightweight props were inspired by the papery winged pods of a samara, or helicopter seed, which relies on the wind to disperse its seed. During my visit Crowner also shared a digital playlist that she was listening to at the time of the commission. Frank Ocean, Blood Orange, Brian Eno, Cluster, and other contemporary avant-gardists, whose music she described as "emotionally stirring, lyrical," had set the sonic stage for her work in the studio on the ballet.

There is another note to carry forward from the concatenation of correspondences between Goeritz's 1953 manifesto and Crowner's art today that resounds in the material of history itself. Goeritz's emotional architecture was of a piece with many strands of modernism that mingled disciplines of making—by one or many hands—into boundless forms of painterly abstraction. Thus could a wall become a sculpture when it is painted, a room could become a sanctuary when it is suffused with color, spaces could become chromatic when filled with music, and a floor could become a painting for dancing on. Throughout her work, Crowner actively engages with such pasts by working in dialogue with specific artists and objects that make present painting's ongoing potential to move.

Curtain (Vidas Perfectas) incarnates another theater curtain, this one made in Kraków by Maria Jarema, an artist so avant-garde in appearance alone (picture a 1930s woman in a handmade patchwork sheepskin coat and a wedge of cropped hair) that people reputedly shouted at her in the streets. Sewn in 1956, Jarema's curtain was itself something of a reincarnation of the abstract sets and costumes she had designed for the original Cricot Theater company, which was founded in 1933 to foster a culture of experimentation that World War II would bring to an end, and the subsequent Cricot 2, which was created by Jarema and others. A geometric patchwork of peach, beige, and brown linens, the curtain, which was hidden for many years in the theater's archive, now hangs in the National Museum in Kraków. However, for Crowner, it was seeing a poor reproduction of the curtain in a book that made her wonder enough about its colors to fashion her own. Following Jarema's original composition like a pattern, but with colors so saturated and contrasts so bright, Crowner's new work leaves no doubt a curtain can be a painting and a painting can be a curtain.[10]

Crowner credits learning about Maria Jarema to Paulina Olowska, for whom the Polish modernist is an admired national figure and inspiration for Olowska's own foray into puppet making. Crowner and Olowska met as artists in residence at the ARCO art fair in Lisbon in 1999 and have exhibited, collaborated, and championed one another's work since. A 2017 mural designed by Crowner in Nairobi came about through the Kraków-based Razem Pamoja, a foundation supporting social activism through art and learning that was started by Olowska's husband. Its bold, bright pattern literally puts a wrap on the renovation of Mathare Advanced Community Core Organization School, a

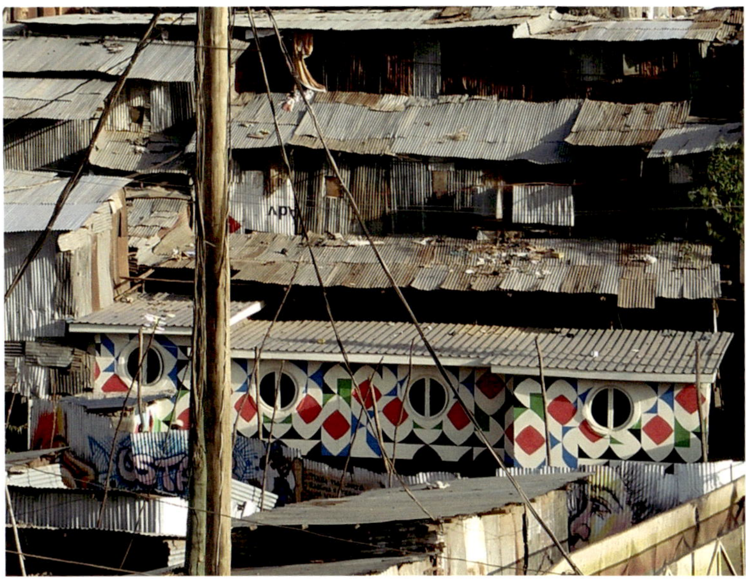

Mural for MACCO School, 2017. Wall painting. Mathare Advanced Community Core Organization School, Nairobi, Kenya, 2017

hub of the slum community that the foundation serves. When asked in 2016 to spotlight a work of art at the Frieze Masters art fair in London, Crowner chose Carol Rama's 1951 painting *Le Amiche* (The Friends). Why? "They *become* pattern," Crowner said of the thick impasto portrait of two friends rendered as "saturated bodies of color banging into each other," which she found to be "very complex, personal, and moving."[11] Wondering where the two figures might be off to, she mused, "Some kind of adventure, perhaps."

Friendships among artists lie at the heart of interdisciplinary movements and moments. How else would dance, painting, and music; textiles and sculpture; fashion and architecture; and theater and design all come together were it not for radically and aesthetically like-minded people seeking to interact? There is also love. The story of Paulina pointing her friend Sarah in the direction of Maria's art ends with an embrace, an enfolding of Jarema's curtain into Crowner's painting. And so do many of Crowner's works begin with an encounter that leads to falling in love with something, someone, someplace in the world. Her art increasingly brings opportunities to travel and explore. Trips to Venice over the years for the Biennale accrued into the "Scarpa platform," as Crowner calls the elegant wooden platform with semicircular cutouts that shaped the gallery floor of her 2018 exhibition *Weeds* at Casey Kaplan, New York. To relate more closely with her paintings, viewers could step onto this eccentric pedestal, which for some may have also functioned as a subtle means of transport—a hovercraft to memories of being in the garden Carlo Scarpa designed for the Central Pavilion in Venice in 1952, with its curvaceous concrete slab canopy floating over the courtyard's pools and plantings.

Volumes of Sophie Taeuber-Arp

For Crowner, a meaningful encounter may also happen via a reproduction. She has a Proustian remembrance from the early 2000s of her friend David Senior, then the librarian at the Museum of Modern Art,

RIGHT Installation view, *Weeds*, Casey Kaplan Gallery, New York, 2018

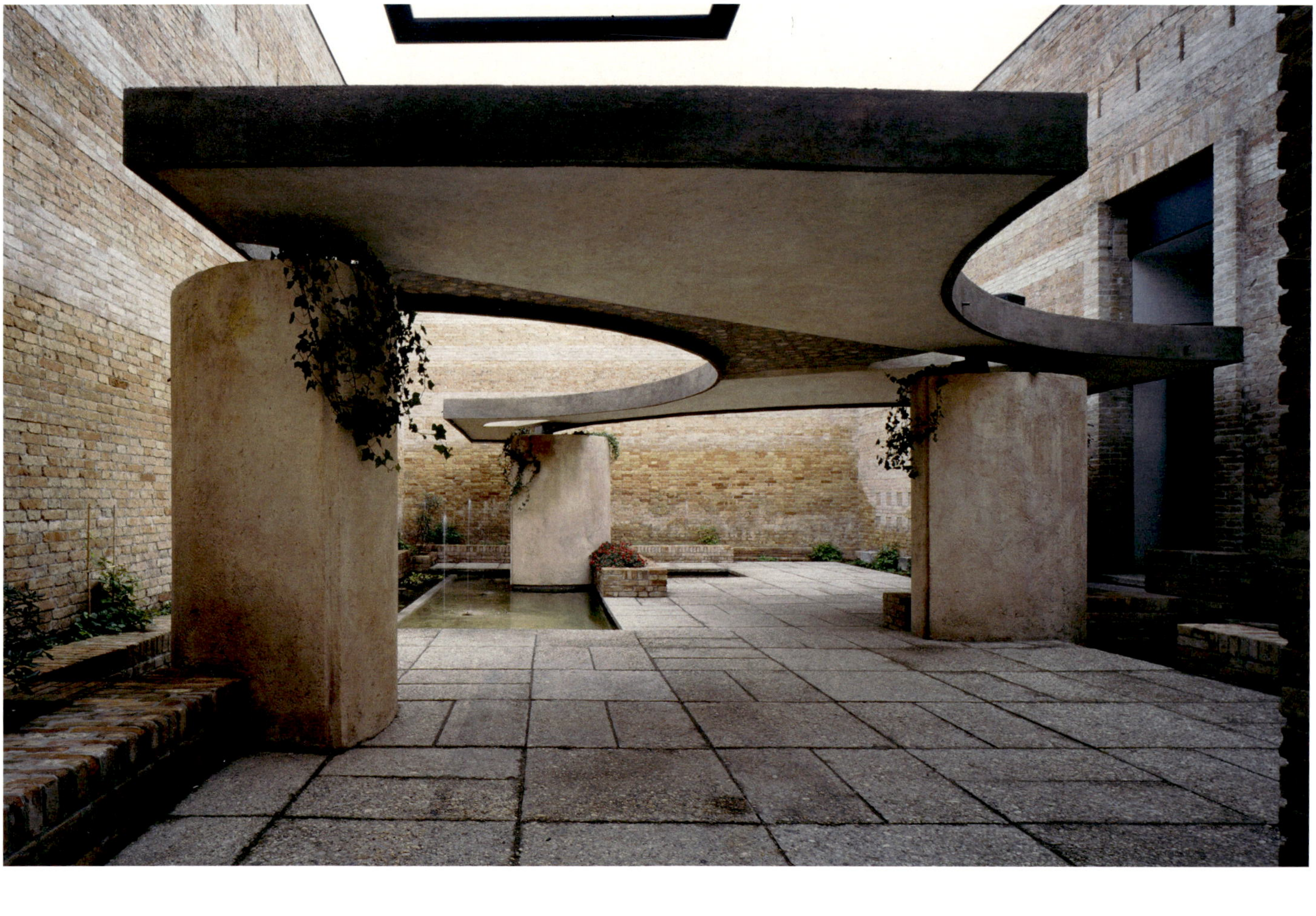

BELOW Carlo Scarpa, garden of the Central Pavilion, Venice, 1952

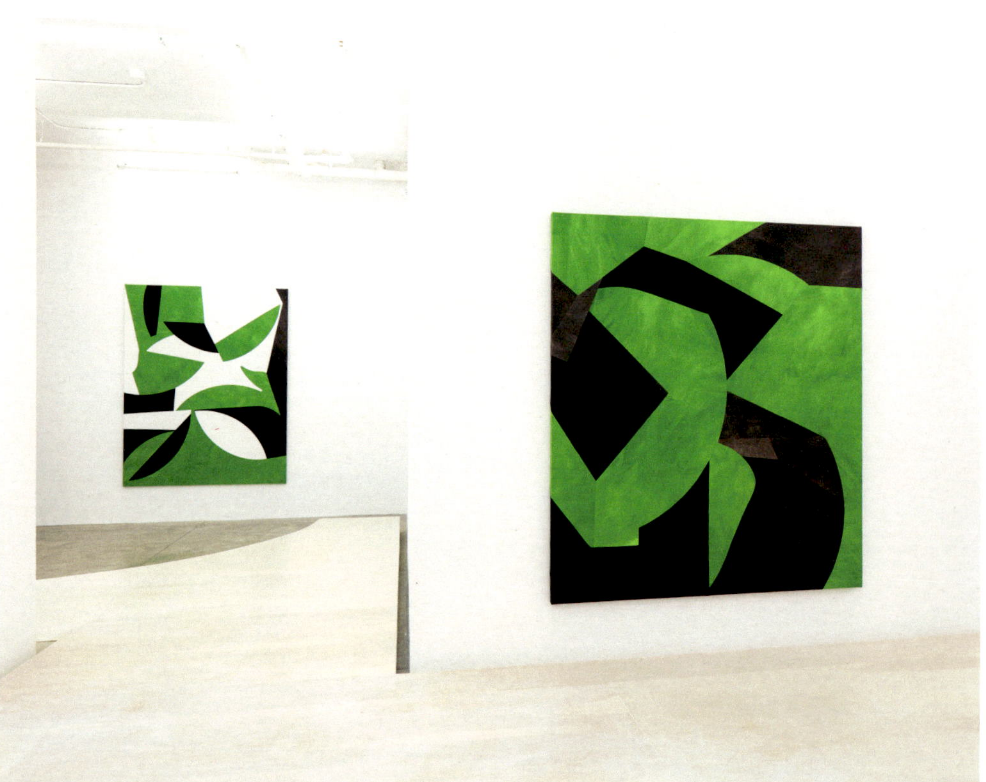

showing her an issue of *Plastique*, the 1937 journal dedicated to abstraction. "I can still remember the smell and the touch of the paper." It was also her first contact with the work of Sophie Taeuber-Arp. "Whenever I'm stuck, I always go to her work,"[12] she says of the supremely multidisciplined modernist, whose paintings, performances, pillows, purses, puppets, sculpture, furniture, interiors, and graphic design Crowner has been studying for over a decade. A signatory of the 1918 "Dada Manifesto" and a teacher of textiles, Taeuber-Arp studied movement with Rudolf von Laban ("full of spikes and fish-bones" was Hugo Ball's admiring description of her dance in cubist costume at the Café Voltaire[13]) and collaborated on what is considered to be the first modernist public space to fully integrate abstract art, the Café Aubette in Strasbourg. "And since the image itself does not change, it is the spectator who lets himself be transformed by the image,"[14] her friend Emmy Hennings wrote of the experience of inhabiting Taeuber-Arp's wall and ceiling paintings. Possibly the first work of hers to be shown in America was a tablecloth.[15]

"Yes," affirmed Crowner, "I'm attracted to artists and designers who have a more open practice as it related to painting like [Sonia] Delaunay, Eileen Gray, certain Neo-Concrete artists in Brazil in the 1950s like Lygia Clark and Hélio Oiticica, as well as the artists and architects of the Bauhaus era or the Weiner Werkstätte."[16] In the ever-growing playbook of artists who have contributed ideas and motifs to Crowner's painting and abstraction, as well as a good amount of pragmatism about how shapes can take form, Taeuber-Arp continues to provide volumes.

Art historian Briony Fer detects a playful refusal to be still in Taeuber-Arp's geometric abstractions—the protagonists of which were sticks, circles, dots, and squiggles. "The paintings simply will not settle," Fer writes of work "that seems to be finding its own state of balance as you look at it."[17] Even Taeuber-Arp's most nearly monolithic of compositions, the *Gradation* series of 1934, with its modular stack of winged curves, has the humorous precarity of looking like seven equilibrists—some thin, some fat, all with arms outstretched—delicately balanced on each other's bellies. Entering the game almost a century later, Crowner made the next move by abstracting the negative shapes from the margins of Taeuber-Arp's composition and spinning them on edge into elongated forms in a 2016 series of stitched paintings. One of these

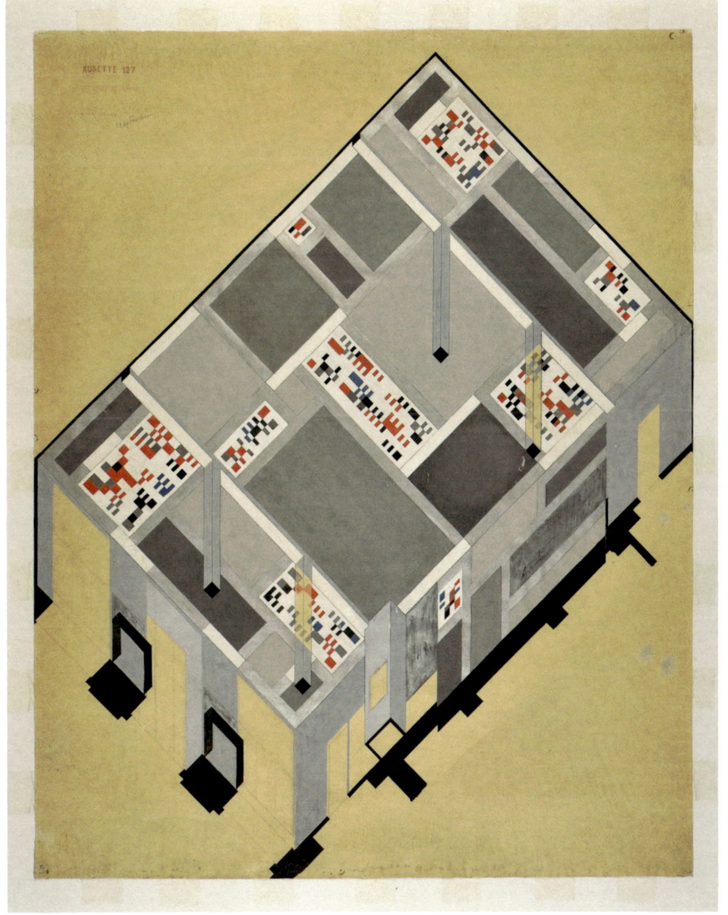

Sophie Taeuber-Arp, *Aubette 127*, 1927. Axonometric drawing of the "Five O'Clock" tearoom in the Aubette, Strasbourg, France. Gouache, metallic paint, ink, and pencil on diazotype; 48⁷⁄₁₆ × 39 in. (123 × 99.1 cm). Strasbourg Museum of Modern and Contemporary Art

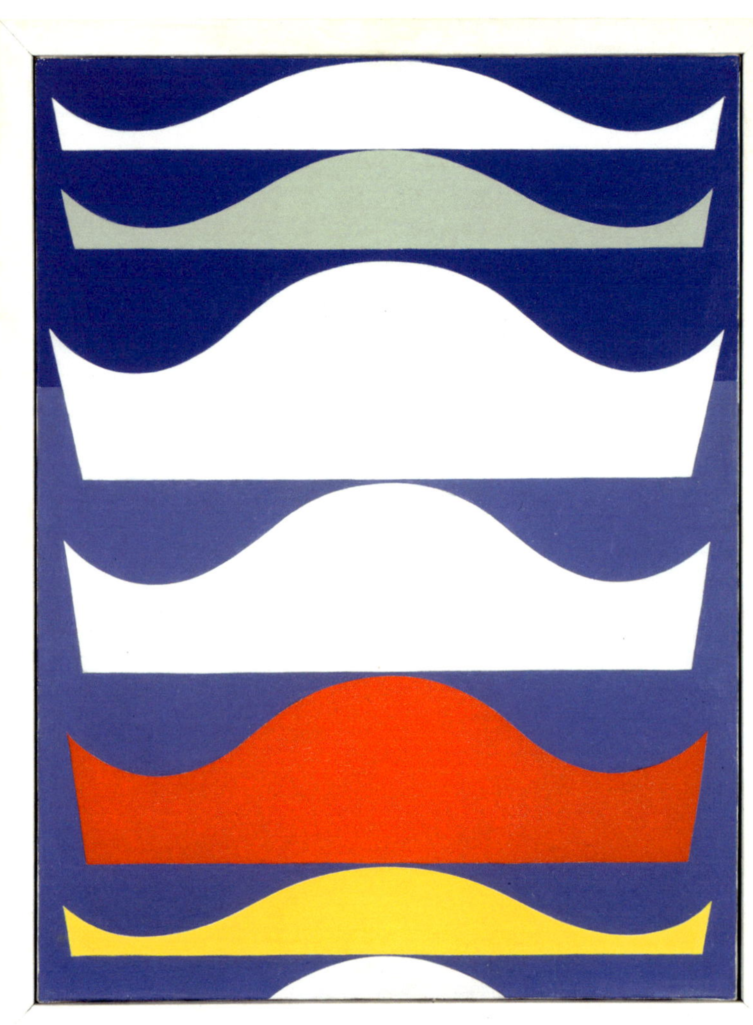

Sophie Taeuber-Arp, *Colored Gradation*, 1939. Oil on canvas; 25½ × 19¹¹⁄₁₆ in. (64.8 × 50 cm). Kunstmuseum Bern. Gift of Marguerite Arp-Hagenbach

Stretched Stems appears in the photograph we were studying earlier, of Carolyn Schoerner performing *Post Tree*, her own limbs outstretched from her stem of a body.

In Taeuber-Arp, Fer finds the wobble of doubt in the purity of abstraction that would open up destabilizing new possibilities for a postwar generation of artists who were seeking more material connections to life through form.[18] Specifically, Ellsworth Kelly "must surely have been at least partly triggered by her modular arrangements when he began his sustained engagement with chance."[19] More sweepingly, there is the reception of Taeuber-Arp's art in Brazil. After her accidental death in 1943 at the age of fifty-three, the dissemination of her work led, among other places, to substantial presentations in 1950 and 1951 at the São Paulo Biennial and from there, Fer speculates, to "a larger and more expansive modernist trajectory exemplified by Brazilian artists . . . who were similarly preoccupied by forms in movement."[20] References to Hélio Oiticica's *Metaesquemas* (1957–58) and Lygia Pape's *Neo-Concrete Ballets* (1958–59) loop back to the pages of Crowner's playbook of art history, in which Kelly also figures. Swivel and turn from *Stretched Stems* to face a wall in the same installation that is largely empty, save for a small square canvas that holds a wedge of Kelly's orange.

Art's Devotions

Crowner's interactions with artists and their work over time constitutes a form of reverence. "I love and appreciate these objects,"[21] she said, speaking specifically of ceramics to generally open even wider the embrace of her art's devotions. Crowner assembled a constellation of objects for the 2018 exhibition *Clay Bodies* in Louisville from collections around Kentucky: a tiny bowl by an Acoma potter, a footed bowl by Beatrice Wood, a juice cup produced by an industrial pottery in Tennessee, four goblets formed by Gerard Ferrari, sculptures by Ken Price, Ester Kislin's glaze archive, a collection of Doyle Lane tiles, an eared cooking pot from Mexico, Wedgwood. The installation was staged as a series of tableaux, with display furniture, wall colors, and a theatrical backdrop of sky (by Scenic Art Studios in Newburgh, New York), all

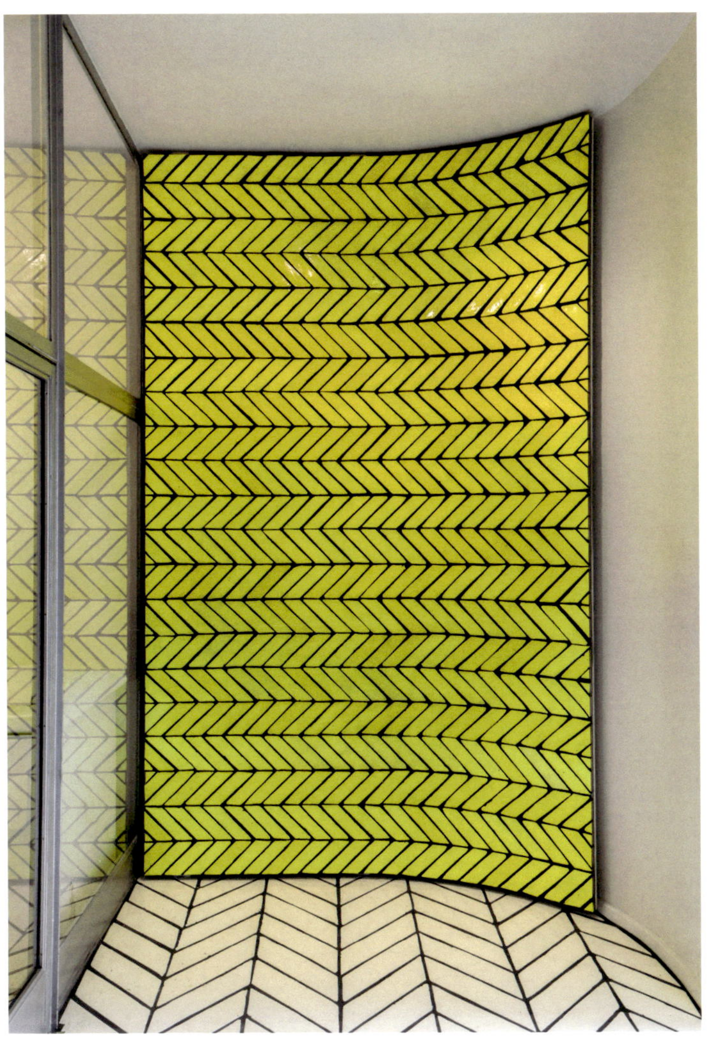

Wall (Yellow Terracotta), 2017. Glazed terracotta tiles and grout; dimensions variable. Solomon R. Guggenheim Museum, New York. Purchased with funds contributed by the International Director's Council and additional funds contributed by Mr. and Mrs. J. Tomilson Hill, 2017.46

designed by Crowner, whose own works in clay and canvas were also part of the mix. Overall, the exhibition appeared to frame "a deep and primeval urge to make the things we own more beautiful."[22] These words were formulated in 1922 by Taeuber-Arp in answer to herself. Against the rupture of world war and the rumbling of global unrest, she asked: "In our complicated times, why conceive ornaments and color combinations when there are so many more practical and especially more necessary things to do?"[23]

Do we run from feelings to make our lives less complicated? Or do we embrace the dictum of the avant-garde dancer, choreographer, and filmmaker Yvonne Rainer, who titled her 2006 memoir *Feelings Are Facts*, and welcome emotion to make our lives more real? In her pursuit of form as feeling, Crowner approaches her work with a complete lack of pretense. "Irony, to me, is not important . . . I see it as a crutch, or even a curtain to hide behind. I feel it is more daring to be sincere."[24]

Back in the studio, a worktable covered with prototypes, material samples, models, and drawings sits adjacent to Crowner's desk. There are a paint set and brushes next to a pair of loose watercolor sketches with collage elements that relate to a recent trip to São Paulo, where Crowner visited the transparent glass house of Lina Bo Bardi (1950–52) and the opaque Casa Millán (1970–74), a concrete house designed by Paulo Mendes da Rocha. By expressing connections through her own work, she calls these sketches "wishes" in hopes of engaging with these places in an actual way someday. As for projects that have come true, there are the handmade ceramic cups that Crowner designed and produced for the restaurant Eleven Madison Park in New York, which, inasmuch as they conjure Taeuber-Arp's designs for Café Aubette, also tap into Crowner's 2017 installation for the Wright. For this boîte of a museum café at the Guggenheim, she created multiple elements, including an immersive abstract painting, which she titled *Backdrop (after Rodhe, 1961)* in reference to a wool tapestry by the Swedish artist Lennart Rodhe for the restaurant Operakällaren in Stockholm that served as a study for Crowner's almost textile-like ceramic tile installation. Covering the walls and floor in geometric pattern and tactile color, the handmade terracotta tiles in Frank Lloyd Wright's spiraling monument take us right back to Mexico—by way of Brooklyn.

FOLLOWING PAGES *Backdrop (after Rodhe, 1961)*, 2017. Acrylic on canvas, sewn; panel 1: 61 × 53 × 5 in. (154.9 × 134.6 × 12.7 cm); panel 2: 61 × 95 × 5 in. (154.9 × 241.3 × 12.7 cm); panel 3: 61 × 121 × 5 in. (154.9 × 307.3 × 12.7 cm). Solomon R. Guggenheim Museum, New York. Purchased with funds contributed by the International Director's Council and additional funds contributed by Mr. and Mrs. J. Tomilson Hill, 2017

Puebla

On a table in Crowner's studio sat a miniature construction of the courtyard and galleries her art will occupy at the museum in Puebla. Like many artists in the process of creating an exhibition, she uses architectural models to help spatialize her work. Among the postage stamps–sized reproductions of her paintings at play was an itty-bitty version of *Medusa* (2020). Named for the snake-haired Gorgon, whose gaze had the power to turn a person to stone, the composition is a

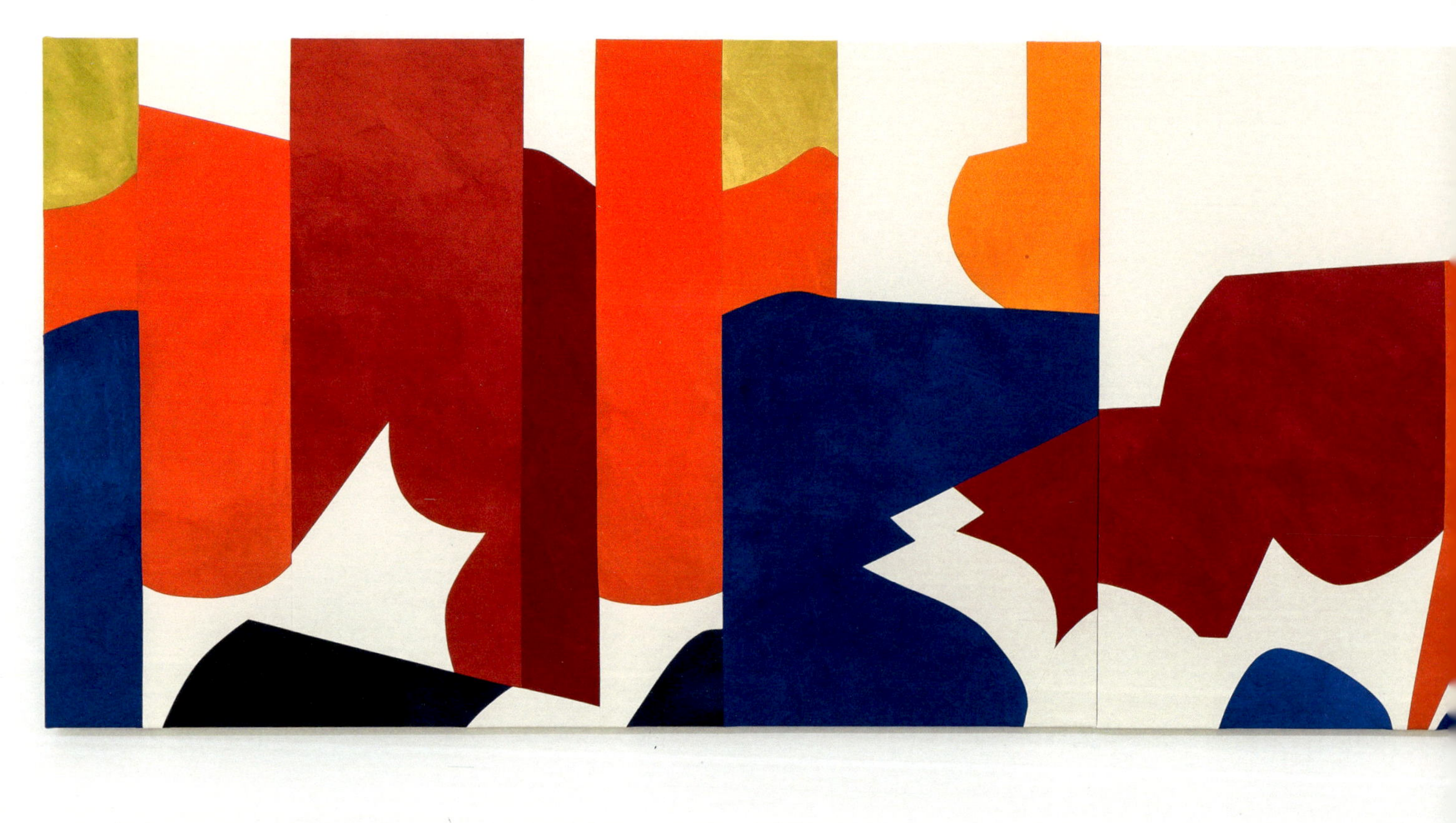

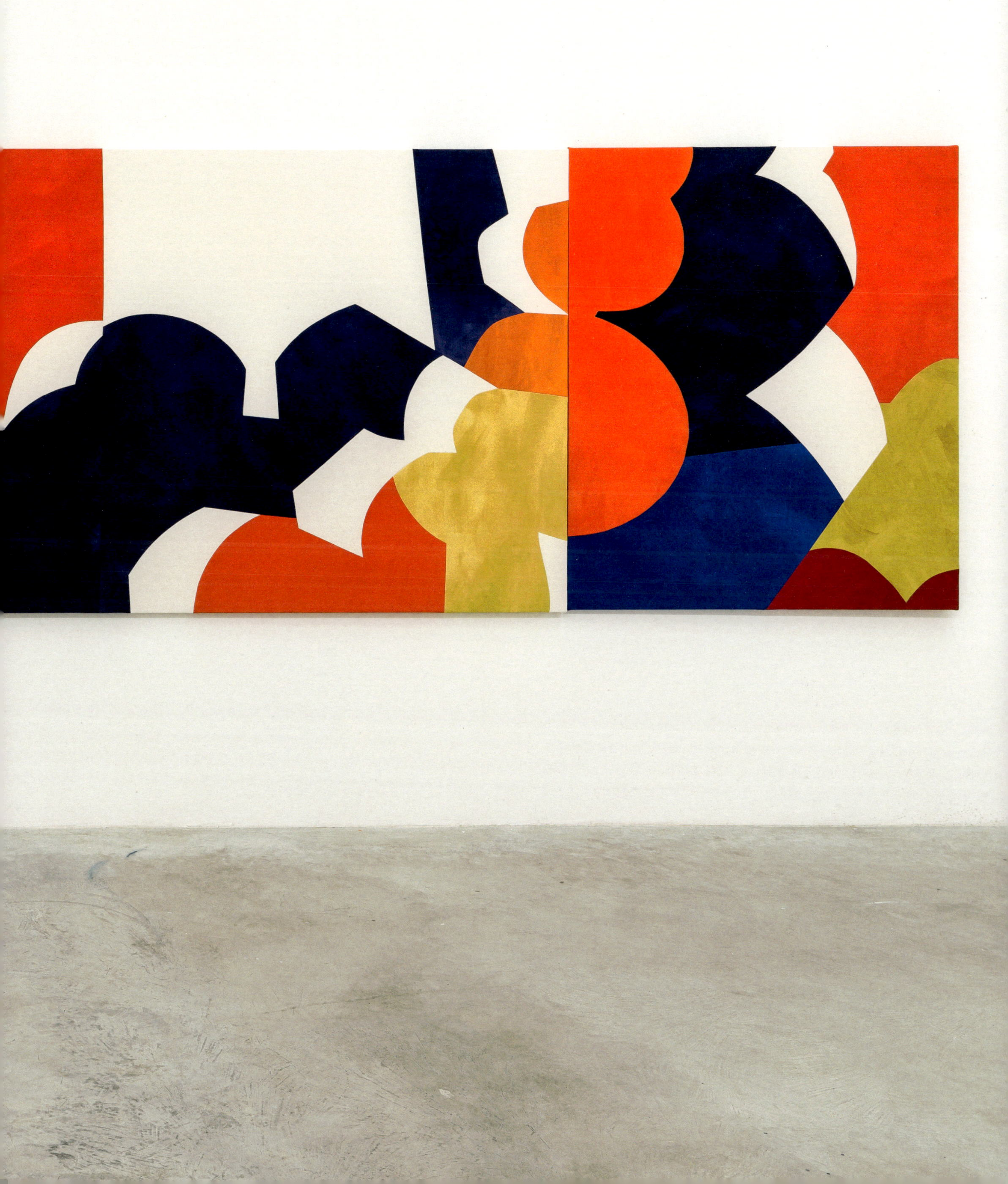

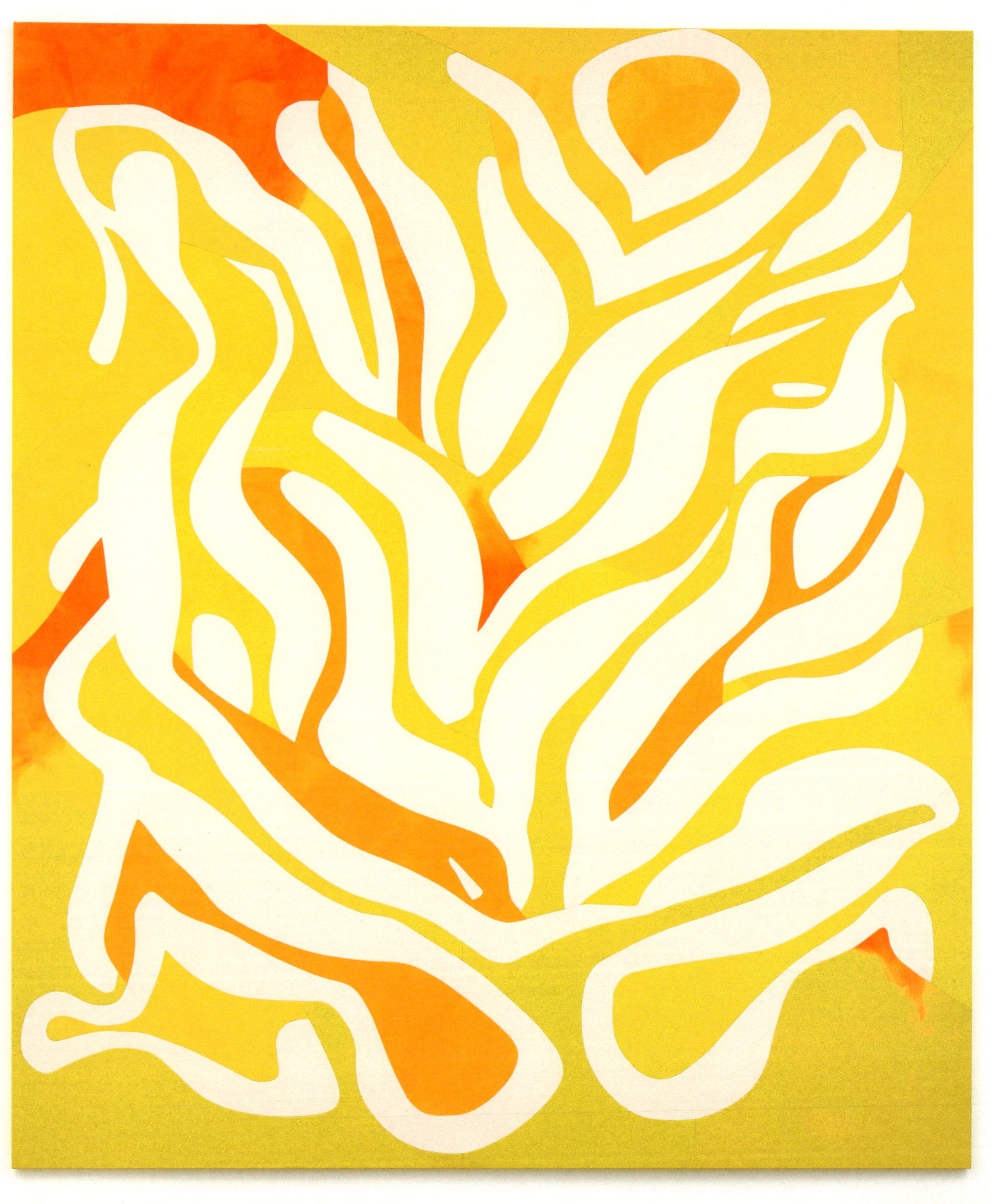

OPPOSITE *Solar Medusa*, 2021. Acrylic on canvas, sewn; 120 × 104 in. (304.8 × 264.2 cm). The Nancy A. Nasher and David J. Haemisegger Collection, Dallas, TX

FOLLOWING PAGES Installation views, *Platform (Blue Green terracotta for JC)*, Chinati Foundation, Marfa, TX, 2022. John Chamberlain, *Gone to Marfa*, 1977 (painted and chromium-plated steel; 76 × 23 × 29 in. [193 × 58.4 × 73.7 cm])

squiggling bundle of linear shapes forming an anemone of raw canvas against a vivid magenta ground. The energy comes from Rome, where as a recent fellow at the American Academy Crowner spent days wandering a city that struck her as alive with classical, medieval, and baroque sculptures of animals, serpents, and "writhing stone."

Housed in two colonial-era buildings, in a city renowned for traditional Talavera tilework that has roots outside of Toledo, Spain, the Museo Amparo is one of Mexico's most significant historic museums. Crowner's exhibition will take place in the central and largest of three interior courtyards, which has a fountain in the middle of it, as well as in three adjacent galleries. Judging from what was going on with the model, Crowner was in the middle of figuring out a problem that, not unlike the plan of the Museo Experimental El Eco, was full of dramatic potential. How to create a discrete experience in the galleries—which are tall, narrow, and relatively compressed interiors—that could hold its own and be contiguous with the impact of her tile platform painting in the exterior space?

In the smallest of the three galleries, she was experimenting with the possibility of working with objects from the museum's encyclopedic collection. The Amparo has collected the work of Graciela Iturbide in great depth, and Crowner was particularly drawn to a set of the photographer's contact sheets that features studies of snake skeletons. So heavily marked and covered with lines by Iturbide, they appear practically as drawings. Crowner's thoughts of putting her own work in dialogue with these "sketches" by Iturbide were still far from certain. What was concrete, however, was her idea of the courtyard as a liquid space.

Ever since her 2014 installation at Barragán's Casa Franco in Guadalajara, Crowner has consistently realized new work with Cerámica Suro and José Noé Suro Salceda, whose father founded the Guadalajara-based tile manufactory in the 1950s. She is currently at work on a tile platform that will also be a viewing platform for photographs by the sculptor John Chamberlain. The pairing will take place as a special exhibition at the Chinati Foundation, the museum founded by Donald Judd in Marfa, Texas. Filling the bridge of an enormous U-shaped building, Crowner's painting is conceived as an expansive pool of light and color and is sure to be experienced as a brilliant infusion of coolness to the Chihuahuan Desert that visibly surrounds. For the Fundación Casa Proal, an artists' residency in Veracruz, she designed an actual swimming pool (see pp. 18–19): a basin of deep blue tile, framed by a deck of unglazed terracotta and shaped like a stylized wave.

At the Museo Amparo, Crowner imagines her tiled platform flooding the courtyard with a pool of saturated blues, sparkling with reflected sunlight, zigzagging with movement, and brightening every sound, to make voices and footsteps and the fountain's splashing water all part of the experience of the painting. If a painting could look at Medusa, from whose head snakes poured like tresses, this one destined for Mexico was already turning to stone. In the studio, Crowner picked up a sample of one of the ceramic tiles. It was shaped like a very large scale on a snake's skin. Serpent. *Serpiente*. *Serpentear*, which in Spanish means to meander, to loop, to follow a winding path. To go back to our journey's beginning, this is how it all comes together.

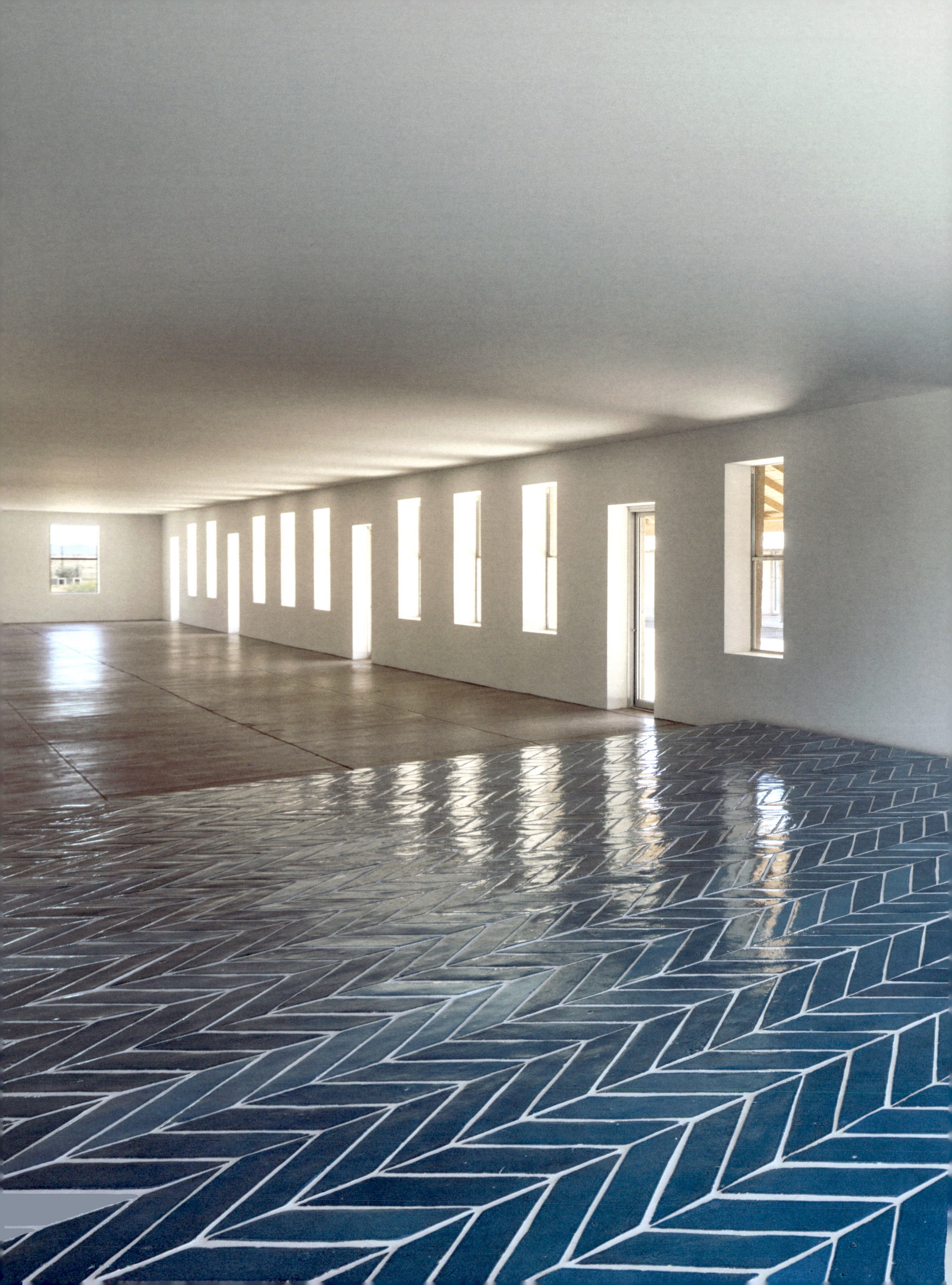

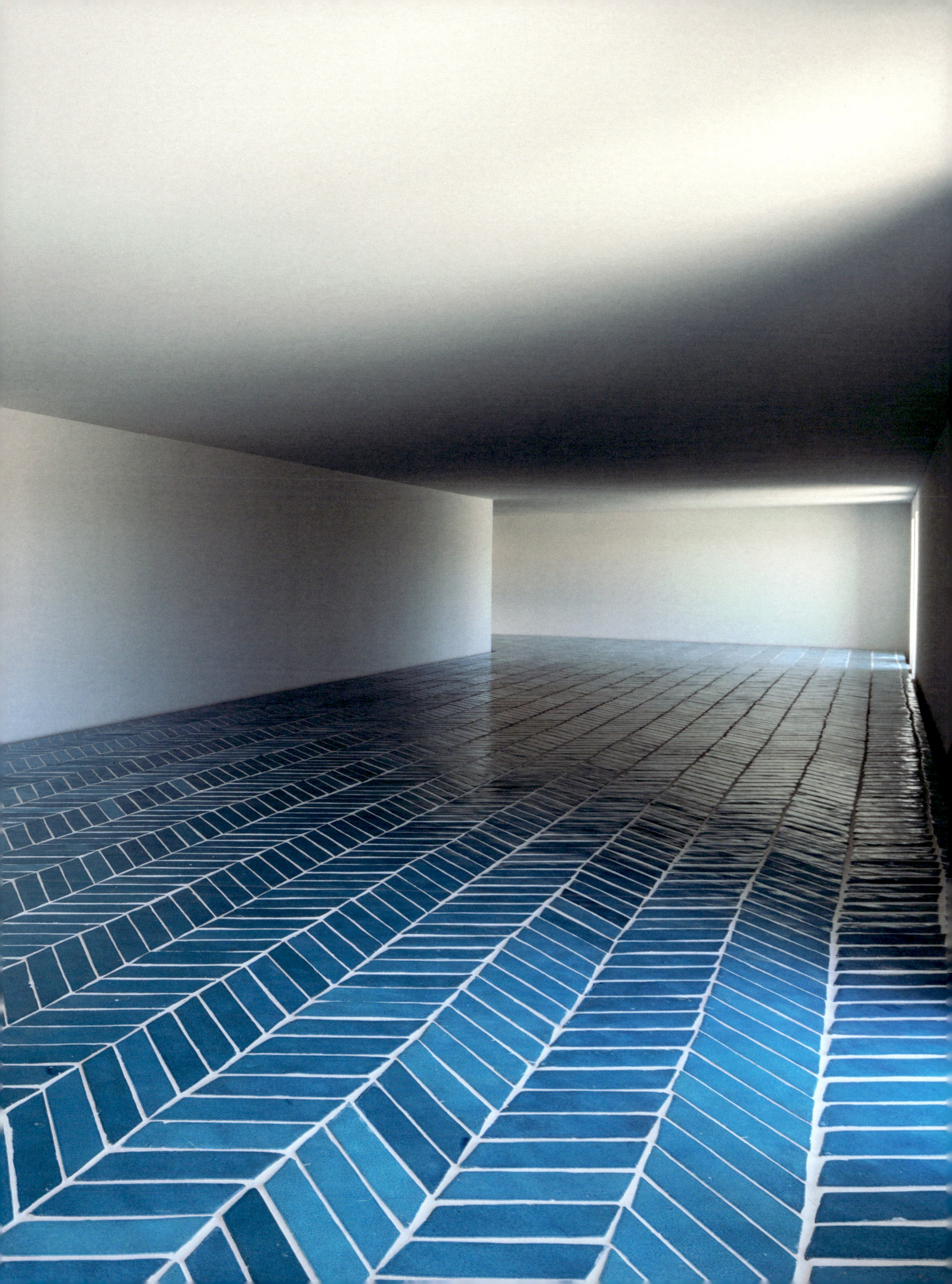

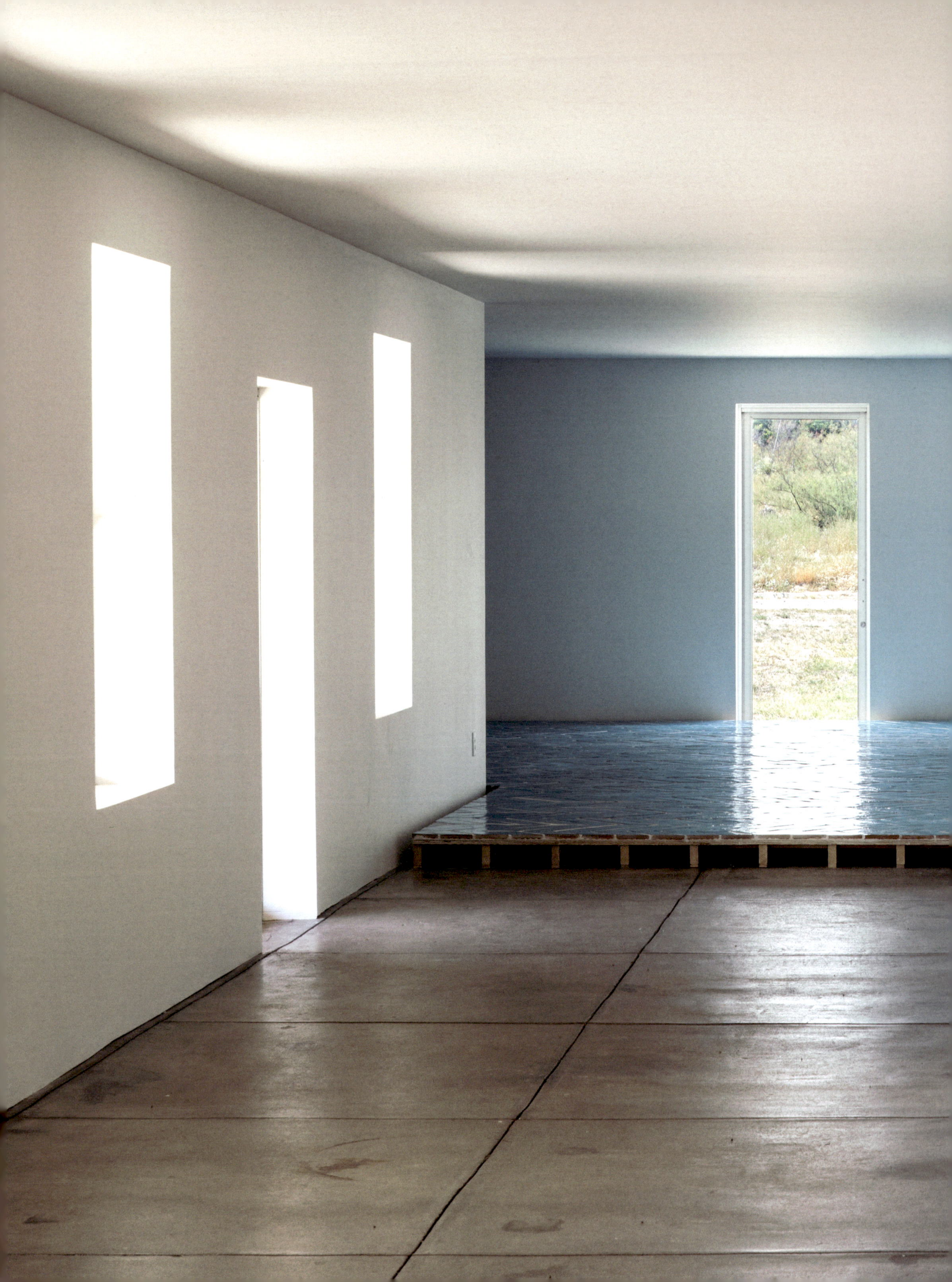

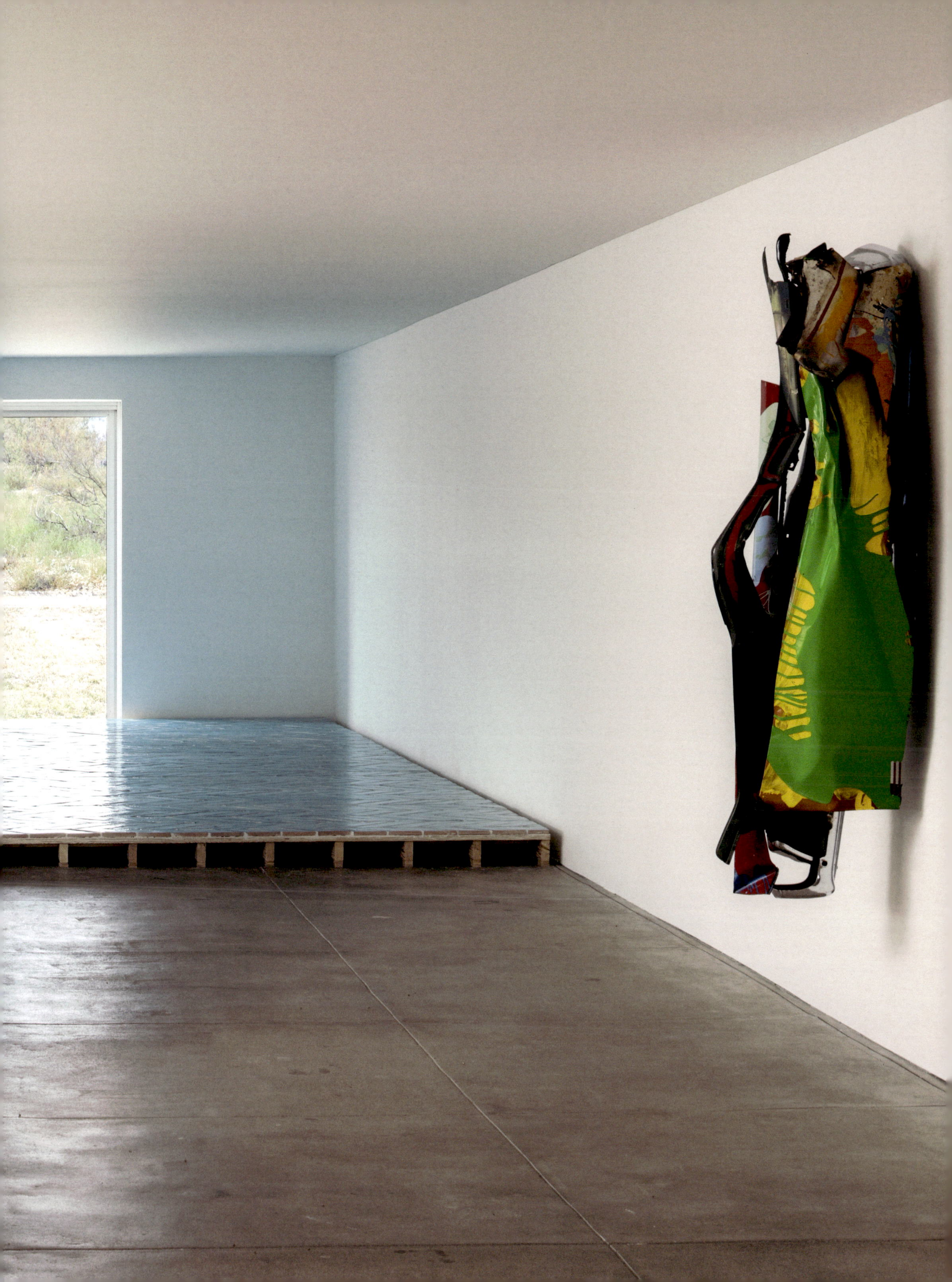

NOTES

1. Mathias Goeritz wrote his "Manifesto of Emotional Architecture" in 1953 after the completion of his Museo Experimental El Eco. For an excellent history of the manifesto, the museum, and the German-born sculptor and designer, who transplanted to Mexico in 1949, see Jennifer Josten, *Mathias Goeritz: Modernist Art and Architecture in Cold War Mexico* (New Haven, CT: Yale University Press, 2018).
2. All unattributed quotes of Goeritz in this paragraph are from his 1953 manifesto, available at https://designmanifestos.org/mathias-goeritz-emotional-architecture-manifesto/#:~:text=The%20new%20El%20Eco%20Experimental,whose%20main%20function%20is%20emotion.
3. All unattributed quotes of Crowner are from my studio visit with the artist, November 30, 2021.
4. Crowner's exhibition *Post Jacaranda* was on view at Galerie Nordenhake in Mexico City from May 18 to June 15, 2019. The exhibition was accompanied by a limited-edition artist's book.
5. "Sarah, I believe you may have created the first wheelchair-accessible painting," said curator Bartholomew Ryan of the artist's tiled platform and ramp for her 2016 exhibition *Beetle in the Leaves*. In Ryan, "Medium as Medium: A Conversation with Sarah Crowner," in *Sarah Crowner*, exh. cat. (North Adams, MA: Massachusetts Museum of Contemporary Art; and New York: DelMonico Books/Prestel, 2017), 21.
6. Elizabeth Karp-Evans, "Sarah Crowner: Touch the Tile," *Guernica*, May 16, 2016. Online publication accessed February 23, 2022, https://www.guernicamag.com/touch-the-tile.
7. Lauren O'Neill-Butler, "500 Words: Sarah Crowner," *Artforum* online, September 5, 2011. Accessed February 23, 2022, http://artforum.com/words/id=28886.
8. A protegé of the pioneer of Black dance Katherine Dunham, Walter Nicks formed his small company El Ballet Negro in Mexico City in 1953. Back in New York by the mid-1950s, as director of the Walter Nicks Dance Company, he was an internationally renowned dancer, teacher, and choreographer.
9. See Susan Cross, "Beetle in the Leaves," in *Sarah Crowner* (2017), 43.
10. *Curtain (Vidas Perfectas)* and *Kurtyna Teatru (After Maria Jarema)* are nearly identical works from 2012. Like *Curtain*, which, following its appearance on stage in Brooklyn, held leading roles in projects at the Institute of Contemporary Art, University of Pennsylvania, in Philadelphia and at the Museum of Fine Arts, Boston, *Kurtyna Teatru* has its own exhibition and performance history. After its debut in Stockholm at Galerie Nordenhake, Crowner's *Kurtyna Teatru* traveled to Warsaw to appear in the 2013 group show *The Splendor of Textiles* at the Zachęta National Gallery of Art, where it also occasioned a dance performance by Iza Szostak.
11. Crowner encountered the painting as part of a "mini lesson in the Italian avant-garde Carol Rama's life and work" at Galerie Isabella Bortolozzi's booth. Crowner, "An Artist's Eye: Sarah Crowner," *Frieze* online, October 19, 2016. Accessed February 23, 2022, https://www.frieze.com/article/artists-eye-sarah-crowner.
12. Crowner, in conversation with the author, November 30, 2021.
13. Hugo Ball, quoted in the chronology (1917) prepared by Laura Braverman with Walburga Krupp for Anne Umland, Walburga Krupp, and Charlotte Healy, eds., *Sophie Taeuber-Arp: Living Abstraction*, exh. cat. (New York: The Museum of Modern Art, 2021), 306.
14. Quoted in Carolyn Lanchner, *Sophie Taeuber-Arp* (New York: The Museum of Modern Art, 1981), 13.
15. Sophie Taeuber-Arp's tablecloth *Cross on Red Ground* (1924) was part of the *International Exhibition of Modern Tapestries* at the Toledo Museum of Art, Ohio, in 1930–31, which traveled to the Brooklyn Museum, New York.
16. Crowner, in Ryan, "Medium as Medium," 27.
17. Briony Fer, "Balancing Act," in *Sophie Taeuber-Arp* (2021), 170.
18. Fer, "Balancing Act," 173.
19. Fer notes that Ellsworth Kelly visited Jean Arp in Paris around 1950, when he would have seen "Taeuber-Arp's works still on the walls and her studio as she had left it." Fer, "Balancing Act," 173.
20. Fer, "Balancing Act," 173.
21. Crowner, quoted in Brian Sholis's essay "From the Ground Up," in *Sarah Crowner: Clay Bodies*, exh. cat. (Louisville, KY: Kentucky Museum of Art and Craft, 2019), n.p. The exhibition took place December 15, 2018 to April 7, 2019, and was curated by Aldy Milliken.
22. Sophie Taeuber-Arp, "Remarks on Instruction in Ornamental Design," (1922) in *Sophie Taeuber-Arp* (2021), 24.
23. Ibid., 162.
24. Crowner, interviewed by Eleftheria Ioannidou on the occasion of her exhibition *Zig Zag and Curves* at Helena Papadopoulos Gallery in Athens, for *Ozon*, June 25, 2011. Accessed February 23, 2021, https://en.ozonweb.com/culture/art-design/interview-sarah-crowner.

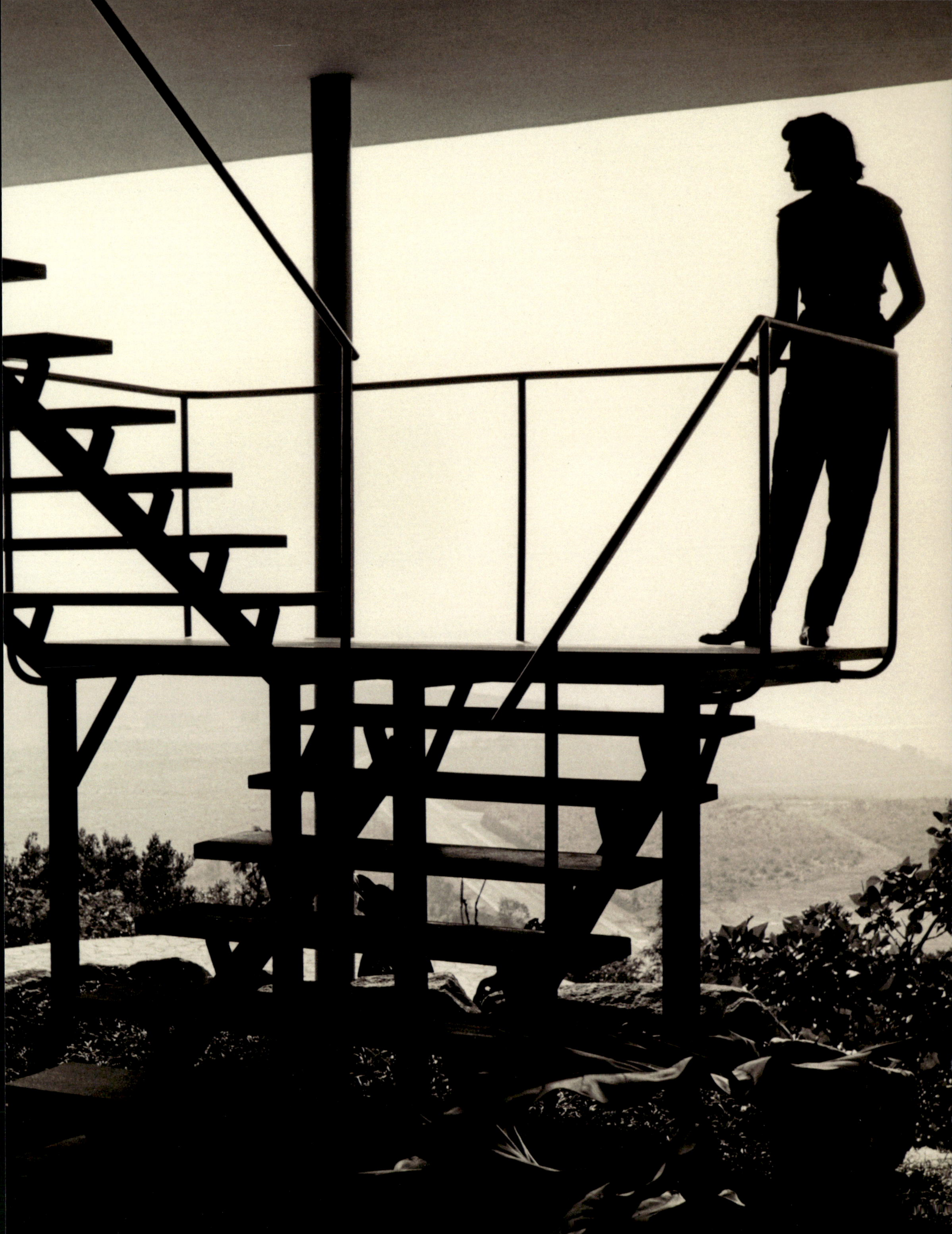

Diego Matos

Blues in Greens, Greens in Blues

Color as Shape, Painting as Architecture

Para a folha: verde Para o céu: azul Para a rosa: rosa Para o mar: azul	For the leaf: green For the sky: blue For the rose: rose For the sea: blue
Para a cinza: cinza Para a areia: ouro Para a terra: pardo Para a terra: azul	For the gray: gray For the sand: gold For the earth: brown For the earth: blue
(Quais são as cores que são suas cores de predileção?)	(What colors are your favorite colors?)

—Caetano Veloso, "Rai das Cores"
(Rai of Colors, 1989)

SARAH CROWNER'S FIRST EXHIBITION IN BRAZIL is mounted concurrently in two São Paulo venues: Instituto Bardi, in the famous Casa de Vidro (Glass House) designed by Italian-Brazilian architect Lina Bo Bardi and completed in 1952, and auroras, an exhibition space housed in a residence designed by Italian-Brazilian architect Giancarlo Gasperini in 1957. Both of these modernist houses feature myriad architectural devices that provide visitors with a merged experience of the interior and exterior worlds they create and occupy. Crowner's work features a modulating, choreographic, and seductive relationship between material and technique, as well as shape and composition—certainly key functions of all great architecture—resulting in artworks that complement the spaces of their Brazilian venues.

Crowner manages to undermine the traditional roles that landscape and architecture serve, tipping architecture's mediating nature (public/private and visible/invisible, among many other dualities) to a place that lands just a bit off balance. Two of the works presented in the auroras space, *Greens Window (Brazil)* and *Another Green World 2*, become windows into her artistic and natural world. Both works can be seen from the edge of a window frame, or from the threshold of a door. In

Lina Bo Bardi at Casa de Vidro, São Paulo, 1952

another work, *Blues with Red Margin*, the reflection of the sky on the mirrored surface of the outdoor pool appears, with red alluding to a kind of delineation, an intermediate place of her painting and the surrounding architectural forms. For Bo Bardi's Glass House, Crowner made *Blues for Lina*, a large painting that is in sync with the horizontality and transparency of the house, with its cool, light-blue tiled floor and views of the house's surrounding dense, green forest. The blues and greens in *Blues for Lina* shift throughout the day with the changing light, in constant dialogue with the natural world outside and the manmade space, forming a unique intimacy with Bo Bardi's architecture.

These artworks are not merely ornamental; they are borne from an inquiry that has preoccupied art history for more than a century, examining the spaces between art and architecture. Crowner has a completely intuitive awareness of architecture, and her installation of seven paintings in the auroras space (one of which is a diptych) gives the presentation a dynamic, performative feel. Crowner's technical acuity questions the language of painting, sidestepping its historical tendency toward storytelling while still matching the scale and purpose of panels or murals. This advancement, from an initial sense of curiosity and wonder toward some sort of functional condition of the work of art, is one of her most significant gestures.

In *Lovers Up and Down*, a two-panel artwork presented on opposite sides of a shared wall, Crowner works with spatial volume and painting's relationship with the viewer—a theme she has been exploring over the past decade in her various exhibitions. For example, in her solo exhibition at the Massachusetts Museum of Contemporary Art in 2016, the artist showed two-dimensional works that referenced the patterns of the tiled floor installed with them, while at the same time engaging in a dialogue with the architecture of the venue.

Mostly produced after the artist's first visit to Brazil in 2022, Crowner's canvas panels on view at auroras and their respective titles reveal the artist's connection to the landscape and the way in which color plays a leading role: *Aurora*, *Greens Window (Brazil)*, *Rising Violet*, *Lovers Up and Down*, *Another Green World 2*, *Blue Descending Staircase*, and *Blues with Red Margin*. Here, seduction through synesthesia underscores the importance of color in both form and volume. And in this synesthetic tendency we can see in Crowner's artworks something akin to what is found in "Rai das Cores" (Rai of Colors), a 1989 song by Caetano Veloso. There is an interesting poetic parallel here—a transmutation that at times occurs between music and painting, between melodic modulation and the modulation of color. The song itself is a quasi-visual poem, in which the world around us is associated with colors in a sort of ode to its very plasticity. The works installed by Crowner provide a visual and material dance of colors: blues, greens, reds, pinks, yellows, oranges, magentas, whites, and beiges. We can find a possible amalgam between colors and sounds, sounds and colors: a poetic path. It is said that the term *rai*, a form of Algerian popular music dating to the 1920s, is a hub that aggregates the colors alluding to folkloric Arab-Algerian music, but it also can be literally translated as an opinion or thought. The artist's body of work is, in this sense, a *rai* of colors.

OPPOSITE *Blue Descending Staircase*, 2021. Acrylic on canvas, sewn; 70 × 48 in. (177.8 × 122 cm)

FOLLOWING PAGES *Blues for Lina*, 2022. Acrylic on canvas, sewn; overall 78 × 220 in. (198.1 × 558.8 cm). Hall Collection

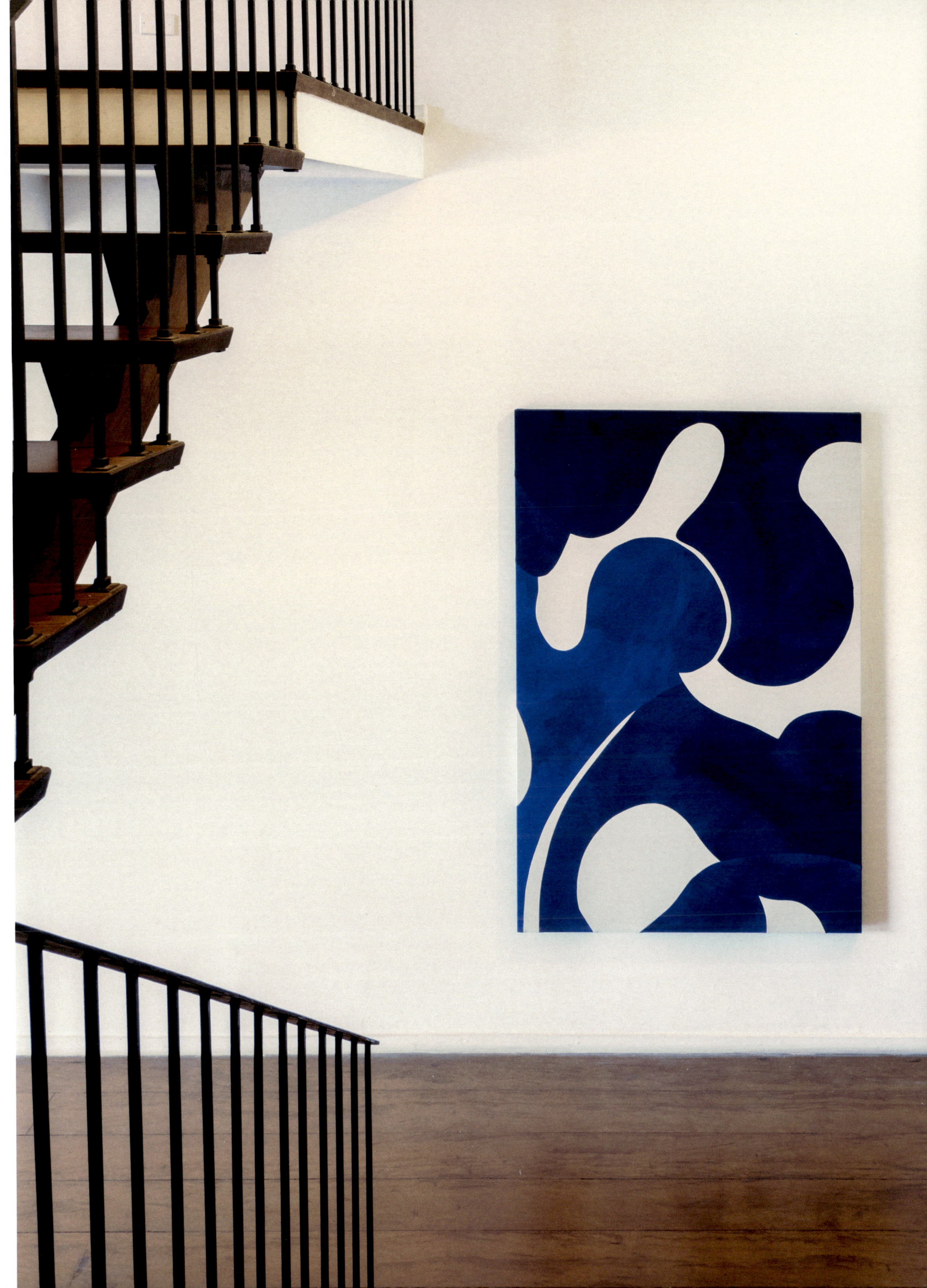

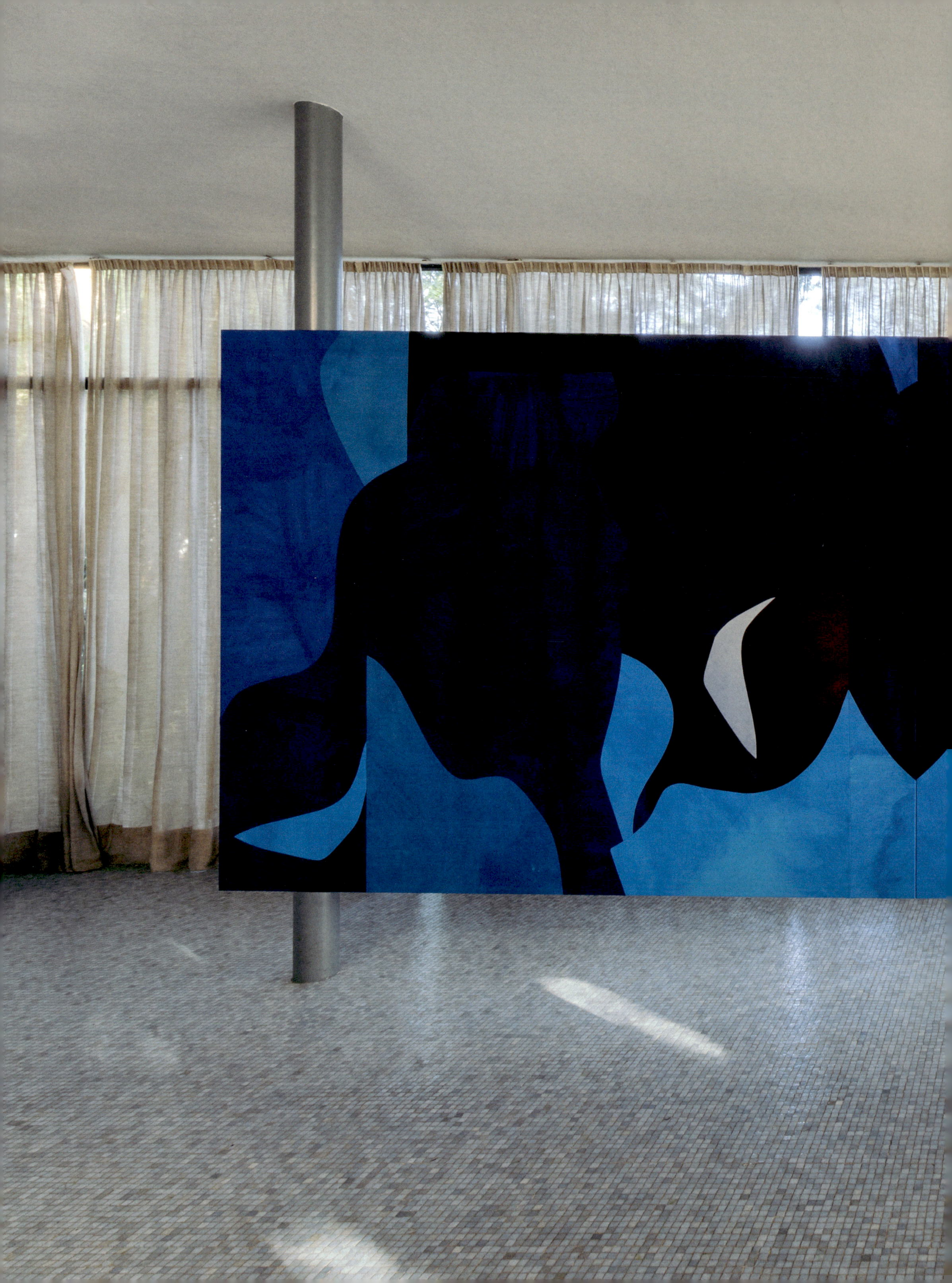

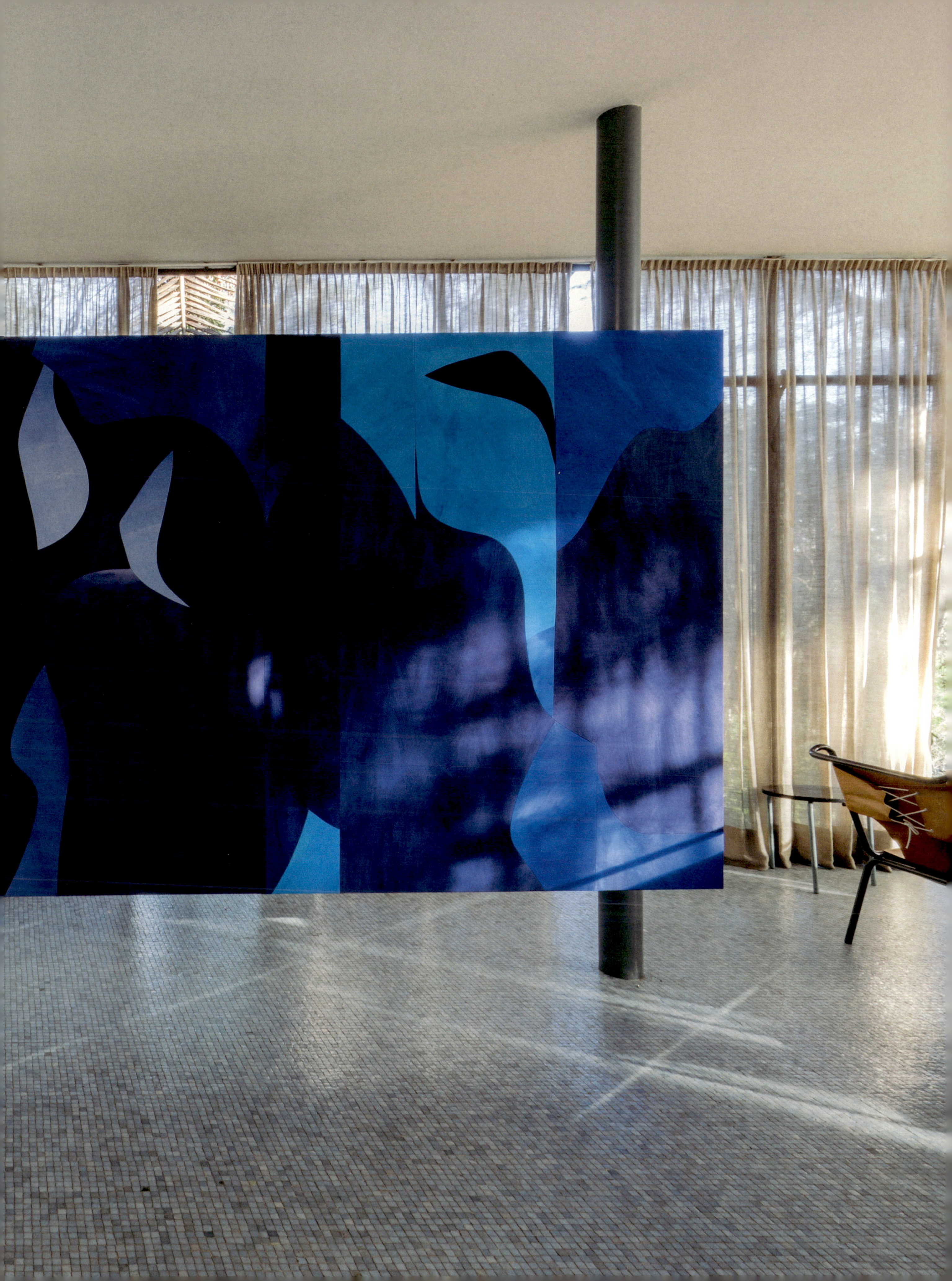

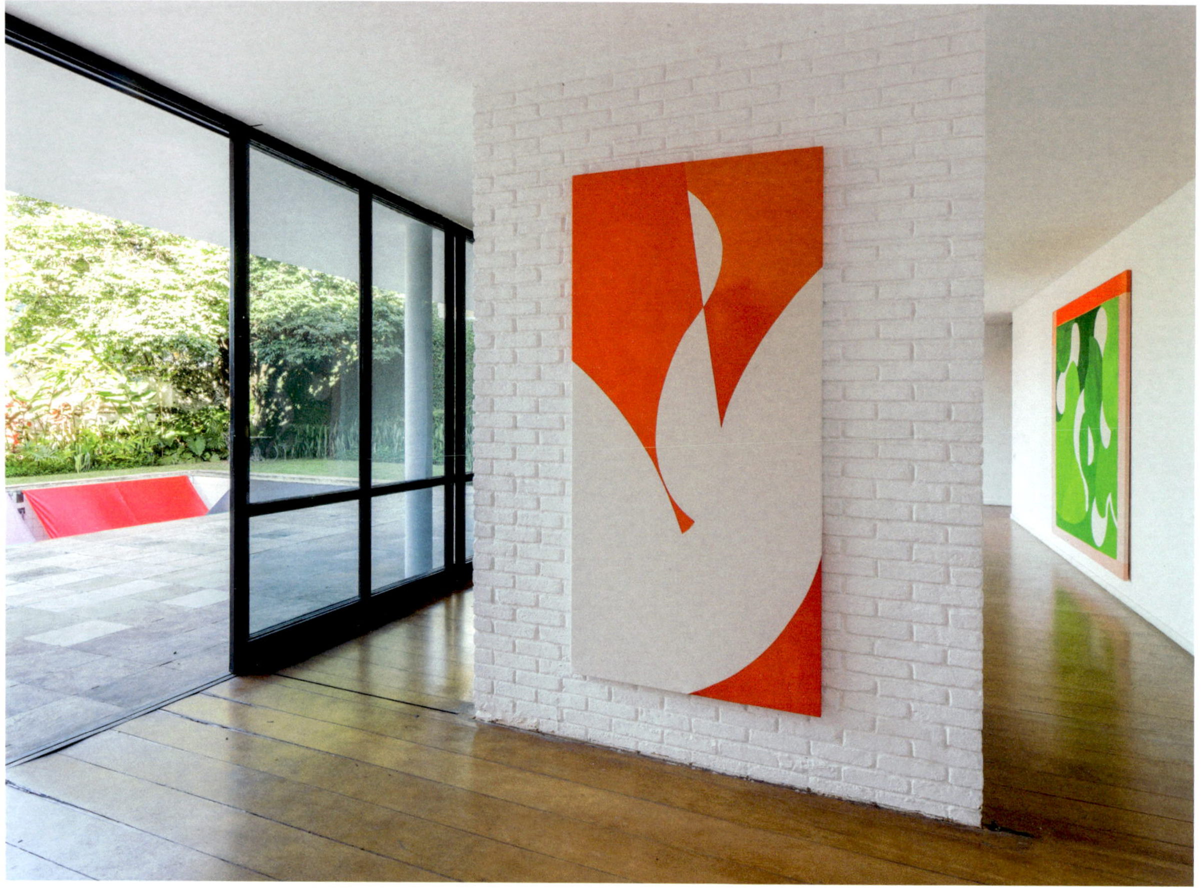

Lovers Up and Down (detail), 2022. Acrylic on canvas, sewn; two panels, each 80 × 40 in. (203.5 × 102 cm)

The titles of the exhibitions, *Blues in Greens* at Casa de Vidro and *Greens in Blues* at auroras, form an immediate association with "Blue in Green" by Miles Davis and Bill Evans, a ballad that was part of the revolution that Davis's *Kind of Blue* (1959) embarked upon.[1] One of the great innovations of modal jazz—the stylistic movement of this record's moment, which radically departed from the complex harmonic changes in the improvisational structure of bebop—was that improvisation could happen on top of simple melodic lines in a dizzying variety of ways, letting moods build into more sinuous musical movements. This opening of fluid possibilities even led to new synesthetic play and the destructuring of sequences and tempos. It is an endless mantra, and there is the very same feeling of expansiveness in Crowner's artistic work.

In English, the color blue (and the use of the word "blue") sums up a mood in which nostalgia, a certain sadness, and calm are triangulated. Yet when blue is introduced to green, it gains a peaceful feeling. If "Blue in Green" can be a feeling, a melodic arrangement, or an artistic composition, it is color that cuts through this protagonism of meanings: of a sound to a sentiment, of a sentiment to an excitement of color, of a color to a musical expression. It is therefore color gestated as an appropriate form.

However, with poetic license, each work of Crowner's Brazilian presentation opens up like a window of color(s), providing a vision of the artist's intuitive perception regarding formal and functional issues

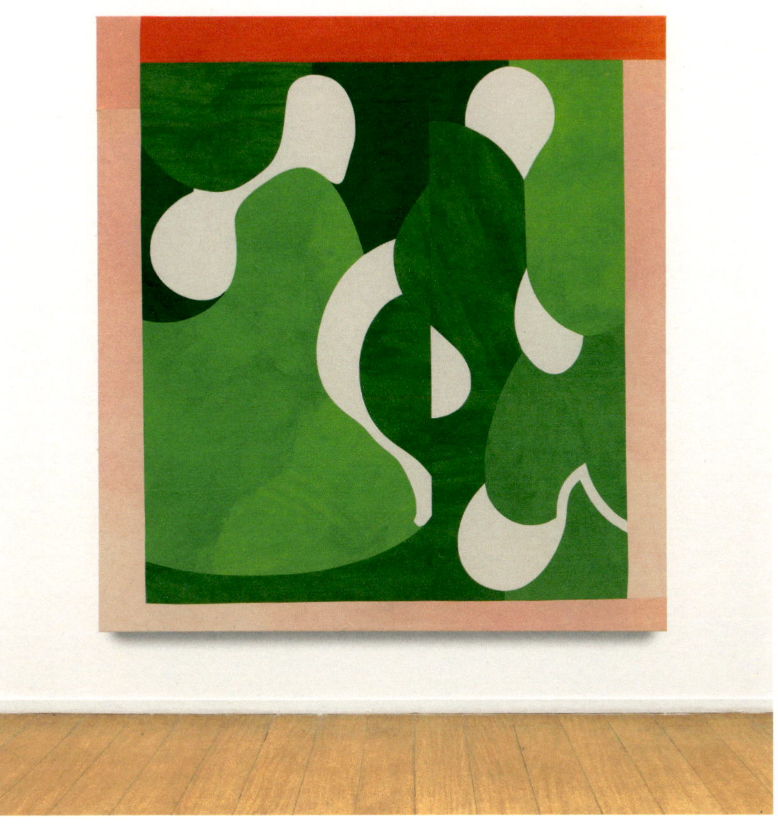

Greens Window (Brazil), 2022. Acrylic on canvas, sewn; 90 × 86 in. (228.5 × 218.5 cm)

of the architecture with which the work is in dialogue. Sometimes intuition is perceived as uncontrollable, or lacking in rigor, yet Crowner shows us precisely the opposite: rigor and intuition walk hand in hand in connection—albeit transitory—with the architecture that houses it.

Sarah Crowner's practice expands the field of painting with intuitive sensitivity in the way she combines abstract parts within, and emanating from, her compositions. They are perfectly fused parts, where any frames, profiles, or even the edge of the flat canvas itself functions as a border point between the work and the world—a frontier that may someday overflow, appropriating a place that belongs to architecture. This is not a desire, a conceptual objective, but rather a wish to establish a specialized zone that qualifies as, and feeds back into, the artist's research. *Blues in Greens, Greens in Blues* are color as form, painting as architecture: poetic and formal meetings imagined by the artist, for now, in Brazil.

NOTE

1. The album *Kind of Blue* is one of the most successful and influential jazz records, celebrated for its experimentation in weaving together a musical genre, modal jazz, and its approximations with popular music and other forms of artistic expression.

FOLLOWING PAGES Studio view, Rauschenberg Residency, Captiva Island, FL, 2019

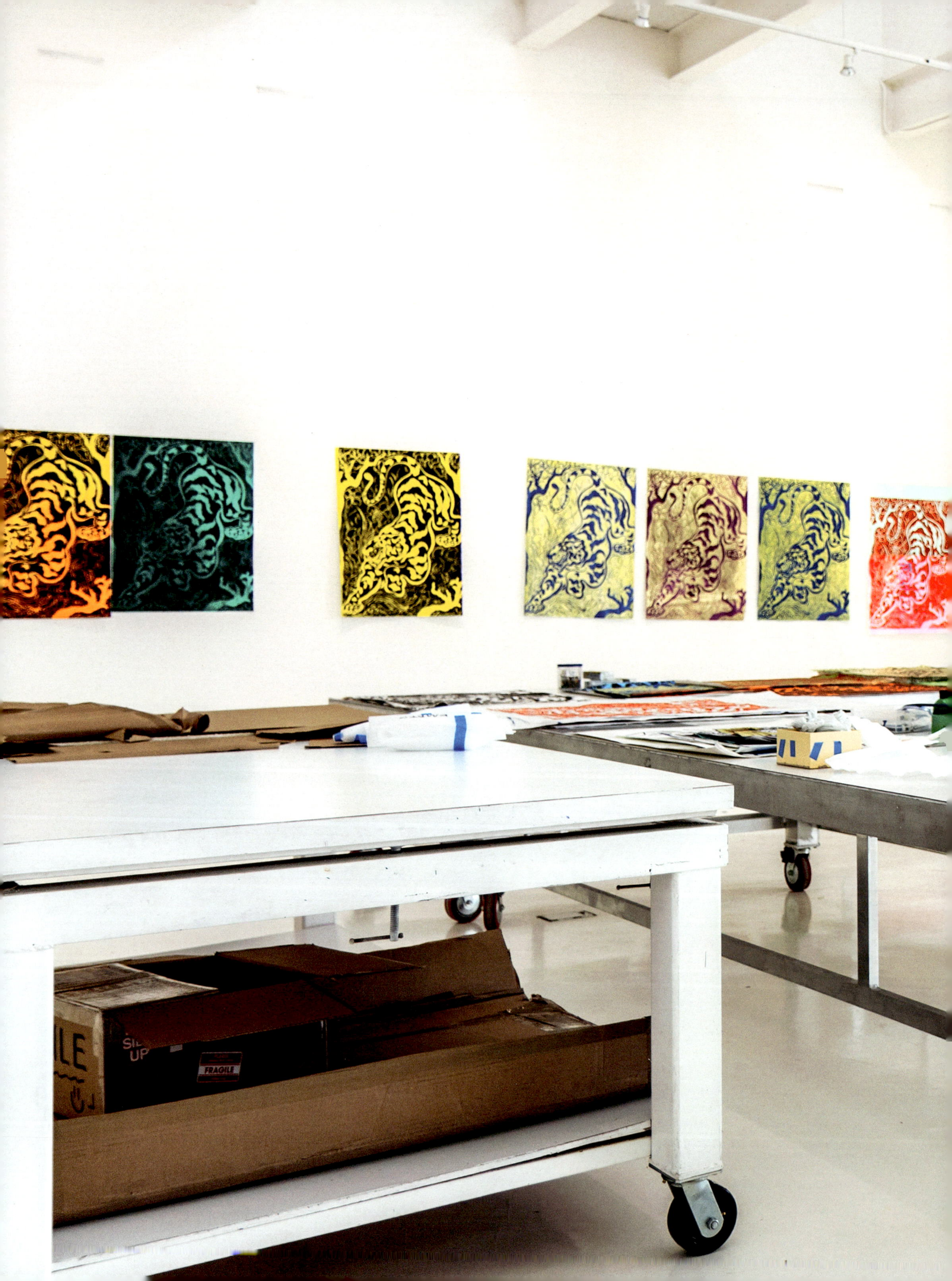
FRAGILE

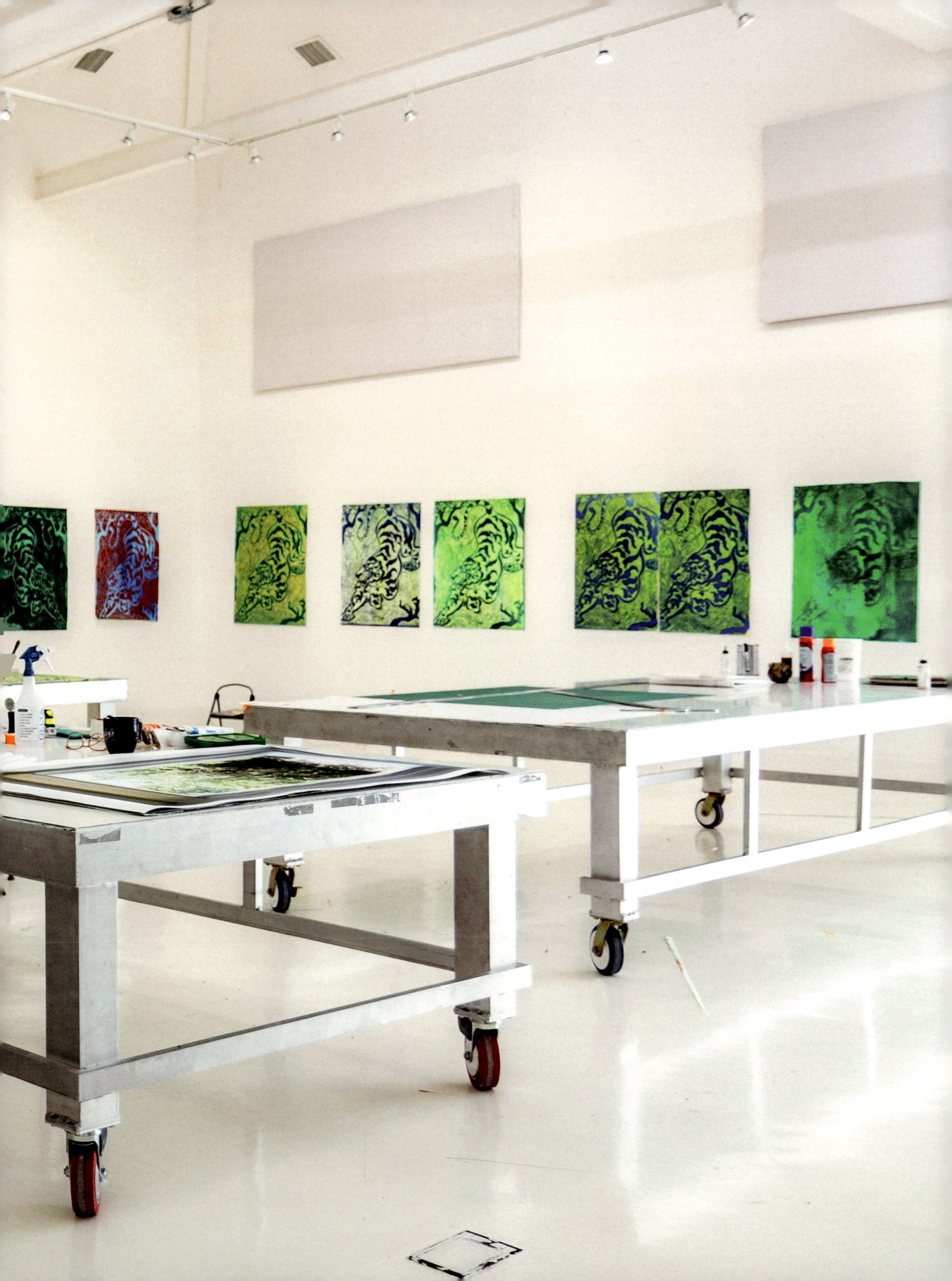

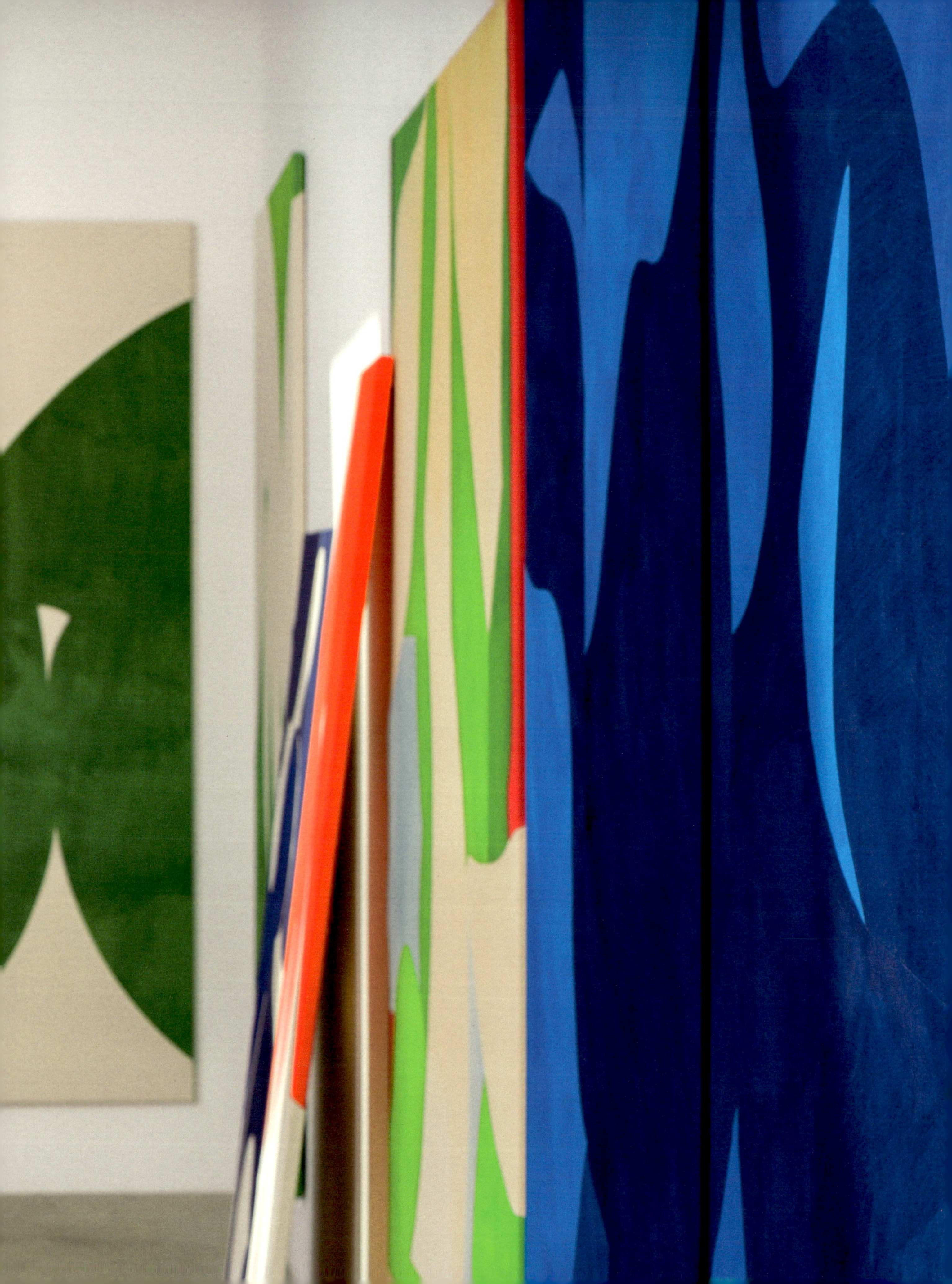

Contributors

Nikki Columbus is a writer, curator, and editor based in New York. Her writing and programming focus on museums and social justice, performance, and contemporary art of the Middle East. She has written for *n+1* and numerous art publications, organized public forums for the Graduate Center of the City University of New York and the Vera List Center for Art and Politics, held editorial posts at *Parkett* and *Artforum*, and curated at Townhouse Gallery in Cairo. She is currently working on a book about maternal discrimination.

Quinn Latimer is a poet, critic, and editor whose work often explores feminist economies of writing, reading, and image production. Her publications include *Like a Woman: Essays, Readings, Poems* (2017), *Sarah Lucas: Describe This Distance* (2013), and *Rumored Animals* (2012). Her writings have appeared in *Artforum*, the *Paris Review*, the *White Review*, and *Texte zur Kunst*, and her performance and language-based works have been featured widely. She is the editor or coeditor of various publications, including *Amazonia: Anthology as Cosmology* (2021), *Simone Forti: The Bear in the Mirror* (2019), *The documenta 14 Reader* (2017), and *Pamela Rosenkranz: No Core* (2012). Previously, Latimer was editor-in-chief of publications for documenta 14 in Athens and Kassel. She is now head of the master's program at the Institute Art Gender Nature in Basel, where, with Chus Martínez, she organizes a semiannual symposia series on questions of gender, language, social justice, and artistic practice. She lives and works in Basel and Athens.

Ana Elena Mallet is a Mexico City–based curator specializing in modern and contemporary design. She is currently a distinguished lecturer at the School of Architecture, Art and Design of the Tecnológico de Monterrey. A member of the acquisitions committee of the department of architecture and design of the Museum of Modern Art in New York, she has collaborated as curatorial advisor and member of advisory and acquisitions boards with many museums and university collections. Mallet has held positions as curator at the Museo Soumaya and Museo de Arte Carrillo Gil, as deputy director of programming at the Museo Rufino Tamayo, and as chief curator of the Museo del Objeto del Objeto. As an independent curator she has organized exhibitions for various museums in Mexico and abroad.

Diego Matos is a São Paulo–based researcher, professor, and curator specializing in the fields of art and architecture. In 2021, with Márcio Seligmann-Silva, he co-organized the permanent exhibition *MemoriAntonia: For an Active Memory in the Service of Human Rights* at the Maria Antonia Center, University of São Paulo. Matos was chief curator of the Brazilian Museum of Sculpture and Ecology (2022–23) and the primary author and guest editor of *Cahiers d'Art*'s edition dedicated to the Brazilian artist Cildo Meireles in 2022. Matos holds PhD and master's degrees from the Architecture and Urbanism College, University of São Paulo.

Ingrid Schaffner is curator at the Chinati Foundation / La Fundación Chinati in Marfa, Texas. In 2018, she organized the *Carnegie International, 57th Edition* at the Carnegie Museum of Art, Pittsburgh. From 2001 to 2015, she was chief curator at the Institute of Contemporary Art, University of Pennsylvania, Philadelphia, where she organized many exhibitions, including *Anne Tyng: Inhabiting Geometry* (2011), *Queer Voice* (2010), and *Dirt on Delight: Impulses That Form Clay* (with Jenelle Porter in 2009). Schaffner is currently at work on a history of Skowhegan School of Painting and Sculpture, the summer residency program founded in 1946 by artists for artists.

Studio view, Brooklyn, NY, 2022

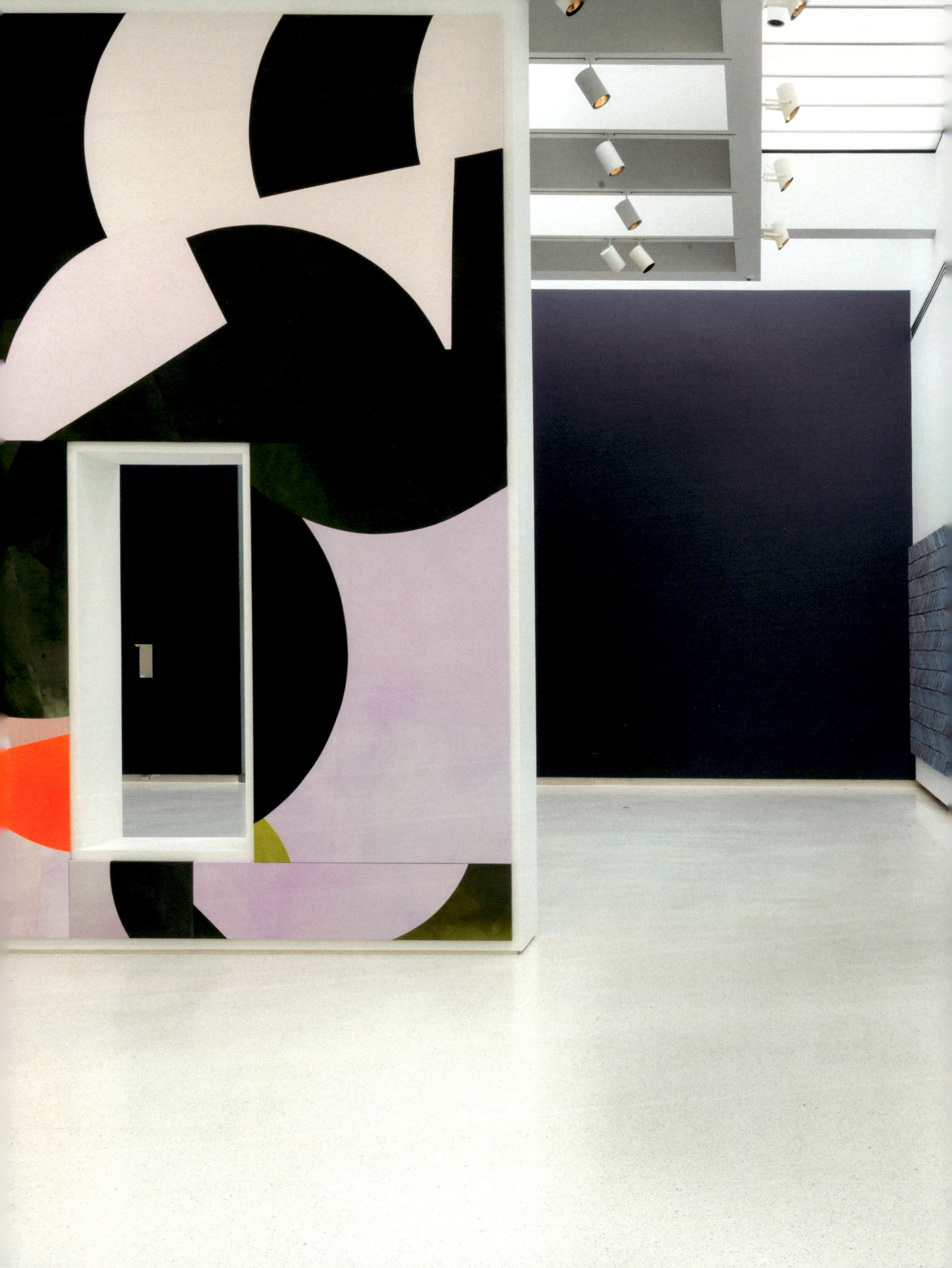

Selected Exhibition History

Born in Philadelphia, 1974
Lives and works in Brooklyn, NY

Solo Exhibitions

2023 *Blues in Greens*, Casa de Vidro Lina Bo Bardi and *Greens in Blues*, auroras, São Paulo

Galerie Nordenhake, Stockholm

Pulitzer Arts Foundation, St. Louis

Hill Art Foundation, New York

2022 *Platform (Blue Green Terracotta for JC)*, Chinati Foundation, Marfa, TX

Serpentear, Museo Amparo, Puebla, Mexico

2021 *Landscape*, Kayne Griffin, Los Angeles

Plant Based, Galerie Nordenhake, Berlin

2020 *Sarah Crowner*, Casey Kaplan Gallery, New York

2019 *Paintings for the Stage*, Simon Lee Gallery, Hong Kong

Post Jacaranda, Galerie Nordenhake, Mexico City

Three Concrete Sculptures, Kayne Griffin Corcoran, Los Angeles

2018 *Clay Bodies: Moving Through Ceramics*, Kentucky Museum of Art and Craft, Louisville [curatorial project]

Weeds, Casey Kaplan, New York

2016 *Beetle in the Leaves*, Massachusetts Museum of Contemporary Art, North Adams, MA

Installation view, *Carnegie International, 57th Edition*, Carnegie Museum of Art, Pittsburgh, PA, 2018

Sarah Crowner / Tutsi Baskets, Galerie Nordenhake, Stockholm

Plastic Memory, Simon Lee Gallery, London

2015 *Everywhere the Line Is Looser*, Casey Kaplan, New York

2014 *Interiores*, Travesía Cuatro, Guadalajara, Mexico

Motifs, Galerie Catherine Bastide, Brussels

Sunday in the Park, Locust Projects, Miami [curatorial project]

The Wave, Nicelle Beauchene Gallery, New York

2012 *Geometric Park*, SAKS Galerie, Geneva

Rehearsal, Galerie Nordenhake, Stockholm

2011 *Acrobat*, Nicelle Beauchene Gallery, New York

Ballet Plastique, Galerie Catherine Bastide, Brussels

Zig Zags and Curves, Helena Papadopoulos, Athens

2009 *Paintings and Pots*, Nicelle Beauchene Gallery, New York

2008 *Handbuilt Vessels*, Nice + Fit Gallery, Berlin

Group Exhibitions

2023 *The Future Won't Be Long Now*, Someday, New York

2022 *New Abstracts: Recent Acquisitions*, Los Angeles County Museum of Art

No Forms, Hill Art Foundation, New York

2021 *Cerámica Suro: A Story of Collaboration, Production, and Collecting in the Contemporary Arts*, Museo de Arte de Zapopan, Mexico

Contemporary Art + Design: New Acquisitions, Dallas Museum of Art

Field of Vision, Peter Blum Gallery, New York

New to the Collection, Carnegie Museum of Art, Pittsburgh, PA

2020 *Must Dream About Blue Tonight*, Sifang Art Museum, Nanjing, China

Painting, Kayne Griffin Corcoran, Los Angeles

Sculpture, Kayne Griffin Corcoran, Los Angeles

2019 *Abstract, Representational, and so forth*, Gladstone Gallery, New York

Hinge Pictures: Eight Women Artists Occupy the Third Dimension, Contemporary Arts Center, New Orleans

Notebook, 56 Henry, New York

2018 *2018 Invitational Exhibition of Visual Arts*, American Academy of Arts and Letters, New York

Carnegie International, 57th Edition, Carnegie Museum of Art, Pittsburgh, PA

Hog's Curve, Halsey McKay, New York

Painting/Object, Flag Art Foundation, New York

2017 *99 Cents or Less*, Museum of Contemporary Art Detroit

Building 6 / Summer Season, Massachusetts Museum of Contemporary Art, North Adams, MA

Für Barbara, Hall Art Foundation | Kunstmuseum Schloss Derneburg, Germany

Mauvaises Herbes: Sarah Crowner, Caitlin Keogh, Paulina Olowska, Simon Lee Gallery, Hong Kong

Salon Hang, Kunstverein, Amsterdam

The Centre Cannot Hold, Near East, Istanbul

You Should Be an Artist, Galerie Catherine Bastide, Brussels

2016 *If Only Bella Abzug Were Here*, Marc Straus, New York

We Are Not Things, Invisible-Exports, New York

2015 *Faux Amis*, Simon Lee Gallery, London

Matthew Brannon's Skirting the Issue, Casey Kaplan, New York

Repetition and Difference, Jewish Museum, New York

Space Between, The Flag Art Foundation, New York

Surface Tension, The Flag Art Foundation, New York

2014 *Conversation Piece*, Museum of Fine Arts, Boston

From Pre-History to Post-Evening, Sean Kelly Gallery, New York

2013 *Abstract Generation: Now in Print*, The Museum of Modern Art, New York

Beyond the Object, Brand New Gallery, Milan

DNA: Strands of Abstraction, Loretta Howard Gallery, New York

Edge, Order, Rupture, Galerie Lelong, New York

Excursus IV: Primary Information, Institute of Contemporary Art, Philadelphia

Experienz #2, Wiels, Contemporary Art Centre, Brussels

Larry Bell and Sarah Crowner, Meet Marlow Moss, Kunstverein, Amsterdam

Painter Painter, Walker Art Center, Minneapolis

Pathfinder: And to End, -1, Paris

Questioning the Canvas, Guekens & De Vil, Knokke, Belgium

Splendor Tkaniny, Zachęta National Gallery of Art, Warsaw

Work, Klaus von Nichtssagend Gallery, New York

2012 *a gathering*, Athens Festival, Athens

Material Occupation, University Art Museum, State University of New York at Albany

Surface in Volume, Luce Gallery, Turin, Italy

2011 *New Shadow Old Legs*, Eleven Rivington, New York

Paying a Visit to Mary Part 2, Kunstverein, Amsterdam

We Regret to Inform You There Is Currently No Space or Place for Abstract Painting, Martos Gallery, New York

2010 *Creeds, Colors and Combinations*, Nicelle Beauchene Gallery, New York

Owl Stretching Time, Nordenhake, Berlin

Peter Saville: Accessories to an Artwork, Glenn Horowitz Bookseller, East Hampton, NY

Whitney Biennial 2010, Whitney Museum of American Art, New York

2009 *For the blind man in the dark room looking for the black cat that isn't there*, Contemporary Art Museum St. Louis; Institute of Contemporary Arts, London; Museum of Contemporary Art Detroit; de Appel, Amsterdam; and Culturgest, Lisbon

Cave Painting: Installment #1, Gresham's Ghost, New York

Looking Back: The White Columns Annual, White Columns, New York

Sarah Crowner and Yiannis Moralis: Conversations Part I, Nice + Fit Gallery

2008 *Ceramics and Other Things*, DAAD Galerie, Berlin

Opportunity as Community: Artists Select Artists, Part Two, Dieu Donné, New York

Special Projects

2022 US Embassy of Honduras, Tegucigalpa, Honduras

2019 Site-specific commission, Park House, Dallas

2018 *Garden Blue*, sets and costumes by Sarah Crowner, choreography by Jessica Lang, American Ballet Theatre, New York

Site-specific commission, David H. Koch Center, New York–Presbyterian Hospital, New York

2017 Site-specific installation, The Wright Restaurant, Solomon R. Guggenheim Museum, New York

2011 *Vidas Perfectas*, set design by Sarah Crowner for stage production, The Irondale Center, Brooklyn, NY; Serpentine Gallery, London (2012); *Whitney Biennial*, Whitney Museum of American Art, New York (2014); and Ballroom Marfa, Marfa, TX (2014)

Selected Bibliography

Monographs and Artist Books

2020 *Stripes*. Self-published. [edition of 200]

2019 *Post Jacaranda*. Exh. cat. Mexico City: Galerie Nordenhake. [edition of 400]

2018 *Patterns*. Brooklyn, NY: Primary Information.

2017 *Sarah Crowner*. Exh. cat. North Adams, MA: Massachusetts Museum of Contemporary Art; and New York: DelMonico/Prestel.

2015 *Everywhere the Line Is Looser*. Exh. cat. New York: Casey Kaplan.

2013 *Flying Paintings*. Self-published. [edition of 100, signed]

2012 *Format*. New York: Primary Information.

2009 *Selective Geometries*. New York: Anteprojects and Olney Press.

2008 *Beatrice's Library*. Exh. cat. Self-published.

The Blind Man, nos. 1 and 2. Facsimile project for Whitney Biennial. New York: Dexter Sinister.

Group Exhibition Catalogues and Other Publications

2021 Crowner, Sarah. "Hantaï: Color, Shape, Indecision, La Marche du Crabe." In *Simon Hantaï*, 26–30. Philadelphia: ER Publishing.

2019 *Dispatch: Carnegie International, 57th Edition*. Exh. cat. Pittsburgh, PA: Carnegie Museum of Art, 2019.

Hinge Pictures: Eight Women Artists Occupy the Third Dimension, 72–82. Exh. cat. Catskill, NY: Siglio Press.

2018 *The Guide: Carnegie International, 57th Edition*, 56–57. Exh. cat. Pittsburgh, PA: Carnegie Museum of Art.

Hoffmann, Jens. *99 Cents or Less*, 90–91. Exh. cat. New York: Karma.

2015 Hoffmann, Jens, and Susan L. Braunstein. *Repetition and Difference*. Exh. cat. New York: Jewish Museum.

Hudson, Suzanne Perling. *Painting Now*. London: Thames and Hudson.

2014 *Excursus I–IV*. Exh. cat. Philadelphia: Institute of Contemporary Art.

2013 Dumbadze, Alexander, and Suzanne Hudson, eds. *Contemporary Art: 1989 to the Present*. Chichester: Wiley-Blackwell.

Jachula, Michal, and Marta Kowalewska, eds. *The Splendor of Textiles*. Exh. cat. Warsaw: Zachęta National Gallery of Art.

Painter Painter: Notes for an Exhibition. Exh. cat. Minneapolis: Walker Art Center.

2012 *Material Occupation*, 8–11. Exh. cat. Albany: University Art Museum, State University of New York at Albany.

2011 Cashdan, Marina. "Sarah Crowner." In *Vitamin P2: New Perspectives in Painting*, 76–79. London: Phaidon.

2010 Bonami, Francesco, and Gary Carrion-Murayari, eds. *2010: Whitney Biennial*. Exh. cat. New York: Whitney Museum of American Art.

2009 Huberman, Anthony. *For the blind man in the dark room looking for the black cat that isn't there*. Exh. cat. Saint Louis, MO: Contemporary Art Museum St. Louis.

Studio view, Brooklyn, NY, 2022

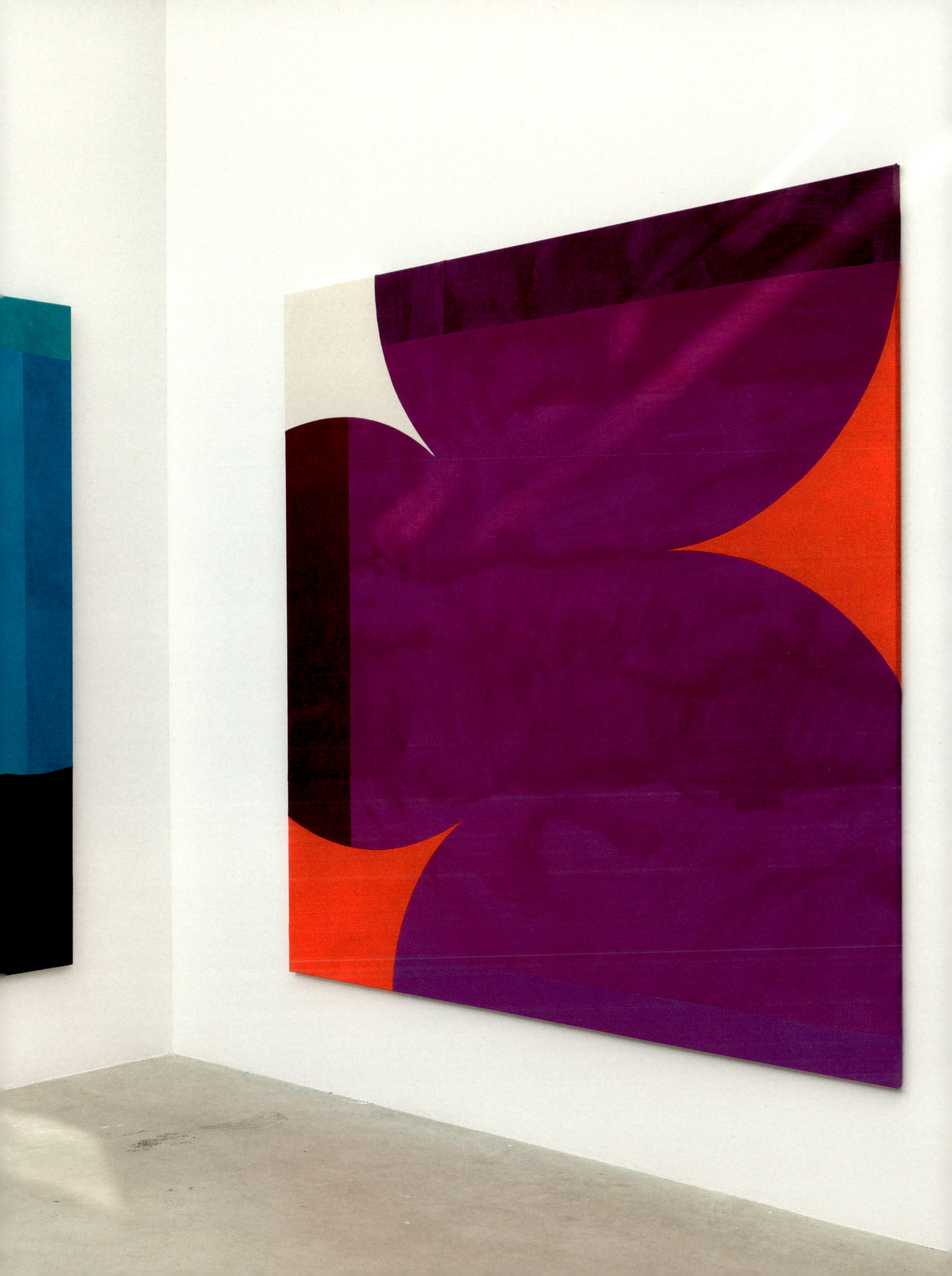

Artist's Acknowledgments

Tatiana Bilbao
Nikki Columbus
Marcos Dau
Laura Estévez
Sergio Flores
María José Fresneda
Alex Gibson
Fabian Gosselin
Hill Art Foundation
Casey Kaplan Gallery
Ricardo Kugelmas
Quinn Latimer
Luhring Augustine Gallery
Supriya Malik
Ana Elena Mallet
Ramiro Martínez Estrada
Diego Matos
Kelsey Knight Mohr
Nancy A. Nasher and
David J. Haemisegger
Galerie Nordenhake
Ryan Polich
Paloma Gómez Puente
Carolina Rojas
Toni Sadurni
Karina Salcido
Ingrid Schaffner
Cerámica Suro
José Noé Suro
Donna Wingate
Akiha Yamakami

The Sarah Crowner commission at Chinati was made possible with dedicated support from Bob Ackerley, Joseph DiCristina, Galerie Nordenhake, Hauser & Wirth, Hill Art Foundation, The Kraus Family Foundation, Kathleen Irvin Loughlin and Christopher Loughlin, Lawrence Luhring and Roland Augustine, Nancy A. Nasher and David J. Haemisegger Collection, and Christian and Rebecca Patry.

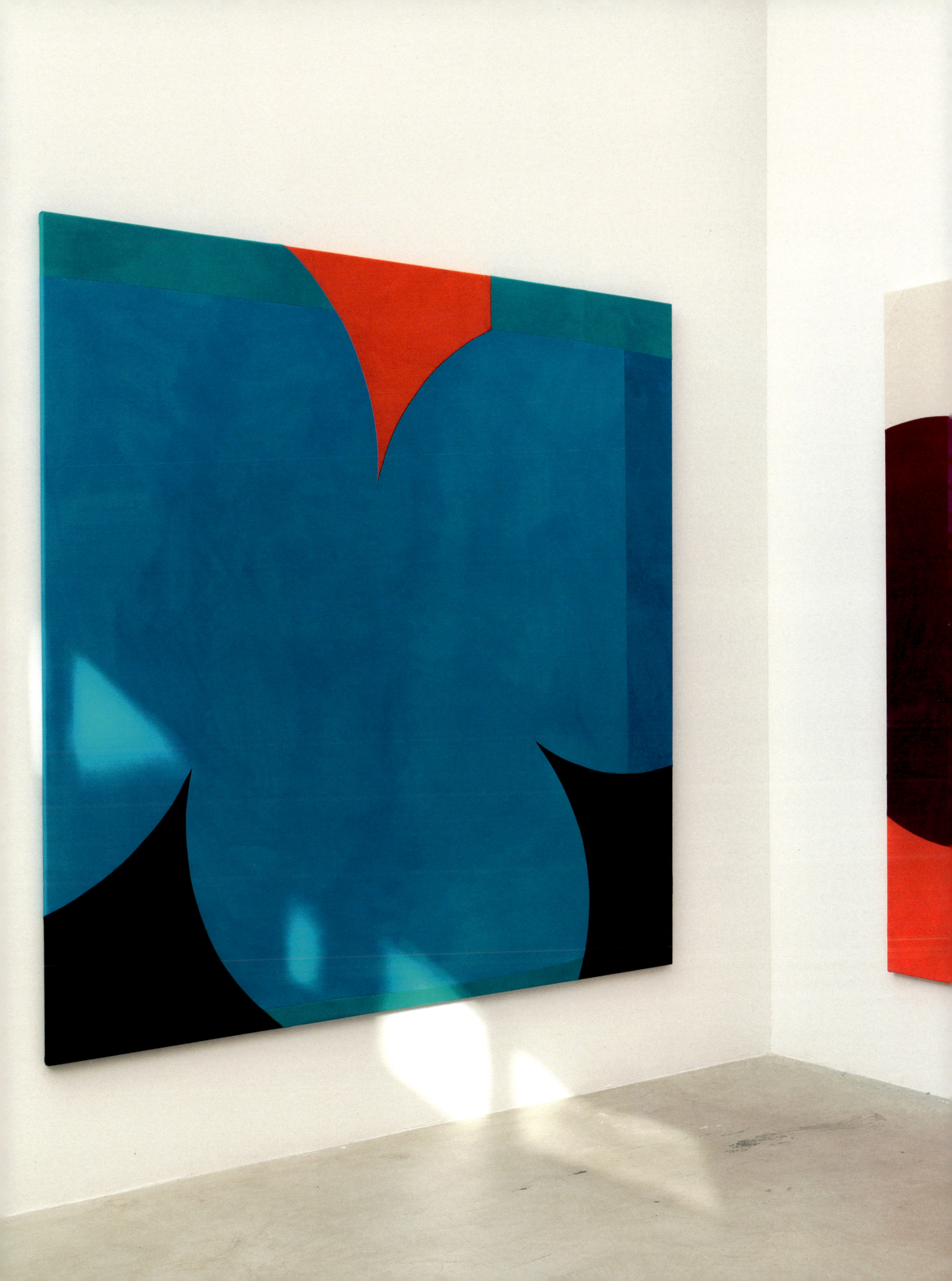

Photography Credits

The copyright holders, photographers, and sources of visual material other than the owners indicated in the captions are listed below. Every reasonable effort has been made to supply complete and correct credits; if there are errors or omissions, please contact the publisher so that corrections can be addressed in any subsequent edition.

Frontispiece, pages 20, 24–25, 50: photographs © Luis Gallardo/ LGM Studio. Courtesy Galerie Nordenhake

Pages 4, 17, 33: photographs by Sarah Crowner

Pages 8–14: photographs by Carlos Varillas / Museo Amparo

Pages 16, 92: photographs by Bryan Conley

Pages 18–19: photographs by Alexander Barrios

Page 22 (left): © 2023 The Josef and Anni Albers Foundation / Artists Rights Society (ARS), New York. Photograph by Tim Nighswander/Imaging4Art

Page 22 (right): © 2023 The Josef and Anni Albers Foundation/Artists Rights Society (ARS), New York

Pages 26, 36, 38: photographs by Rosalie O'Connor, courtesy American Ballet Theatre. ABT Dancers: Stella Abrera, Joo Won Ahn, Aran Bell, Misty Copeland, Herman Cornejo, Thomas Forster, Blaine Hoven, Hee Seo, Christine Shevchenko, James Whiteside, Katherine Williams

Pages 28, 31: photographs by Isabelle Arthuis, courtesy the artist and Catherine Bastide, Brussels

Page 29: photograph by Jason Mandella, courtesy the artist and Nicelle Beauchene Gallery, New York

Page 32: photograph by David Dashiell, courtesy MASS MoCA

Page 34: photograph by Olga Khvan, courtesy Museum of Fine Arts, Boston

Page 35: photograph by Børre Saethre

Pages 46–47: photograph by Gerhard Kassner

Page 49: © Fundació Joan Brossa, VEGAP, Barcelona. Photograph by FotoGasull, courtesy MACBA Museu d'Art Contemporani de Barcelona

Page 56: © 2022 Fairweather & Fairweather LTD / Artists Rights Society (ARS), New York, courtesy The Chinati Foundation. Photograph by Alex Marks

Page 59 (left and right): © 2022 Barragán Foundation, Switzerland / Artists Rights Society (ARS), New York. Photographs by Armando Salas Portugal

Pages 65–67, 99, 107, 109: photographs by Charles Benton

Pages 68–69: photographs by Marcia Prentice, courtesy of Travesía Cuatro

Pages 70–71: photographs by Marianne Goeritz

Page 73: photograph by Bartoz Przybl Olowski

Page 74 (top): photograph by Jason Wyche, courtesy the artist and Casey Kaplan, New York

Page 74: (bottom): photograph by Orsenigo Chemollo

Page 75: © 2022 Stiftung Arp e.V., Berlin/ Rolandswerth / Artists Rights Society (ARS), New York, Strasbourg Museum of Modern and Contemporary Art, photo Museums of Strasbourg, M. Bertola

Page 76: © 2022 Stiftung Arp e.V., Berlin/ Rolandswerth / Artists Rights Society (ARS), New York, image courtesy Kunstmuseum Bern

Page 77: photograph by David Heald © Solomon R. Guggenheim Foundation, New York

Pages 78–79: photograph by Kristopher McKay © Solomon R. Guggenheim Foundation, New York

Pages 82–85: © 2022 Fairweather & Fairweather LTD / Artists Rights Society (ARS), New York. Courtesy The Chinati Foundation. Photographs by Alex Marks

Page 88: © Instituto Lina Bo e P.M. Bardl / Casa de Vidro. Photograph by Francisco Albuquerque

Pages 91–95: photographs by Ding Musa, courtesy of auroras, São Paulo

This book is published on the occasion of the exhibition *Sarah Crowner: Serpentear* at the Museo Amparo, Puebla, Mexico, December 10, 2022–April 17, 2023.

Museo Amparo
Av 2 Sur 708
Centro, 72000
Puebla, Pue., Mexico

Published by
Turner
Diego de León 30
28006 Madrid
www.turnerlibros.com

Distributed by
TURNER
www.turnerlibros.com

United States
DAP
orders@dapinc.com
www.artbook.com

Europe
ACC
sales@antique-acc.com
www.accdistribution.com/uk

SPANISH EDITION AVAILABLE

Spain
Machado Grupo de Distribución
machadolibros@machadolibros.com

Latin America
Océano
info@oceano.com
www.oceano.com

© 2023 Turner
Texts © 2023 the authors
All artwork by Sarah Crowner © 2023 Sarah Crowner

ISBN: 978-84-18895-14-2
DL: M-11601-2023

Designer: Ryan Polich, Marquand Books, Seattle
Editor: Donna Wingate
Coeditor: Marc Joseph Berg
Copyeditor: Jane Hyun
Typesetter: Brynn Warriner
Proofreader: Janice Lee
Translator: Kurt Hollander
Production manager: María José Fresneda
Color management: I/O Color, Seattle
Printed and bound in Spain by Artes Gráficas Palermo

Jacket: Studio view, Brooklyn, NY, 2022. Photograph by Charles Benton

Frontispiece: *Ceiling (Stretched Pentagons)* (detail), 2022. Glazed terracotta tiles, plywood, aluminum, mortar, and grout; dimensions variable. Valhalla (house), Punta Mita, Mexico, architecture by Tatiana Bilbao Estudio. Photograph © Luis Gallardo/ LGM Studio, courtesy Galerie Nordenhake

Page 4: Studio view, Brooklyn, NY, 2022

Pages 8–14: Installation views of *Sarah Crowner: Serpentear* and *Platform (Cobalt Snakeskin)*, Museo Amparo, Puebla, Mexico, 2022. Photographs by Carlos Varillas / Museo Amparo

Page 49: Joan Brossa, *Poema visual*, 1970/1978. Silkscreen on paper; 19½ × 14⅞ in. (49.5 × 37.7 cm). MACBA Collection and Consortium, Fundación Joan Brossa

Page 50: *Ceiling (Stretched Pentagons)*, 2022. Glazed terracotta tiles, plywood, aluminum, mortar, and grout; dimensions variable. Valhalla (house), Punta Mita, Mexico, architecture by Tatiana Bilbao Estudio. Photograph © Luis Gallardo/ LGM Studio, courtesy Galerie Nordenhake

Page 51: Graciela Iturbide, *Pescaditos de Oaxaca, Mexico*, 1992. Collection of the artist

Pages 52–53, top: Graciela Iturbide, *Autorretrato con serpiente, Brasil*, ca. 1990. Silver gelatin contact sheet. Museo Amparo Collection

Pages 52–53, bottom: Studio views, Brooklyn, NY, 2022. Photograph by Charles Benton

Page 54: Graciela Iturbide, *Benarés, India*, 2000. Collection of the artist

Page 55: Studio views, Brooklyn, NY, 2022. Photograph by Charles Benton